TRANSITIONS IN TAIWAN

Transitions in Taiwan

Stories of the White Terror

EDITED BY
Ian Rowen

Literature from Taiwan Series
in collaboration with
the National Museum of Taiwan Literature,
National Taiwan Normal University, and
the National Human Rights Museum
General Editor: Nikky Lin

Amherst, New York

Copyright 2021 Cambria Press,
the National Museum of Taiwan Literature,
and the National Human Rights Museum

All rights reserved.
No part of this publication may be reproduced, stored in or introduced into a retrieval system, or transmitted, in any form, or by any means (electronic, mechanical, photocopying, recording, or otherwise), without the prior permission of the publisher.

Requests for permission should be directed to permissions@cambriapress.com, or mailed to:
Cambria Press
100 Corporate Parkway, Suite 128
Amherst, New York 14226, USA

ISBN 9781621966975

Front cover image is *Before the light* by Ou Young Wen, reproduced by permission of Nan Gallery.

Table of Contents

Foreword vii

Note from Series Editor ix

Introduction: Stories about the White Terror
    Ian Rowen 1

1: Long, Long Ago There was an Urashima Taro
    Chu Tien-hsin (translated by Sylvia Li-chun Lin and
    Howard Goldblatt) 17

2: The Taste of Apples
    Huang Chun-ming (translated by Howard Goldblatt) 51

3: Rice Diary
    Sung Tse-lai (translated by Ian Rowen) 79

4: Dixson's Idioms
    Huang Chong-kai (translated by Brian Skerratt) 165

5: Beef Noodles
    Li Ang (translated by Sylvia Li-chun Lin) 197

6: Disappearing Manhood
    Wu Chin-fa (translated by Chris Wen-chao Li) 215

7: My Second Brother, the Deserter
    Wu He (translated by Terence Russell) 245

About the Editor 273

About the Translators 275

Cambria Literature in Taiwan Series 277

Foreword

Taiwanese literature, like its history, reflects the island's hybrid ethnic diversity and unique culture. Due to its geographical proximity to the Chinese Empire, Taiwanese literature has been greatly influenced by the ancient tradition of classical Chinese literature.

In 1895, Taiwan's fifty-one years of Japanese colonial rule began. During this period, the groundwork for the development of modern Taiwanese literature was laid. The end of World War II also meant the end of Japanese rule, but it was not a time of peace for Taiwan, which found itself caught in the escalation of the Cold War. The result of this was thirty-eight years of martial law. However, through political activism and the persistent efforts of the Taiwanese people who sought to revolutionize and refine the island's political system, martial law ended in 1987 and the island was transformed into Asia's most liberal country, and one with a strong, democratic political system. The struggle for democracy also set the tone for increased responsiveness and acceptance in the literary sphere.

As such, it is important that the world learns about the distinctive brand into which Taiwan literature has evolved. This book is part of the Literature from Taiwan Series, which comprises a varied selection of literary works showcasing exemplary Taiwan literature. It is part of a systematic and measured attempt to introduce Taiwan's distinctiveness to the rest of the world.

All the literary creations featured in the series have been composed by writers who were afflicted or confined by the societal pressures of their time. If one reads a single work of Taiwanese literature, one can easily sense the exuberance of Taiwan's literary masters. However, when one reads a collection, one can experience the force that is driving Taiwan forward.

Since the Taiwan Ministry of Culture's launch of its promotional project, "Books From Taiwan (BFT)" in 2016, the Taiwanese Ministry of Culture has taken on a proactive role in establishing an international copyright information platform and has been an active presence at international book fairs. The Ministry of Culture, furthermore, has been inviting international translators to Taiwan and assisting in the facilitation of translations of Taiwanese books into various languages, measures which have proven fruitful thus far. The National Museum of Taiwan Literature (NMTL) is affiliated with the Ministry of Culture and its structural organization/structural mechanism aligns with that of the BFT, with both parties focusing on the promotion of important Taiwan literary creations.

In addition to this book series, the NMTL has been working on creating a long-term database of translators of Taiwanese literature. It has also conducted a Taiwanese literary survey in various countries with the aim of promoting Taiwanese literature internationally as well as raising awareness for Taiwan's literary excellence, thus giving it a well-deserved voice on the international stage of world literature.

—Su Shuo-Bin,
Director,
National Museum of Taiwan Literature

Note from Series Editor

The inset painting on this book's front cover is *Before the Light* (2001) by Ou Young Wen. Ou Young Wen was born in 1924 during the Japanese colonial era on Chiayi Street in the prefecture of Tainan (now known as Chiayi City). He was a Western-style artist and photographer who fell victim to Taiwan's White Terror. The lilies depicted in the painting symbolize Taiwan's democracy, while the barbed wire is a metaphor representing authoritarian control. The details in the painting are testament to the relentless spirit of the Taiwanese people in the face of authoritarian rule. Reproduced by permission of Nan Gallery; copyright restrictions apply.

I would like to thank Yi-Chia Lee, Kirsten Klitsch, and Chein-Sen Peng for their assistance on this project.

—Nikky Lin,
General Editor,
Literature from Taiwan Series

Transitions in Taiwan

Introduction

Stories about the White Terror

Ian Rowen

Violence composes a fundament of modern Taiwan's history, and a legacy that continues to influence its contemporary society. "The terrible human rights record of Taiwan under martial law," as scholar Mark Harrison notes, "has left unspoken stories of suffering, personal betrayals and death in the family memories of the Taiwanese." Such stories have been reimagined and retold by writers, often from the margins, who "understand that violence is foundational to that experience [of Taiwanese modernity]."[1] The bloodiest and most readily bounded episode of violence in modern Taiwan is undoubtedly the 228 Incident, which took place on February 28, 1947, and has been memorialized in monuments across the country. The highly repressive period that followed, known as the White Terror, lasted for decades and is the focus of this volume.

The stories in this volume recount the violence and oppression conducted under the flag of the Republic of China (ROC), which took control of Taiwan in 1945 and continues to be the flag under which now-democratic contemporary Taiwan is governed. The 228 Incident, a most shocking episode is named for the day after policemen struck a female cigarette vendor and killed a bystander in the crowd that had gathered to defend the woman. As Taiwanese rose up across the island in rebellion, the ROC, under the control of the Chinese Nationalist Party (Kuomintang or the KMT), declared martial law and killed approximately 10,000 people and wounded perhaps another 30,000. Many of those targeted were educated elites.

The White Terror period that followed is difficult to date definitively, but what is certain is that during this time the KMT consolidated its military/police party-state rule, attempted to legitimize it through anti-communist and nationalist Chinese ideological campaigns, and that thousands more were killed or imprisoned.[2] State violence was aimed at alleged proponents of Taiwanese independence as well as supposed communist collaborators. During this time, the KMT systematically favored mainland Chinese over native-born Taiwanese and reserved most military, educational, and police positions for the former. Taiwanese, who had been under Japanese rule for 50 years, were forcibly "re-educated" as Chinese subjects. China-centric national history curricula enforced Mandarin-language pedagogy and media, and the renaming of streets and public spaces after places in China further enforced a representational regime of Chineseness, which was implemented to legitimize the authority of the KMT. These campaigns wiped out an entire generation of intellectuals—both native-born Taiwanese as well as mainland Chinese exiles were subject to imprisonment, torture, and execution.

In her pathbreaking book, *Representing Atrocity in Taiwan*, Sylvia Lin (whose translations are included in this volume), proposes a chronology of three periods in the literary and cinematic representation of the 228

Stories about the White Terror

Incident and the White Terror. The first, she suggests, began shortly after the 228 Incident and consists of short stories, many of which were buried for the most repressive years that followed. The second period began in the early 1980s, coinciding with newly energized social movements that advocated democratization. The third period began after the lifting of martial law in 1987, when writers tested the waters and gained confidence that they were in fact able to publish without fear of legal repercussions. Surveying the field in the mid-2000s, Lin tentatively posits that there may have then already been a fourth period underway, typified by a self-reflexive style more attuned to the "(im)possibility of recapturing the past and discovering the truth."[3]

Given increasing global attention to the literature of Taiwan as manifest in this and related publications, Lin's posited fourth period of cultural production may someday be characterized not only by doubt and self-reflexivity but also by increased attention to the transnationalism and translingualism already—and always—present in the representation of Taiwan's history. While the events narrated in this volume all take place in Taiwan, the stories make clear that that the White Terror and authoritarian rule operated transnationally. The KMT regime arrived from China and was supported financially and militarily by the United States, a relationship that is at the foreground of Huang Chun-ming's story and in the background of several others that feature peripheral characters with American connections.

Transnational circuits of memory and mobility—and their import for the present and future of Taiwan—are salient not only for the writers, characters, and readers of these of stories but also for the increasingly high-profile writings of the contemporary diaspora, which attend as well to violence and trauma. For example, Chang Ti-han writes that Shawna Yang Ryan's *Green Island*, which stages its family saga across three distinct settings (including the United States), contributes to the "worlding of Taiwanese literature" and raises "a critical question of how we imagine a postcolonial-society-yet-to-come beyond its geopolitical boundary."[4] Related questions haunt the pages of this volume, not only for the writers whose work appears here, all of whom wrote about Taiwan from within it, but also for (im)migrants and others entangled in the changing inscriptions of its geopolitical and cultural boundaries.

This anthology brings together selections from a four-volume collection of stories about the White Terror period, published in 2020 with the support of Taiwan's National Human Rights Museum.[5] This collection comes on the heels of a state-backed transitional justice project announced during the 2016 inauguration speech of President Tsai Ing-wen. This project included the formation of several transitional justice commissions that were still active at the time of writing. Although this process was eventually backed from the highest levels of the state, it only gained traction following decades of activism by activists, academics, artists, and other advocates from within Taiwan's civil society.[6] Using a language of "truth and reconciliation" drawn from transnational social justice movements, these commissions and the grassroots campaigns that preceded them have focused on investigations, exonerations for the wrongfully convicted, and to a far lesser extent, reparations.

Although this publication is spurred in part by domestic attention to as well as state financial support for such projects, the stories here may also be usefully seen in light of the themes of hybridity that characterize their production, as well as their increasingly transnational circulation and consumption. This owes as much to the changing circumstances of their writers and publishers, as it does to the increasingly global stage on which Taiwan—*as Taiwan* (and not as the ROC or "Free China")—is playing. In this sense, this volume signifies a new political wave as much as an artistic one—channeled through civil society and amplified through state support—to enroll cultural production into an ongoing national project explicitly named as *transitional*.

This volume's thread of transition begins with Zhu Tianxin's "Long, Long Ago there was an Urashima Taro," first published in a *China Times* literary supplement in November 1990. It tells the tale of one Li Jiazheng, who was held for 30 years as a political prisoner on a never-named island that no doubt refers to Green Island.[7] Even after his release from prison, Li remains convinced that he is still being monitored by secret agents, and he writes reports and letters and sends them to any agency or official that he thinks may pay attention. While his son works in a different city, Li takes his bright grandson Junjun to and from school every day, changing routes every time for fear of being tracked by spies.

The story is as much a portrait of Li's disjointed daily life as it is a nostalgic reflection on the passing of time. The protagonist recollects the books he used to read, the songs he once sang, the river and mountain paths he used to walk, and slowly comes to terms with the 30 years that already passed, the grandchildren who were born, the wife he barely recognizes (and who is now older than his mother was when he saw her last), and the ravages of age on his own body. The story shows us glimpses of his wizened, scrawny frame in the mirror, the proddings of his one remaining friend (also a fellow captive), and finally, the surprise discovery of an unforwarded cache of letters which pushes him to begin to truly apprehend his loss.

Zhu Tianxin (Chu T'ien-hsin) was born in 1958 in Fengshan, Kaohsiung, and raised in a military village. Her father was Zhu Xining, a well-known writer born in Shandong, China, and her mother, the translator Liu Musa, was born of Hakka parentage in Miaoli, Taiwan. A graduate of the History Department of National Taiwan University, she is the second of three famous Zhu sisters (the other two being Zhu Tianwen and Zhu Tianyi) who were personally tutored and deeply influenced by writer Hu Lancheng (the first husband of Eileen Chang, who had lived next door to the Zhu family for several years in the 1970s. Zhu Tianxin served as the editor-in-chief of *Three Three Magazine*, a late-1970s literary periodical that was named to invoke both Sun Yat-sen's Three Principles of the People and the Christian trinity.[8] Her many writings have explored the lives of mainlanders and military villages, among other themes, and include *The Old Capital: A Novel of Taipei*, translated by Howard

Goldblatt, who also co-translated, with Sylvia Li-chun Lin, Zhu's story "Long, Long Ago There was an Urashima Taro" in this volume.

The next story, "The Taste of Apples," by Huang Chun-ming, was first published in a *China Times* literary supplement in December 1972 and is also translated by Howard Goldblatt. The story examines the relationship between Taiwan and the United States through an allegorical and darkly comic lens. A seemingly straightforward but terribly tragic fairy tale, "The Taste of Apples" sardonically sends up Taiwan's acclimation to American military domination and financial aid during the Cold War period. It also illuminates Taiwan's social and spatial divisions, particularly the plight of impoverished migrants from the rural south.

The tale begins with a car accident in which an American military officer crashes into Ah-fa, a poor laborer who has brought his family of seven to Taipei in search of a better life but instead finds that they struggle to get by as they live in a slum. Before the accident, Ah-fa even considered selling his mute daughter to make some extra money. However, the accident, in which he and his bicycle are hit by the careless and irresponsible colonel, makes this unnecessary. The family members are swiftly picked up by military police—their first time riding in a car—and brought to the gleaming, pearly white Catholic-run hospital, where an angelic American nurse dazzles the youngsters. The contrite colonel, flanked by local military colleagues, promises not only a large cash payout but also offers to send Ah-fa's daughter to a school in America.

Ah-fa's windfall makes him the envy of his coworkers and superiors, even though it comes at the cost of a broken body. This grotesquely crippling approximation of "the good life" proves just how severe his family's poverty and how unlikely it was that they could have escaped it. The story concludes with the family at the hospital eating apples—an otherwise unaffordable and exotic luxury. The apples are beautiful yet tasteless and maybe even toxic. No longer an object of aspiration, the fruit found its way to them, albeit not in a way they would have wanted.

Stories about the White Terror

Huang Chun-ming was born in 1935 in Luodong, Yilan County. Huang has written in a variety of formats, including novels, essays, and plays. Between 2012 and 2015, he ran a café and literary salon in Yilan. His works have also been translated and published in multiple languages and adapted into films, including "The Sandwich Man" (1983). "The Taste of Apples" has previously appeared in several collections that were also translated by Howard Goldblatt.

The next story in this volume, "Rice Diary," deals as well with food, or rather the conditions of its production. Written by Sung Tse-lai, it was first published on October 25, 1979, in the second issue of the avant-garde series, *Formosa Tomorrow* (*Fuermusha de Mingtian* 福爾摩沙的明天), and I have translated it. Part of a series about Daniunan, a village in Yunlin County, it is structured as a diary of everyday happenings, including the weather. This particular story of a disastrous rainy rice harvest sheds light on the multiple and overlapping regimes of exploitation that long extracted wealth from central and southern farmers to serve the state and northern urban centers. In so doing, the story effectively dramatizes the broader processes of island-wide socioeconomic and environmental change.

The village of Daniunan is split into several factions, each with their own gathering places and distinct characteristics. The first is the land-owning class that clusters around the temple by the main road at the front of the village. The second, a nimbler and more socially mobile group, hangs out by the barber shop and general store in the middle of the village. Finally, toward the rear of the village is one of the few remaining stands of cottonwood trees, which provides shade for the poorer and less-educated farmers to gossip, gamble, and rest in-between working the fields. Although the three classes collect in specific places, the inclusion of civil servants and teachers as members of a distinct and spatially flexible class that lives betwixt and between these groups was a peculiar characteristic of KMT rule, which relied on these constituencies to shore up support. While this class had traditionally been dominated by mainlanders, their presence and importance in Daniunan shows how such realignments penetrated a Hoklo village where ethnic division would otherwise go unmentioned.

At first blush the story seems to center on an act of fraud perpetrated by a wealthy villager who had moved to the city long before, but it covers much more. The villagers getting defrauded by the former neighbor is a profound tragedy, but it is not without a silver lining for some residents. The decline of the village's remaining major landlord, who has also been cheated, proves to be a boon for his offspring, who become freer to pursue their own paths. Likewise, the middle- and lower-class villagers also now have opportunities to become more socially mobile.

More than anything, the tale demonstrates the irrational, if emotionally necessary, optimism and resilience of rural laborers and landlords, who all have to deal with an unaccountable state authority and face an uncertain future. Corrupt institutions such as the county government and the Farmers Association are implicated, but so are the dynastic family politics and economies of unequal land distribution that preceded the KMT regime. The villagers here are not much more angelic than the state and industry players that exploit them. There are no heroes in this tale, but how could there be?

Sung Tse-lai is the pen name for Liao Weijun, born in 1952 of Hakka parentage in Yunlin County. After gaining literary renown, he went on to earn a PhD from the program in Taiwanese Literature at Cheng Kung University. Fitting for the author of a story about Taiwan's many transitions, Sung and his body of work have also undergone multiple linguistic and religious transitions. His earlier stories, such as this one, were written in a relatively standard register of Chinese with some idiomatic Hoklo Taiwanese expressions. He later carried the banner for Hoklo literary production—his novella, "*Kangbao de Damao shi/K'ong-pok* e p'ah-niau tsi" (translated variously as "The city of Damao in revolt" or "The violent protest of P'ah-niau City"), which focuses on the 228 Incident and its aftermath, was published in 1987 and was among the first and most thoroughly researched works to be written entirely in that language. Questions of faith, spirituality, and superstition are prominent in these stories as well as in Sung's life, as he had professed faith in various forms of Buddhism before later converting to Christianity. His genre shifts are no less extraordinary; they include experimentations with modernism, nativism, realism, and even science fiction such as his 1985 diary novel, *Wasteland Taiwan*.

The next story, Huang Chong-kai's "Dixson's Idioms," adopts a radically different structural motif. Translated by Brian Skerratt, it arranges its narrative through a series of English idiom lessons compiled, translated, and transmitted by juxtaposed literary figures and their families. Each section puts a specific phrase to use, piecing together parallel fragments of life in Cold War America and White Terror Taiwan. Using such literary devices, the story relates the young author's own experiences mastering politicized forms of language with those of Ko Chi-hua, a real-life Taiwanese teacher, writer, and political prisoner who learned from and then translated the English-teaching books of Robert Dixson, an American who taught English to Puerto Rican laborers.

Told through the eyes of multiple characters, the story examines the role of language in building, maintaining, and threatening family relationships, as well as for forging and transmitting memories. As it happens, Dixson's English teaching, as well as Ko's literary endeavors, was motivated in part by a personal commitment to emancipatory politics. Through Ko's work, which was later reedited and published by Lai Shih-hsiung, the celebrity founder of the company Ivy English, Dixson's book became so widespread that its author's surname almost served as a metonym for English education. The story ends with a very personal reflection of the writer's own experience studying English, and his discovery of his uncle's 1981 copy of one of Ko's English-teaching books.

The story underscores the changing role of language for the characters who, depending on the time and place, speak and think variously in English, Spanish, Japanese, Mandarin, and Taiwanese. It connects these experiences to the policies of different state regimes, such as the KMT, which included the forcible suppression of Hoklo, Hakka, Japanese, and indigenous Austronesian languages in favor of Mandarin. English only comes alive when channeled for the cause of emancipation by a skilled and passionate orator like Martin Luther King, Jr., whose "I Had A Dream Speech" is played on a portable stereo by the author's schoolteacher, providing a rare moment of catharsis for the classroom. Elsewhere in the story, the same speech moves both Ko (whose own children immigrated to the United States) and Lolita Dixson, Robert's wife, adding transnational context for struggle and solidarity.

By far the youngest writer to have their work appear in this collection, Huang Chong-Kai was born in 1981 in Yunlin. A graduate of the history program at National Taiwan University, he has also been a writer-in-residence at the University of Iowa and long-time member of Alphabet Lab, a collective of experimental writers and critical theorists in Taiwan. In addition to four novels, he has also written a collection of stories, *The Content of the Times*, in which "Dixson's Idioms" first appeared—this collection received the Taipei International Book Exhibition award and the Wu Chuo-Liu Award Grand Prize.

The next story, Li Ang's "Beef Noodles," appeared in her 2007 collection, *Yuanyang Chun Shan* 鴛鴦春膳 (*An Erotic Feast for Lovebirds*), and is translated by Sylvia Li-chun Lin. It plumbs the history of a famous noodle soup to tell the hybridity, creativity, and violence that constitute the identity of one of contemporary Taiwan's most popular culinary delights and cultural exports. The protagonist is a political prisoner serving time in a jail where, thanks to financial support from his family, a bowl of beef noodles is among his few affordable delicacies. In this prison, inmates are regularly executed with little to no warning. The story begins with the protagonist feeling regret for not buying a bowl as a gift for an arrival who was executed before ever having a chance to enjoy a taste.

Although the story provides a vivid portrait of prison life, "Beef Noodles" is as much about the creative cultural and material refashioning of Taiwan's national identity as it is about the pain of incarceration or the finality of death. The protagonist, like his fellow prisoners, wrongly assumed that so-called "Sichuan beef noodles" were brought from that province by the KMT regime and mainlanders and were a faithful reproduction of their namesake. But as he discovers after visiting Sichuan long after his release, the dish is not from there at all. Rather, it is a quintessentially Taiwanese composite cooked by people hailing from a variety of provinces who arrived in Taiwan and adapted it based on their hometown memories and access to ingredients. In this sense, Sichuan beef noodles are a sort of simulacrum, a culinary copy without an original. The name stuck even as its style diversified. After the dish became popular abroad, particularly in Europe and North America, chefs began simply calling the dish "Taiwan beef noodles" to distinguish its actual place of origin. Coming to terms with the hybrid identity of this dish is a way for the narrator to come to terms with the hybrid identity of Taiwan as a whole.

Li Ang, born Shih Shu-tuan in 1952 in Lukang, Changhua, studied philosophy at the Chinese Cultural University and theater at the University of Oregon. Like Zhu Tianxin, she belongs to a family of writers, which includes her older sisters Shih Shu and Shih Shu-ching. Li Ang published her first story, "Flower Season," at the age of sixteen, around the same time she first met Taiwan's pioneering feminist activist, Annette Lu, who went on to serve as vice president from 2000 to 2008. Arguably Taiwan's highest-profile and most prolific feminist writer, Li Ang is well-known for her frank, forceful, and insightful examinations of sexuality and society. In addition to writing extensively about the pre-1949 feminist-communist Taiwanese activist, Xie Xuehong, Li Ang met a variety of dissidents in the 1970s and 1980s and donated money to *Formosa Magazine*, a publication that played a pivotal role in Taiwan's democratization movements. Some of her best-known works include *The Butcher's Wife* and *The Lost Garden*, also translated into English by Howard Goldblatt and Sylvia Li-chun Lin. In 2007, "Beef Noodles" was adapted for a theatrical production performed by le Théâtre de l'Opprimé in Paris. More recently, 2019 saw the opening of a permanent exhibit dedicated to her work and housed at the library of National Chung Hsing University in Taichung.

The next story, Wu Chin-fa's "Disappearing Manhood," translated by Chris Wen-chao Li, employs a magical and metaphorical style to depict the psychological reconstitution and dissolution of a writer facing state repression and social and intellectual frustration. The protagonist, poet and former teacher Wilfred Lee, discovers bird feathers growing from his skin, but no doctors are able to help. Even a celebrated psychiatrist can do little more than cryptically diagnose the problem as a "flight response." Wilfred's physical condition penetrates his unconscious—when he sleeps, he chirps and caws and dreams that he is a bird in flight.

Wilfred's problems turn out to be as much about politics as they are about poetry. Neither domain is under his control. Once popular with both the public and students, he fell into disrepute after his edited poetry anthologies offended a number of writers and institutions. To move on from the trauma, he begins researching birds, learning their flight patterns, and photographing them wherever he can. His studies take him toward a bird habitat by a military barracks, where he is detained by officers and interrogated as a suspected security threat. Although he is released, the experience pushes him to want to escape even more. He dreams that he has become a bird again and wakes up to find that the dream has become reality. From that night on, no one sees any trace of the poet Wilfred Lee.

The mythical style of the story imbues it with parodic and ambiguous elements. Most obviously, the story explores the limitations and pressures of the post-war political and literary atmosphere. As the pressure increases, the poet and critic has little choice but to transform literally into a bird, to fly away and disappear. More obliquely, Wilfred's professional struggles could very well be referring to those of the author, or any number of his contemporaries, including Sung Tse-lai, who pursued cultural production in the face of social opprobrium and political controversy.

Stories about the White Terror

Wu Chin-fa was born in 1954 of mixed Hakka and indigenous ancestry in Meinung, Kaohsiung. "Disappearing Manhood" was first published in the November 1985 issue of the Taiwanese literary quarterly *Wenxue Jie* 文學界 (Literary realm). His books include *Street of Crying Swallows*, *Spring and Autumn Tea House*, *A Boyhood Trilogy*, and *The Autumn Chrysanthemum*, which was adapted into the film *Youth Without Regret*. These works examine conflicts between ethnic groups, with particular attention on youth experiences. Wu also worked in newspaper and film companies and served as vice chairman of the Council of Cultural Affairs from 2004 to 2008 and later as Director of the Cultural Office of Pingtung County Government.

The final, and perhaps most stylistically and thematically challenging, story of this volume, is Wu He's "My Second Brother, the Deserter," translated by Terence Russell. It uses a years-long cat-and-mouse game between the narrator's brother, an army deserter, and the "hunters" who come to capture him again and again as he flees from home to home, to reflect on the seductions of freedom and the perversions of repression. The first-person narrator, a university student, is also drafted into the army, where he discovers the strange strictures of political warfare officers, the furtive ubiquity of gambling rings, and the ever-present lechery and corruption on base. Much of his time is spent undergoing ideological reform because opportunities for more interesting work were sidelined due to his expression of undesirable thoughts. He tests out the prospects of desertion before remembering what became of his brother.

Sex, anomie, and absurdity animate the recounting, which flits between stream-of-consciousness and only slightly more straightforward accounts of the narrator's exploits. The protagonist eventually locates his second brother, who has hidden himself away in a sex worker's bedroom for nine months, mumbling in a cryptic language of his own design. During this encounter in a squalid boudoir, he comes face-to-face not only with his brother but also with deeper existential questions. Who, he wonders, is freer—himself still dancing, however reluctantly, to the monotonous military tune, or his brother, trapped behind layers of reinforced concrete but free from the gaze of the state? What might it mean to trade places?

Wu He (Dancing Crane) is the pen name of Chen Guocheng, born in Chiayi in 1951 and a graduate of the Chinese Department of Cheng Kung University, where he initially studied engineering. This story was first published in 1991 in *Taiwan Wenyi* 臺灣文藝 (Taiwan literature and art) and republished ten years later in a book collection. Like the deserter brother of the story, the author is no stranger to seclusion—after ending his own military service, he spent ten years in a soft form of it in Tamsui beginning in 1981, during which he wrote this story and many others.[9] He went on to win nearly every literary award in Taiwan, including the Wu Chuo-liu Literature Award and the Lai He Literature Award.

Wu He's elliptical and fragmented approach serves as a fine coda for a collection of literature that considers the persistence of the past in the present. Wu He is not concerned, as he told a fellow novelist, "to give an objective account of the historical present... [which] is a project that is essentially 'fictional' and 'impossible.' The fact is that historical past and present reality always interpenetrate and interfuse."[10] Such an observation is particularly pertinent for this volume, which interprets, translates, and temporalizes a variety of affects and encounters that may not converge on a singular "truth," even as activists rightly seek resolution for atrocities that exceed the bounds of representation, much less restitution.

Therefore, as much as this volume points to the persistence of the past in Taiwan, the vignettes, scenarios, and dramatic throughlines here also reveal the enduring layers of injustices committed through the longer *duree* in Taiwanese history, including Japanese imperial and Han settler colonial projects. In so doing, they enrich and point toward what we might, following Chang Ti-han's observation, imagine as Taiwan's postcolonial society that is yet to come.

Notes

1. Mark Harrison, "Art, Violence and Memory in Taiwan: Telling the Story of the Beautiful Island," *Thesis Eleven* 146, no. 1 (2018): 18, https://doi.org/10.1177/0725513618776665.
2. Steven E. Phillips, *Between Independence and Assimiliation: The Taiwanese Encounter Nationalist China* (Stanford: Stanford University Press, 2003).
3. Sylvia Li-chun Lin, *Representing Atrocity in Taiwan: The 2/28 Incident and White Terror in Fiction and Film* (New York: Columbia University Press, 2007), 16.
4. Ti-han Chang, "Writing History within / Outside of Taiwan: A Postcolonial Perspective on Shawna Yang Ryan's Green Island (2016) and Wu Ming-Yi's The Stolen Bicycle (2015)," *Taiwan Insight*, January 2020; Kuei-fen Chiu, "'Worlding' World Literature from the Literary Periphery: Four Taiwanese Models," *Modern Chinese Literature and Culture* 30, no. 1 (2020): 13–41.
5. 胡淑雯 [Hu Shuwen] and 童偉格 [Tong Wei-ger], eds., 讓過去成為此刻：臺灣白色恐怖小說選 套書 [Let the past become this moment: Selected works of the white terror period in Taiwan] (Spring Hill Publishing, 2020).
6. For a seminal account of the pre-institutional history, see Naiteh Wu, "Transition without Justice, or Justice without History: Transitional Justice in Taiwan," *Taiwan Journal of Democracy* 1, no. 1 (2005): 77–102. For international and geopolitical dimensions, see Ian Rowen and Jamie Rowen, "Taiwan's Truth and Reconciliation Committee: The Geopolitics of Transitional Justice in a Contested State," *International Journal of Transitional Justice* 11, no. 1 (2017): 92–112; For an account of its legal implementation, see Chang-Liao, Nien-chung, and Yu-jie Chen. "Transitional Justice in Taiwan: Changes and Challenges." *Washington International Law Journal* 28, no. 3 (2019).
7. The translations presented in this volume employ a variety of inconsistent romanization schemes. This reflects the unruly orthography of Taiwan's place and personal names, which include idiosyncratic and shifting uses of Wade-Giles, Hanyu Pinyin, Tongyong Pinyin, and Taiwanese Romanization System, as much as it does the varied sensibilities of a diverse set of translators. Rather than attempting to standardize

these styles, I have generally deferred to the translators' decisions and trust that the interested reader will be able to use contextual clues or consult the source texts for further information.

8. Rosemary Haddon, "Being/Not Being at Home in the Writing of Zhu Tianxin," in *Cultural, Ethnic, and Political Nationalism in Contemporary Taiwan*, ed. John Makeham and A-chin Hsiau (Palgrave Macmillan, 2005), 103–123.
9. Sebastian Veg, "Surviving Civilization: Rereading the History of Taiwan and Modernity," *China Perspectives* 1, no. September 2020 (2012): 69–72, https://doi.org/10.4000/chinaperspectives.5831.
10. For this quote and further discussion of *Remains of Life*, see "Imaginary reality in Wuhe's 'The Life that Remains'" by Julian Chih-Wei Yang. https://taiwaninsight.org/2020/01/29/imaginary-reality-in-wuhes-the-life-that-remains/.

1

Long, Long Ago There was an Urashima Taro

Chu Tien-hsin
(translated by Sylvia Li-chun Lin and Howard Goldblatt)

In the fall, when days and nights were the same length, he came back to the city.

He did not need to look twice to see that it was a haphazard city that people had carelessly thrown up with maximum effort.

In a continuing quest for self-protection, he'd become adept at writing denunciation letters, which, of course, he called "letters of questions and dissent." He sent them to various addressees, starting with the district police (before long he discovered that a policeman in the station had him under surveillance); his next recipient was a certain city councilman. He sent the same letter six times before the councilman responded by mailing him a lavishly printed campaign pamphlet that was out of date.

So, for the moment, he focused on two addressees, a newly elected legislator from his district and a former college classmate, Professor Huang Xinrong, who taught in the political science department at a public university.

After spending plenty on stamps and photocopying (he scrupulously kept copies of everything), he concluded that the local post office in his district was not to be trusted, since mail he was supposed to receive did not reach him, and he believed that even double-registered postal items did not get out.

He wrote a complaint against his local post office, and, as a deviation from his normal routine, once he was sure he wasn't being followed, went to the all-night post office at the North Gate. But he spent a long night racking his brains trying to figure out to whom to send the complaint. The most logical person would be the Postal Authority General Director. Yet he was fully aware of how officials cover for each other, so, even if he sent it to the Premier, he wasn't sure if the intelligence agency had bought off or at least was in control of the officials. Not wanting to miss the last bus of the night, he scribbled an unfamiliar government office address on the envelope.

After joining the line at the registered mail window, he caught sight of an old mainlander up ahead who was holding an envelope neatly addressed to "Honorable Chiang Ching-kuo, Office of the President, Taipei City." The man's calm demeanor as he waited astonished him and had him wondering if the younger Chiang's death two years before was real or was just a dream. He walked off before reaching the window; people holding envelopes all seemed to be quietly queuing up to buy a ticket for the underworld.

Maybe it was best to ask Old Cai to drop this into one of the ordinary green roadside mailboxes. He did not believe the intelligence agency could be so efficient as to keep watch over every mailbox in the city.

Long, Long Ago There was an Urashima Taro 19

That night he made two copies of the letter "Oppose the twelve-year compulsory education," which he had sent off many times recently, one copy to the Party newspaper (so his motivation wouldn't be smeared or labeled red), the other to the legislator representing his district. No matter what, he had to do whatever was necessary to put a stop to the policy before it was implemented. Otherwise, when the new educational policy went into effect, his grandson, Junjun, would be unfairly and unduly victimized because of his grandfather's record. Junjun was smart enough to test into a good high school, but agents could collude with his teachers to give him an unfavorable evaluation and prevent him from receiving more schooling.

He could not sleep that night, once again overcome by an attack of fear and anger, so after an absent-minded visit to the toilet, he went back to the opinion letters he'd been working on lately, regarding homosexual relationships, fetishism, masturbation, oral sex, bestiality ... all common matters in his former world, openly practiced in the city he'd left thirty years before, though none of which he had any trouble with. From the perspective of population control, they were all capable of giving vent to sexual desire without resulting in a population explosion. But he did have trouble with celibacy, suicide, imprisonment, castration (contraception), all with the same effect and intensity. Celibates and castrati, for example, must be the cautious type, with a pessimistic view of the future of humanity. Suicides demonstrate that they have the ability to take responsibility for their own lives, to exert self-control, and to self-reflect. As for those who were imprisoned, viewed from the perspective of the human animal, they were a rare group of individuals with variant characteristics who still had the animalistic instinct to brave all dangers and hardships. Nonetheless, these individuals (celibates, suicides, and prisoners) were doomed to decrease in numbers and eventually disappear; bad money driving out good money, we'd be left with a world of weaker people, and so ...

And so, he mulled things over for several days, but no solution emerged, just as he found no conclusive answers when he thought about what he should stand for and what he should oppose, and he ended up spending most of his time worrying about the appropriate place to send his appeal, who might share his interests and viewpoint, and with whom he might come into conflict. Naturally, he needed first to fight off those omnipresent intelligence agencies that opposed and were trying to stifle him.

At four in the morning, he heard the usual rustling noise, like skittering rats or sneaky thieves. It was time for his wife to get up. Most nights she and Junjun went to bed right after the eight-o'clock drama episode. Just after four in the morning, but no later than daybreak, he and his wife, like a changing of the guard, would pass one another in the hallway by the dining room without turning on a light, uttering a single word, or touching. He never learned what his wife did after he went to bed. It was too early for the market to open; he didn't know if she was even in the house, and he didn't think he ought to find out, any more than he should know how his wife and son had gotten through those thirty years. He had lived every minute over the past two years making sure that no one's life would be inconvenienced or changed by his sudden reappearance.

He seldom slept more than four hours a night, but they were restful, dreamless hours.

This meant he woke up without having to struggle out of fitful, perplexing dreams. A bibbed Junjun would be standing at the foot of his bed, after finishing his breakfast, shaking his grandfather's legs as hard as he could, the worried look on his face abruptly replaced by a smile when he saw that his grandfather was awake. Maybe even a six-year-old would be scared by impermanence and death, when he could not rouse the slumbering, gaunt old man.

It was already the third year since he'd begun taking Junjun to day care.

At first, to give the agent following him the slip, he took a different route every day, though there was only limited variation in the twenty-minute walks. Eventually, it became routine: Route A on Mondays; Route B on Tuesdays; through the C construction site on Wednesdays; past the D old market (a peddler of goldfish showed up on the same day each week) on Thursdays; and especially on Fridays, because at one intersection there was an underpass that had yet to be completed after two years, a vegetable garden being converted into a seven-story apartment building with an elevator, and an alley closed off by someone to open a scooter repair shop, all of which ate up half his walkable space.

At first, his attention was divided as he cajoled Junjun, who cried and resisted going to the school. With the boy in his arms, he kept looking around, like a refugee, concerned that the child's wails would bring back the secret agent he'd possibly just dodged. One time, anxiety made him misjudge the distance when jumping over a manure pit in a vegetable garden, and he'd landed in a clump of weeds. His sudden move had so frightened Junjun that he abruptly stopped crying, while he was dazed by a powerful familiar smell, assailed by a toxic odor from the foliage he'd crushed. Entranced, he was unable to move for a long time; curiosity drove him to contemplate: small, unripe star fruits rotting on the ground; light green eucalyptus juice; Chinese juniper trees doomed to be frequently trimmed into spires; grass flattened by angry feet; a pond abloom with Indian lotus; his youngest sister and a neighbor girl looking up with their invitations, unconcerned about rejection, to a meal of Japanese catnip plated on a red roof tile, rice made of betel nut tassels, chicken legs fashioned out of woven bamboo leaves, a miso soup of slushy yellow mud, and rice noodles from viscous spider lily leaves, followed by a post-meal fruit platter of unripe longans, bright red berries from orange jasmine, black and white seeds of canna lilies, semi-transparent sap scraped off a peach tree (covered in prints of fingers forcefully rolling them into round balls), and sweet, dark berries of black nightshades (the only real, edible item), salt and sugar from fine dirt outside an anthill in two empty bottles stolen out of Father's clinic, as well as a bottle of soy sauce that looked real, likely snatched from the kitchen ...

He walked on, not stopping by the girls, keenly aware of the powerful scent from tormented plants pleading for help. More often, however, he lay on the second-floor tatami mat, which the sunlight could reach, to read sheet music. If he turned his head to the side, he could easily spot his father on the eucalyptus trees, where the older man, having acquired many Japanese habits, mimicked their annual custom of trimming a fir to a straight shape. Almost angered by the unruly, stubborn growth of the subtropical vegetation, his father spent nearly all the spare time from his disciplined daily routine on constantly snipping and lopping the thirty-some eucalyptus trees outside their fence, as if in a fit of pique. He accepted no help and forbade his wife from standing at the bottom of a ladder, looking up with a beseeching face and reminding him he was already in his late forties, pushing fifty.

At the time, he turned over on the tatami to let the sun warm his bare calves. He heaved a contented sigh. Lenin said: "We are bourgeois windbags ..."

The betel nut tree that had grown to the height of his window had just stopped flowering and, baked by the sun, gave off a warm fragrance, seeming to form a concrete web of smell from a whole variety of plants that had just been trimmed. Surrounded by the smell, he looked at his father, up in a tree like a monkey, holding onto a branch with one hand, a saw in the other. The revolutionary axe can chop down trees, so why use it to trim branches? He still recalled how he was violently shaken and excited by the phrase.

On this day he and Junjun chose a major thoroughfare for no other reason than that a new convenience store at the corner was promoting interesting new items with daily price reductions. Junjun would put up a fight going to school if he didn't let him go in and look around.

He would go into the rip-off store only when he had to pay for something, but he softened his attitude for Junjun's sake, muttering "damned capitalists." Not until several days later did he recognize the gray-haired man in the reflection of a window as himself, looking like

Long, Long Ago There was an Urashima Taro 23

a scarecrow in his baggy clothes. He was quite willing to dress more nicely and neatly, like everyone else out on the street, at least to avoid drawing attention, particularly the secret agents who had a tail on him. But there was a problem. He'd wanted to take over his son's old clothes, but the narrow shirt collars and pleated pants with baggy legs were, as he recalled, outfits worn by people of his own father's generation. For a while he thought he was at most in his thirties and Junjun was his son, so he needed to keep reminding himself and tried hard to adjust his emotions, never truly grasping how the feelings between a grandfather and grandson and a father and son were different, nor did he understand his relationship with the retired grade-school teacher with whom he lived and whom he had loved and desired when she was his young wife.

One day not long after his return, he walked back and forth at a busy intersection all afternoon, unable to cross the street, not out of fear of the heavy cross traffic (in fact, when he was young, the traffic in town was as chaotic as street scenes you saw in movies set in India and Africa), but because he had yet to find a kind of order, a consistency—something basic belonging to residents of the city who were willing to follow and make sure others did the same—to take part in.

He had walked the thoroughfare several days in a row, and, possibly because of the busy pedestrian or car traffic he could not make out a single secret agent, which gave him a helpless feeling. Regimes had changed, but not the order to keep him under surveillance. During a phone conversation with Huili, his kid sister, who had also been to college, he told her to be careful with what she said when he detected static on the line, knowing someone was listening in.

Huili replied unsympathetically, "Give me a break. Why would they spy on you? There must be a million Taiwanese ahead of you. What age are you living in, do you even know?"

That's what worried him; what age was it? Their surveillance and entrapment techniques had become impossible to detect and harder to fight against. Like, for instance, the big problem he was facing at the moment—he just learned that there was an issue with the school district for Junjun, who would be entering grade school when summer was over. He'd visited the Household Registration Office three times and was positive that the secret agencies were already involved. So, he went to the local police station to lodge a complaint (the same office in which he discovered that everyone in the station had already been bought off) and was told that his current address was invalid. His wife, who had insisted on accompanying him, forced a smile on her face and reminded him of several things in a soft voice, including the fact that in order to elude the secret agents, he had changed his address several times, the last one being the Chung-li home of his son (Junjun's father), who was a wholesaler of boxed meals.

What he hated most was the gentle, tender smile that his haggard, normally indifferent wife gave him, like she was placating a madman, but he decided not to make a stink over it and turned to go home, to her great surprise.

Now they were targeting Junjun!

From early on, Junjun appeared to be smarter than his brother, which was why his parents were willing to let him stay in Taipei and attend the best school in a top school district, while his older grandson, Xiaowei, stayed with his parents in Chung-li to attend an ordinary school.

He'd grown old without accomplishing a thing in life and was now older than his father had been when he saw him up on the tree from where he lay on the tatami. But he was in good shape physically, despite being quite thin. He'd been thin as a boy, and he'd done physical labor all year round on that island and trained daily for the annual long-distance swimming and running competitions. He believed he would be in better shape than his son, with his modern diseases. He had secretly watched his wife like a teenager with raging hormones, aroused as he quietly followed her while she busied herself around the house. But a few days later, in his exhaustion he discovered that she was older than the mother he remembered, and this cost him his sense of reality.

Long, Long Ago There was an Urashima Taro

As someone who read only political news in the paper, he found to his amazement that the names of prominent figures were the same as back when he went away, as if it were a lifetime ago. None had died, none had aged, the only difference being the appearance of unfamiliar relatives and the disappearance of some of the familiar ones he'd missed. So, except for harassment by the secret agents, he had no reason to complain about the thirty years, because, after he'd left, the world outside somehow seemed to have pressed the pause button, no one faring any better than the other.

Letter of explanation, question, and dissent (plus denunciation) 79 No. 16

> Li Jiazheng is a freelance translator of Japanese who sometimes spends nights away from home (at his son's registered address in Chung-li); if such a situation is considered as a non-registered domicile, according to the principle of the law, then Liu Guozhao and Zhu Gaozheng, who also live in non-registered domiciles, should not be running for the legislature. At any rate, the couple Lü Jinxing and Chen Guizhu (my neighborhood chief and an intelligence agent) conspired to slander "Li Jiazheng as a fugitive, an arsonist, and a wanted man ..." Are these to be considered facts!? Additional questions and dissent as follows:
>
> Q 1. Li Jiazheng has his domicile registered at a property belonging to his son (located at number X X on X X Road in Chung-li, Taoyuan County). Li's wife, Qiu Yulan, and Li's grandson, Li Zongjun have their domicile registered in a house under her name (located on X X floor X X Lane on X X Road in Guting District, Taipei City). But the clerk at the Household Registration Office said, "The rules regarding school districts require husband and wife to be registered at the same address." I would like to know the basis of such a rule. I would consider such a claim an abuse of authority or dereliction of duty.
>
> Q 2. Is there any proof that Li Jiazheng never resided in the house under his wife's name? They have intentionally decided not to check when I am home.

Q 3. If they managed to determine that Li does not reside at this domicile, why did they fail to discover that Li's mail, as well as other personal and official correspondence, were seized illegally, that his motor scooter was vandalized, that this particular neighborhood has many invalid household registrations and illegal structures that occupy construction sites?

Q 4. After midnight on January 19 of this year, two men, one riding a woman's motorbike (plate number 86-6641) and the other a white scooter, brought Lü Jinxing and Chen Guizhu home. If Li does not live at this address, how could he have spotted them? Moreover, how could Li's wife know when and where to verify their household registration?

Q 5. Can the so-called "division of responsibilities" authorize personnel at the household registration office and police station to claim similar powers of a judge and let them enforce the rules without recourse (and refuse Li family's verification request or conduct periodic verifications and forbid the village chief from issuing identity cards)?

June 16, Republican Year 79

Li Jiazheng, Dissenter (denunciation filer)

This was the letter he'd been sending repeatedly to anywhere he could think of, but which seemingly never reached anyone, as he'd tried all possible delivery methods to every government office and person he assumed had not yet been infiltrated or compromised by the secret service (including newspaper reporters and writers, one of whom he reminded that literature was a sacred and responsible public service).

But he never received a single reply, except from the city councilman, which actually seemed suspicious. He racked his brains over the anomaly and finally determined that the councilman might want to recruit him for his campaign four years later. He'd seen how it worked once, during the major election at the end of the previous year. On the podium was his old schoolmate, who was so easy to spot, with his indeterminate age, outdated clothes he'd taken pains to keep clean, and his faltering speech, wishing he could be invisible ... Li nearly teared up when he saw the old friend and told himself that, under no circumstances, absolutely no way would he let himself be a monkey or a recently unearthed relic to be put on display, no matter what party or faction, even if they could restore justice for him.

He was carrying the letter he'd copied. Inattentively, but with unusual patience, he waited for Junjun to pick out the snack he wanted. They conducted their English lesson as they walked. His grandson was attending a bilingual kindergarten and was not only fluent enough to conduct daily conversation but also had a large vocabulary.

Just now the boy was reading a word on the packaging. "What's A-N-T-I-O-X-I-D-A-N-T?"

It was some kind of chemical that was anti something. He didn't want to mouth off an answer to the boy and managed to stop himself from telling Junjun that he didn't need to know the word, for he'd likely never use it in his whole life. He liked to teach the boy the most important matters when Junjun was highly focused, as he was constantly amazed by how children's fresh, supple minds can instantly commit something to memory. He taught his grandson P-E-O-P-L-E, people, in his view, a most beautiful word. Another word was GORKY, and he was nearly trembling as he told the boy a little bit about Mr. Gorky, while struggling to withstand the ever-powerful impact from a name that had emerged toward the end of the nineteenth century.

He was silent for a long time, unable to continue his instruction. He did not want to make decisions for the boy or tell him which word was useful and which he would never use—the future belonged to the boy —antioxidant or Mr. Gorky.

Good day, Mr. Gorky.

There was a time when, like countless Russian youths at the dawn of the twentieth century, he'd eagerly read Gorky's works and was a devoted follower of his actions and ideals. Li had been born on the same day as Chekhov and had grown up in a similarly cheerless, insipid small town, but his background was more like that of Pushkin, the son of an aristocratic landowner. This was why he believed he had to make more sacrifices than any of his peers, and, in an almost sadistic way (in Old Cai's words), to serve the people and learn from the people, for only the people, PEOPLE, were kind, forbearing, and genuinely wise. Contrastively, he himself got to enjoy the social status and wealth that his background and education accorded him, without even trying, which shamed him so much that he did his absolute best to divorce himself from the class from which he emerged.

He'd promised the tenant farmers in the mountains that the day he got his inheritance, he would immediately hand them his land, with no strings attached, except that they must continue to till it and not sell their parcels to anyone who could afford to buy it from them and thus create another landowner. He had made this perfectly clear to them.

Even now he recalled every one of their faces. In those days he'd come to know the faces well—weathered, time-worn, and lined with wisdom, like the Tsar's serfs. Without exception, they had shown no reaction to what he had just said. He was not surprised or disappointed because he'd rehearsed the same scene many times in his head. When Nekhlyudov, the protagonist in Tolstoy's *Resurrection*, announced he'd distribute the land to serfs, they not only did not appreciate his offer but actually flew into a rage, believing that the landowner was plotting something odious to extort more money from them, just in a different way.

At least he wasn't subjected to the kind of suspicion and resistance that confronted Nekhlyudov from these expressionless, silent people under the moonlight. On the drying ground, the cicadas sang from dawn to dusk, forming a silence of its own, while the towering acacia trees around them were tossed this way and that way by the wind. Unable to see the trees clearly, he had the feeling that he was on a farm estate surrounded by white poplar, walnut, and fir trees in early summer, when nightingales sang in the trees and the air was permeated with the fragrance of lilacs, apple flowers, and pine sap ... Naturally, all he could detect was the rancid, sour smell of drying white radishes and pig swill that Sister Ah-fang was cooking on a large stove.

He tried to get them to talk. "In my view, the land should not be bought or sold; otherwise, those with land could make all kind of demands on those without it. So, I want to apologize, on my father's behalf, for having so much land and so many trees. But it's an existing reality, so let us come up with a solution together." He spoke slowly, for it was tough saying all this in Taiwanese.

But he elicited no reactions from them, except to stop a temporary worker, who sat off to the side, from playing his homemade instrument. So, Li had to offer the conclusion he'd prepared, "Therefore, I don't wish to own the land. For now, we can discuss how to divide it up when the time comes."

An old man who could have been from a distant grand uncle's wife's family laughed toothlessly, out of embarrassment, despite himself, and said, "We'll just divide it equally among us, Bao *san*."

Everyone here—man, woman, young and old—addressed him in Japanese and called him Bao *san*. The old man was just humoring him, but it did not deviate much from the book, which made it easy for Li to present a rebuttal that he'd formulated in advance, "If we're to divide it up equally, then those who don't work the land would get a share, is that what you're saying? What about Uncle Ah-li's oldest son, who's a business student at a junior college in Taichung, or Ah-yi, who works in the township office, or Sister Fangxing, who will be married off to Tainan in December? If they all sell their share, then those with money will once again control those who need land."

"Ah, *so desu ne*." So that's what it is, someone finally exclaimed gravelly.

His spirits lifted, he continued with a firm voice, "Therefore, only those who work the land get a share, those who don't get nothing. This is a rule we have to establish now."

Oddly, however, they had nothing to say, except for Ah-huo, Ah-yi's adopted son, who smiled and said, "That's good. That's very good."

Every ten days or two weeks in the summer, Ah-huo would come to the Li house around dusk with a load on a bamboo pole. He always refused to use the main entrance but walked through the side door under a persimmon tree, and never stepped beyond the kitchen, no matter how long he stayed.

Every night after his visit, a large plate of frogs stir-fried with Japanese catnip, river snails, or fried carp tempura would appear on the dining table. Not much grew in the mountainous land, some acacia for charcoal or lemon grass for export to Japan, which was why he found no good circumstance to teach them Henry George's idea of land value tax—his family owned no fertile land to make the distinction worth noting. For the time being, he could not emulate Nekhlyudov, who had no trouble promoting the idea of a farming commune to the serfs. These people, who worked for the Li family, were not as poverty-stricken as the Tsar's serfs, and their tools and production methods were quite primitive and varied, differing with each individual in ways not entirely clear to him. Likewise, he wasn't quite sure about his father's relationship with these tenant farmers or how they paid for their tenancy. To be sure, the way they dealt with his father told him that his father had not been a harsh landowner, but that was hard for him to determine, for their courteous and cordial interactions with his father could have simply been out of necessity, typical of servants and the ruling class. His father might well have been generous and kind, unlike other landowners, but he was still in a dominant position guaranteed by the system.

More often than not, he found himself unconsciously avoiding learning more details, for he also realized that full understanding could lead to wholesale forgiveness and the loss of force.

At moments like that, he worried that an old man or woman might strain to change the subject and say with a smile, "Your little boy must be real cute now, Bao *san*."

He did not know enough to say anything about how cute the little boy was. Besides, he did not like the way they showed concern about his son, as the future heir, so he said, "He's almost three now." Then a quick-witted one would follow up, "Sweet at three, dumb at four, stubborn at five, give him a good spanking at six." Or, "Mr. Li must dote on him. The oldest grandson is always like the youngest son."

Everyone would then relax and laugh, or talk among themselves, as if the baby was a topic closer to them than the previous one.

When that happened, all he could assume was that the land did not belong to him yet, and, naturally, they could not give serious consideration to something that hadn't yet happened.

Still, those were delightful, fulfilling days, more within reach and distinct to the present than anything that happened before and after.

He went only during summer and winter breaks at first. Later, after realizing what he could accomplish, he went whenever he could find time, so long as he managed to satisfy his father, who asked him why he'd returned from his college in Taipei again.

Oftentimes, when he walked down paths he knew like the back of his hand—he had to take a rickety public bus to its terminus and cross the Niubei Stream, whose waters overflowed the wooden bridge whenever it rained, followed by an hour and a half of fast walking that would require double the time if he took it slow—he was usually infused with tranquility and joy. Devoid of human inhabitation, the area had soaring acacias and other assorted trees, yellow dirt paths under his feet that were as hard as if they were paved with concrete, and fallen leaves that emitted a crisp fragrance. Cassava, unknown vines, and seasonal wild flowers mushroomed in empty spots among trees. He recalled, in particular, when purple sunset hibiscus and strings of white, plump shell ginger emitted a pungent smell under the hot sun, an indication that the Dragon Boat Festival was just around the corner and that snakes would begin to emerge.

He would be approaching the wooden bridge by the stream when he finished humming the entire *Pastoral Symphony*. Under the bridge were several large, smooth rocks that had turned alkali white by women washing clothes. Normally, he stood on the bridge for a few moments, though not long enough to distinguish fallen bamboo leaves from fish.

After crossing the bridge, he'd begin to see bamboo groves or white flowers from golden dewdrops, two common fence materials for the residents, along with hibiscus. At this point of his journey, the serene pleasure from the *Pastoral Symphony* would have faded completely and he would sing a rousing song that seemed to be playing:

> Everyone, be united in mind and struggle to herald the dawn. We do not fear death. [spoken] Do not try to frighten us with death. We refuse to be conquered slaves! We want to be the masters of China. Let us form an iron Great Wall and drive out all the bandits. Let us form an iron Great Wall as we march onward down the road to freedom.

He favored Nie Er's music and Tian Han's lyrics, which formed a cheerful, spirited perfect union, one that was easy to teach. Sometimes, halfway through his singing, he would hear someone echoing him from beyond a vegetation fence. He was surprised now and then to discover it was someone's wife spreading medicinal herbs on the drying ground or chopping vegetables for pig's feed, or Uncle So-and-so or a young man fixing tools or taking a nap. In any case, they were all working people, his people.

He once told them that the song came from an opera called *Storm Over the Yang-tze* before telling them the story. He taught them to sing another song from the same opera, *Song of the Dock Workers*: "Sweating all day, shedding blood all day, they built multistory houses on our sweat and blood"... Actually, like them, he never saw the opera, which he'd learned about from his high-school math teacher. The first time he read Gorky's *Mother* was on mimeographed copies made by the same teacher, who had to distribute them to his students in installments.

The math teacher did not come back, not unexpectedly, when he was in his third year in high school, which instantly dispersed members of his volleyball team/study group. Some took the opportunity to stop all activities unrelated to the college entrance exam, while others, like him, were overcome by sadness, like baby animals losing their mothers, left with no choice but to fend for themselves and quietly grow bigger and stronger.

On the drying ground in the evening, he would continue to read out loud Gorky's *Mother* and "The Song of the Stormy Petrel," as well as some short stories. His Chinese copy of the novel, published by Wenxue Liancongshe in 1946, was heavy and soggy from constant handling. The locals, who never had enough rest, seemed to look forward to the evening diversion. One afternoon, he ran into Aunt Ah-nian, who was on her way back from picking wild monk fruit in the mountains. Shyly, she mustered enough courage to ask, "Will Shuya die at the end?"

As they walked the rest of the path together, he eagerly explained to her: "Life and death aren't all that important, since the bodies will perish one day. It's more meaningful if the spirit can continue and contribute to the improvement project of human history."

They were still engaged in a discussion when they sat down on a fallen tree trunk to rest. Aunt Ah-nian showed him how to open the monk fruit, which the locals called cow eggs, with bare hands. As they shared the fruit, they talked about Shuya's life, as if she were a relative of theirs. In his considerable effort to shorten the distance between the old Russia and the locals, he translated Sophia, a common Russian girl's name, as Shuya, and Tanya as Danniang, instantly making them familiar women from the countryside.

He'd never forget the momentary silence each time he finished reading for the night. Several women would make a rustling noise as they dried their eyes, while a few bold men would be overcome by their emotions and make simple comments, some on the right track, while others not quite, some within his expectations, while others surprised him. But most of the time he was tearing up himself, as if he had been living back then, a half century earlier, a time he had learned so much about from books but was forever beyond his reach.

To be sure, he was cautious enough to wait until he was alone facing a vast, open field before singing at the top of his voice, his fists clenched, "Chives bloom to show a single heart/Shear the long hair to join the Red Army." Oddly, his stirring singing voice was easily drowned out by the seemingly placid water flowing over rocks. He had to raise his voice even higher and switch to one the math teacher taught them: "Rise up! Anyone who refuses to be a slave. Use our flesh and blood to build our new great wall," or sing the graduation song taught by the same teacher, for whom he and other students did not have a chance to sing. It was also written by Tian Han and composed by Nie Er:

> All of you, students, rise up
> and shoulder the responsibility for our nation's future.
> Listen. The masses are sighing sadly over and over.
> Look. The country is losing territory year after year.
> Do we choose war or surrender?
> We must be our own masters and die on a battlefield,
> and not be slaves even if it means we could soar into the sky.
> Today we are graduating, tomorrow we will be the pillars of
>   society.
> Today we are singing together, tomorrow we will raise the swell
> of national
>   salvation.
> Swells! Swells! Grow ever bigger.
> All of you, students.
> Everyone, show your strength and shoulder the responsibility

for the world's future.

Today we are singing together; tomorrow we will raise the swell of national salvation. The invigorating melody along with the lyrics raised goose bumps on his arms even now.

He told Old Cai about the upcoming meeting with his college friend, Professor Huang Xinrong. He planned to use the opportunity not only to air his complaint about the harassment and abuse at the hands of the secret service over the past two years but also to make some meaningful suggestions.

"You know he's carved out a bit of media territory in recent years and publishes essays all the time." He told Cai about Huang, who, after getting several letters of complaint and petitions on various matters, finally asked to meet with him for coffee one day.

"Then you should have a shave and a haircut." Cai listened to his litany with a smile while carrying on with his work, as usual. It was hard to know his real views and reactions.

Cai had been released a few years before him, after which he set up a stand at a corner of a busy street to sell fried flatbreads the year round. He made only three types, green onion, shredded radish, and red bean paste. He did everything himself, from preparing the dough and the fillings, to making and frying the flatbreads. Only when necessary did Li jump in to help by giving change and bagging the cakes. He kept making mistakes, messing up the types or quantity, or taking a long time as he did the math in his head. In any case, there was always something.

Cai's business was good, often selling out before the day was over. He was happy to close up and take a rest. Li never tried the product, so he couldn't say if they were any good, but the same items on the stand in the next lane cost twice as much, which could be the main reason for Cai's success.

After Cai closed up, the two of them would sit in the tattered rattan chairs to chat. They never had to put the chairs away, as no one seemed to want them.

Cai was reading the paper that day after the busy lunch hour, when Li took out the letter he wanted his friend to mail for him and read it aloud. Once his reading was interrupted by a young man in jeans with a crew cut coming to buy flatbreads. As usual, the man bought one of each flavor, with a fried egg added to the green onion cake.

Watching the young man walk off, Li said to Cai angrily, "I wish I could lace his with something." He was convinced that the man was on the secret service's mid-day shift to monitor him. He could smell it on the young man, whose army shirt reeked of sweat and mildew that could never be washed off, of a sour, stale smell from canteen breakfasts, and a strong, acrid odor from rifle-cleaning oil. But the one best at concealing his identity was the old man under a nearby building passage (according to Cai), who had started out selling lottery tickets, then switched to chewing gum and betel nuts before settling on fighting fish, Brazilian turtles, and hamsters. The vendor had watched Cai patiently for three years. Strangely, however, business was good for the old man and he didn't get lazy and turn to begging.

He'd thought of bringing the old man over to their side but couldn't come up with persuasive reasons, so he decided to hold off and waged a contest to see which of them survived the other. The man looked to be at least a decade older than him, so he was sure he'd retire in two or three years, if he lived that long.

"So, what do you think?" Li asked, after he finished reading, afraid he might have left something out, and looked at Cai expectantly.

Putting down his newspaper, Cai stirred the filling quite unnecessarily, looking at the basins with such caring tenderness in his eyes that their contents might as well be alive.

"Let it go." Cai paused, but then said, "But I'll post it for you."

He was baffled. An alarm went off in his body-wide security system and sent him into high alert.

Sensing his reaction, Cai glanced at him and said in a quivering voice, "Bao *san*." He didn't know why that term of address had dogged him all his life, but he shook when the Japanese meaning of the term suddenly dawned on him.

"You're getting old, Bao *san*."

He was frightened, panicking even, as his eyes darted frantically all around. He didn't feel like talking to Cai anymore.

From somewhere came the sound of music, too far for him to hear the melody, just the drums. But a commotion broke out on the street, where pedestrians and vehicles scattered anxiously, inconsolably, and aimlessly, like a river sweeping sand and pebbles along after a storm. He grew fearful.

"Don't worry." Cai tugged on his sleeve. "It's just a demonstration. I read about it in the paper."

He helped Cai move the stand farther into the lane to park it outside a laundry. As if worried that his stand would affect the laundry business, Cai immediately apologized to the owner with an explanation. In fact, he had good relations with the shop owners in the area. One or two of them, noticing Cai's fine business, once offered him a spot, but he politely turned them down with a reply that might or might not have been serious: "I would never do anything that would require me to pay taxes."

"Did you hear that?" Cai asked him in Japanese with a smile, no longer concerned about his panicky reaction.

"What's that all about?" He also replied in Japanese, in a disapproving tone, though he was smiling too. He heard it. The demonstrators' vehicle was playing a rousing march of the Japanese navy, which sounded familiar, without eliciting any anger or nostalgia.

Enjoying a quiet moment in the commotion, they sat back down in the chairs. Now and then one of them got up to take care of a customer with a white band tied around his head. Li tried to discern what was written in ink on the head bands and the banner they'd stretched across the street, but he was unable to identify the demonstrators or the target of their protest. A great sense of bewilderment overtook him, because back in his time, the enemy was clear and familiar, such as the Younger Chiang, whom they called Chiang *chan* [Little Chiang], as if he'd been an impish, troublemaker from the younger generation in their own clan.

But now there were no familiar clan members, nor friends or neighbors (despite his battle with the special agent couple, Lü Jinxing and Chen Guizhu, he still could not figure out which faction they belonged to. He used to be able, from the way his interrogator tried to direct his confession, to tell if the man was from the Bureau of Investigation and Statistics, the Central Bureau of Investigation and Statistics, the Bureau of Investigation, or the Garrison Command).

In the blistering heat, he stopped paying attention to the angry, baffling slogans that flowed out, like stagnant marshy water, with the demonstrators and their vehicles under the melaleuca trees whose leaves were tossed by the hot June wind to show their silvery green backside.

He discovered he was spellbindingly lonely.

"Lonely," Cai said emotionally in Japanese. So lonely.

He worked up enough courage to splinter the chaotic cheerlessness and told Cai about a newly invented food therapy for bone chills. On the island, they'd all contracted some minor heath issues, and their monotonous daily routine in isolation magnified the illness to such an extent that the fear changed their views on life. Everyone was so focused on caring for themselves; they had become skillful doctors and passively antiwar.

The demonstrators were gone by the time he finished telling Cai about the nine-part food treatment. Without meaning to, they fell into the trap of nostalgia, as if it were an afternoon fever, but neither tried to fight it off. In fact, they welcomed it privately, which was why they reviewed it every once in a while, concerned that their pasts would be buried in oblivion and their memories would corrode.

Confronted with the passing of time, they turned docile and understanding, and also somewhat listless.

By the lane entrance, children were slowly coming out to play, laughing and shouting. The old man under the walkway not only did not close up for the day, of course, but was actually doing a rousing business. He was showing a customer how to feed and raise fighting fish and quail, while at the time keeping up his surveillance with such skill that he didn't even have to look their way. Cai was also getting more customers. As he wondered why there were so many hungry people, Cai reminded him, "School is out for your Gaoshan. Don't make him wait."

Cai continued to believe that Junjun was called Gaoshan. Back on the island, Li had been one of the few married men. Several months before his oldest grandson, Xiaowei, was born, in every letter home he talked eagerly about naming the boy, an anachronistic expression of a new father's joy that came some thirty years late.

In the end, he decided on Gaozhen. He didn't tell anyone about Gao [from Gorky], except to say he wanted the boy to grow tall [gao], with soaring [gao] aspirations. He chose Zhen, because in life one must try every possible way to pursue the state of *zhen, shan, mei*—truth, good, beauty. The baby would be called Gaomei, if it were a girl.

The name seemed increasingly perfect, more profoundly meaningful, the longer he considered it. So in his subsequent letters, with word limits, he kept expanding on the various connotations of zhen, shan, and mei, giving his explication from philosophical, historical, artistic, even religious perspectives. Cai was already talking about Gaozhen before the baby was born. Then, whenever he got a letter from home, Cai would ask him about the celebration of Gaozhen's first month, about the baby teething, walking, about the three stitches in his head after a fall, about the little sister he'd soon have... they were more interested in lifeforms than anything else.

After turning three, Gaozhen got a little brother, Gaoshan—Junjun, that is.

Cai never got it.

They had a family reunion on the day he was released, and he was immediately treated to the surprise discovery that Gaozhen was called Li Zongwei and Gaoshan was Li Zongjun. With great difficulty, he forced back the names he'd been using for the past six years or so, while wondering why no one in the family had ever said a word about the names to him. He couldn't ask them why they hadn't followed his instructions either. Recalling the dozens of eloquent letters about names, each brimming with his feelings, he had to question why they had ignored his intentions altogether. He began to doubt if they'd read the letters, or if they'd even received them. They were simple, obvious letters to home, so there was no reason to confiscate them.

But soon he saw more and more instances of his family going against his wishes. For example, to his great surprise, his wife owned three houses. He recalled writing urgent letters to stop her from buying a house more than a decade earlier, when she'd mentioned her plan. He'd offered his reasons, concerned that he would unwittingly become a landowner again, even before giving the forest land to the locals.

Another case in point: He'd written repeatedly to tell his son, who was in middle school at the time, to study agriculture or engineering and to never ever go into law or politics. After his release, he was stunned to learn that his son had studied law in college. He had been a small business owner following graduation, but Li was convinced that at a critical moment his son's record of law studies would mean negative repercussions for his grandson. Yet he could not recall whether his son had intentionally kept this a secret. His son might not have because there were no shared topics in letters to and from home, as if they were on a parallel trajectory. In his letters, he instructed his family on ways of living an upright life, but their letters to him showed no signs of his influence as they went about doing whatever they wanted. He had no idea what they were always clamoring about. His sister, Huili, was another example. She had followed his lead in high school by reading a great many translated novels and seemed to be going along with his wishes. Yet in recent years, her phone calls to him were reduced to complaining about her husband, "those Mainlanders," and so on. Huili had suffered a lot when dating her future husband because their parents had objected due to his being a Mainlander. For three years, he did his best to comfort her in every letter and gave her all the advice he could think of (he couldn't remember if he'd told her that romance was important or if he'd said it was utterly insignificant, but he was sure he'd probably sounded too high-minded). Each time Huili complained, he had to stop himself from saying, "Didn't I tell you in my letters ..."

He really didn't want to settle old scores with his family now that everything had changed after so many years. Besides the fact that he didn't want to bother or offend them, he never looked into why they had ignored his views in all matters big and small, even his existence, because he realized that time can wear things down and fissures can develop, until a great many things, important or not, fall through the cracks and become impossible to retrieve.

It was too soon for him to determine whether his discovery was good or bad, whether for them it was a blessing or quite the opposite.

The year before, when he returned to the mountains alone, he strained to keep calm. Nothing much had changed, except that the wooden bridge over the Niubei Stream had been replaced by one made of concrete (even it looked old, the same color as the riverbed rocks, with an inscription at the bridgehead showing it had been completed in 1960). Along the riverbank, the sun baked the water buffalo droppings into a pleasing smell, which quickly called up memories of his long and insipid younger days, reminiscent of a lone rooster crowing in the afternoon.

The same, hard, yellow dirt path ran through the acacia forest, but Beethoven's *Pastoral Symphony* no longer played in his head. Without intending to, he began to sing in Japanese, "Missing home after spending too much time away, quickly saying goodbye to friends to go home, my heart fills with happiness and longing on the way, (I wish I could open) the treasure case from the Dragon Girl."

For the first time, he wondered why that had such a pleasant, compelling melody because what followed was, "Everything had changed when I got home. The old house and the village had vanished, and not a single face on passersby looked familiar." When he was young, his mother had told him only three stories, repeatedly: Momo Taro, the Crane Wife, and Urashima Taro. The last one scared him. When she got to the point where Urashima Taro was having a good time with the princess in the Dragon Palace, savoring delicacies from all over, and seeing untold numbers of rare treasures while the days passed like a dream, he would panic, wanting his mother to stop. "Taro was forlorn and sad, wracked by regret over opening the treasure box, for smoke rose up and he immediately turned into a gray-haired old man."

Once she told the story before turning on a light, and he bawled when she finished.

He gazed at the wild hibiscus and shell ginger blooming quietly on the path, as if in a dream. The sun turned to moonlight in his dreamy state, while he stood silently, unsmiling, trying to subdue his memories in a distracted frame of mind, so he would no longer fear the confusion brought on by the song. No, that wasn't true. Nothing around here had changed. The village with his ancestral home, he was certain, was located in the bamboo grove behind the golden dew fence up ahead. As for the passerby, it was none other than Sister Ah-fang, who was walking his way, effortlessly holding a bulging hemp sack in one hand. Happy tears welled up in his eyes while he waited for her to draw closer before greeting her softly, as if afraid of shattering the dreamy state, "Sister Ah-fang."

Showing no sign of aging, she gave him a shy but curious smile. "I'm Fengmei. Ah-fang is my mother."

Like a sleepwalker, he went deeper into the mountain behind Fengmei, after taking her sack from her, as etiquette required. It sure was light. He asked what was in the sack, and she told him it was filled with cicada shells, which were abundant on acacia trunks at that time of year. The locals gathered the shells to sell to the herbal shop down below, Fengmei explained bashfully, but she never asked who he was. A cool breeze typical before a summer thunderstorm blew over, and tiny, fuzzy acacia flowers the color of goose webbing drifted off acacia trees. It looked like rain.

The familiar but aging faces recognized him right away and called out, "Bao *san*."

A young, familiar face turned to him with a somewhat apologetic smile for not knowing who he was. He couldn't tell where the temporal fissure occurred. A woman was chopping greens for pig food on the edge of the drying ground, and a man was mending bird netting. Sipping the cool sickle pod tea they brewed for him, he noticed that the cup he held steadily in his hand was ugly but new. It was not chipped and had no tea stains, but there was an inscription: "Gift from the County Government on Teacher's Day, 1966." He did not see many chickens or ducks around, but he kept stepping on goat droppings. Brother Ah-yi, no, Brother Ah-yi's son explained that they had more than two hundred goats, which fetched a good price down below, where mutton hotpot was a popular winter dish.

Accepting their invitation, he walked into the main room, which was cool and dark in the middle of the day, and he wouldn't get in the way of the boys doing stunts in the heat and dust on their cross-country motorcycles.

Inside, a young man, clearly on leave from his military service, and an old man were watching a video of a Japanese prankster game show. They were too busy laughing to greet him. He didn't recognize the old man, but the man beside him hurriedly told the old man who he was. After learning he was Mr. Li's oldest son, the old man quickly expressed his gratitude to old Mr. Li for giving them the land without compensation before he died. But then he followed it with a complaint that the forest land was worthless, and they wouldn't have been able to pay the taxes if they hadn't started raising goats. The others tried to stop him, so flustered they looked about to burst into tears, and hurried to offer him cigarettes. Unable to say a thing to him, they just called him, "Bao *san*," reached out, and held his arm.

He was disappointed to see they were as resolute as ever in treating him as a landowner visiting his tenant farmers. Maybe he should be happy about their ignorance, a word that could mean good fortune or bad, but they hadn't been implicated after all.

The trip he made had no effect, neither destructive nor constructive, except he grew visibly gaunter, pale as a pubescent youth whiling away his days with fantasies. The toilet became his favorite place, not to sneak a cigarette or read pornography, to be sure, but he spent a long time in there, doing nothing, not even relieving himself.

Saying good-bye to Cai, he went to the passage and lingered by the old man. He was seriously thinking about buying a little pet for his grandson as a kindergarten graduation present, while signaling to the old man that he could knock off work now—either out of good intentions or mockery.

Imagine his surprise when the old man acted supremely normal and sold him a pair of quails the size of his thumb, at a price that was neither too steep nor too cheap (Junjun had asked for them and told him the cost). Straining to behave naturally, he paid while turning to make eye contact with Cai, who was also busy with the afternoon crowd. They quickly exchanged a look of "all clear," something that only they understood.

Long, Long Ago There was an Urashima Taro   45

Out of a strange tacit understanding, he and Cai lived diligently, not just for themselves but also for the certainty of the other's survival. He had no idea what Cai did besides tending his stand, or even where he lived. The same went for Cai about him; Cai might have his phone number, but he wasn't sure because they'd never spoken over the phone. Yet as long as they still lived in this city, they would appear before each other after an indeterminate interval so the other would know that he was still alive. Day after day, cautiously and earnestly, they showed and maintained their footprints and imprints so the other could find a way to track him down if something were to happen.

Junjun was keyed up from too much excitement that night and found an excuse to stay up, insisting that his grandfather change the quails' cage or find them a box. The old man had asked to put the birds in a clear plastic box that was meant for the fighting fish. At 70 NT a piece, the box was the size of a sugar cube container, but flatter, with a net-like cover for air holes. It was large enough for birds that size, while giving them a view of the birds eating, shitting and, later, mating and giving birth to young ones, from every angle. It seemed perfect to him, like his familiar life of many years.

He started out humoring the boy by pretending to look for a new home for the birds. His wife, like Cinderella at midnight, had gone to bed at nine. The unfamiliar house that he'd lived in for the past two years was just right for exploration.

With his grandson in tow, he opened the room next to his bedroom, where they were immediately overtaken by a new and fun game. Quietly, breathing heavily, they launched into their own search.

Li saw lots of banners and medals, whose inscriptions he had to strain to read under the harsh glare of a very bright lamp, like a warehouse flood light. They were mostly commemorative items given by graduates of this class or that class or from the school for years of educating a new generation of talents. The wall by the window with tightly drawn curtains looked forlorn, with countless black-and-white photos. Only one of them caused him to take a second look, which was how he discovered that the shadowy figure lying on the tatami wearing only underwear, holding a guitar, and raising crossed legs so high the privates were in danger of exposure was ... him. He had no recollection of having this picture taken, nor could he recall where he could have found a guitar to hold and play. He'd briefly studied the violin at one time.

Then from behind the door he found a large department store shopping bag oozing colors that he knew all too well—he had been loyal to purple ball point pens since he'd found them on sale, for the hue closely resembled a familiar, fading blue fountain pen ink. They were letters he'd written, letters he'd thought to have been intercepted; to be sure, these were only a portion of them, sent by regular mail.

How did the letters he'd asked his wife to post for him end up here? The stamps had not been franked. His legs felt wobbly, so he took a deep breath while putting up with the deafening noise of his heart beating violently against his scrawny ribs. Heaven and Earth seemed to shake until he realized it was Junjun tugging on his shirttail, "Grandpa, the phone is ringing."

He picked up the phone and said hello, but heard no reply, which, based on his experience, meant the secret service was calling to see if he was home. He was about to hang up when he heard, "Bao *san*." It was Old Cai.

He wanted to remind Cai to use their codes, no matter how urgent the matter, to keep those monitoring them in the dark. But Cai had never called him before, so he knew, even without hearing the tone of voice, that his friend was in trouble.

"Some people came to talk to me after you left. I don't know what office they work for, but they were in police uniforms. No matter what happens, you have to say you were with me that night and we talked. I didn't kill him. They said they just wanted to know if I'd seen anything or anyone suspicious, but I know they're trying to find a scapegoat and close the case."

Long, Long Ago There was an Urashima Taro   47

"Old Cai! Old Cai!" He was too focused on telling Cai to use Japanese to hear what his friend was saying.

"Bao *san*."

He spoke in Japanese to cheer up Cai and asked him who'd been killed. Cai began to choke up. "An old member of the National Assembly living in one of the apartments in the alley was killed a while ago. Don't you remember? Didn't you say you hoped it was a murder motivated by politics not robbery? You were right, Bao *san*. It has to be political. Otherwise, why would they need a scapegoat?"

"Old Cai!" He shouted to alert his friend but could not stop Cai from chattering on like a man talking in his sleep.

"I suspect it was the old man. So, we were not his targets. It was those ancient members of the National Assembly."

Then he heard nothing but passing cars honking. Cai was using a pay phone. He called out to him a few times before the mental image of his friend being dragged into a vehicle put him on alert. He quickly hung up the phone. "Please don't die, Old Cai," he muttered.

He hurried back to the room, with the intention of getting rid of the bag of unsent letters. After dragging it away, he saw behind it several unsealed boxes from fruit merchants. He randomly opened the topmost one, which advertised first-rate red flesh plums from Zhuolan, sending bits of roach droppings falling along with more letters, some opened, some still sealed. He had to puzzle over the criteria the recipient(s) used to determine which to open and which to ignore, something that struck him as especially curious, the greatest mystery in the universe. Calmly he opened a securely sealed envelope addressed in his handwriting—which had remained surprisingly unchanged over the thirty years, getting neither better nor worse—to Ah-xiang, his son's name. "Ah-xiang, it's summer break now, and I hope you won't spend your time only having fun. Your letter of two months ago said you planned to go mountain climbing with your classmates. In my view, mountain hikes are good physical exercise, but your brain is even more important. You must know that the human brain is more intricately constructed and valuable than any machine. You must take good care of it and not let useless things wear it out or allow trivial, entertaining reading to take up too much of your precious time. Otherwise, where would you put it when more important matters came up? There are many ways to study, of course. I'll give you a list in my next letter and outline steps for you to practice over the summer break. I don't need money now, but please ask your mother to send me a bottle of multivitamins as soon as possible. I already mentioned it in a previous letter. Your Father."

"Huili, did you receive my letter of July 10? Yesterday I got yours from July 22, but you did not respond to my questions or recommendations. Are you really that busy at work? Of course, I know you're dealing with lots of difficult matters, but that's what life is all about. There's a Western saying, 'Someone who's suffering has no right to be pessimistic.' I got the sense that you've become quite pessimistic and have been in low spirits over the past two years. I don't think you have the right to live like that, while your brother here has to carry thirty loads of water every day and walk three hundred meters to water the vegetables. Watching the greens grow by the day, I'm cheered by the vitality alone, not just because of the coming harvest. Please go home and spend time with Mother over the winter and summer breaks. You're married now, but that doesn't mean you have to wait for New Year's to go see her. To be honest with you, Mother has complained about you in her letters. Your husband doesn't speak Taiwanese, but he's part of the family now, so go visit Mother and Father, I'm sure they will be happy to see you both. Please write more, since you paid for the stamps already. Jiazheng."

"Ah-xiang. What age do you think you're living in? Why are there so many requirements with the wedding? I think you ought to have a good talk with your future wife. In my time we had to do it that way for the older generation's sake. I think you should have shared ideals and views on things, which will form a sturdy foundation for the life ahead.

Material extravagance and waste won't do you any good. I hope the bride will understand and comply with the family tradition I've worked hard to develop. Your Father."

"Lan, did you receive my letters of the 11th and 18th? If you haven't bought the vitamin pills yet, why don't you just send the money for it? I owe two hundred pills now. The internees never ask me for them, but it'll be bad for their health if I don't pay them back. Please tell me if you're having difficulty. Don't keep me in the dark and make me wait forever. Jiazheng."

"Ah-xiang. Your baby won't be born for another two months yet, but I'm sure you've made all the necessary preparations for the little one's arrival. I'm pleased that your mother-in-law will come from Kaohsiung to help you out during the first month. Go to your mother's mother and ask her for a type of Japanese tonic for expectant mothers. It's good for the unborn baby too, and it has no side effects. I'm the grandpa, but I can't do anything from here. I do plan to ask for a few tree saplings to plant in the vegetable plot assigned to me. Maybe someday my grandchild will have the opportunity to come visit this island with me. We could sit under these trees and enjoy the ocean breeze. Of course, I have a present for the baby, a meaningful and great-sounding name."

He slumped to the floor, regretting opening the treasure box, a gift from time. All those letters, jabbering on and on like a deranged man's ranting, so embarrassing. At that instant, the countless opened and unopened letters seemed to have swirled and turned into white smoke to rise up into the air. He did not need a mirror or a second look to know he'd become a gray-haired old man.

He wailed, like his childhood self after listening to the story on that evening long ago, before the light was turned on.

2

The Taste of Apples

Huang Chun-ming
(translated by Howard Goldblatt)

The Accident
Early one morning, as rain began to fall from thick layers of clouds, an automobile accident occurred at the intersection where the road from the eastern suburb opened into the city. A dark green sedan with a foreigner's license place crashed into a rickety old bicycle, like a wild animal pouncing on prey, crushing it on the other side of the double-yellow line. A pickaxe was still securely fastened to the bicycle rack, which protruded from under the car, but the contents of a lunch box—rice and a smashed salted egg—which had been tied to the handlebars, lay scattered alongside the safety island.

The hard-falling rain was washing away a puddle of congealed blood in front of the car, as foreign and local military police busily tried to determine exactly what happened.

The Telephone Call

"He won't be in this morning ... uh-huh ... don't worry about it. A junior secretary like me can easily handle a matter like this. Um ... huh? Now hold on a minute, listen to me. Don't forget, we're in Asia now. And the other fellow *is* a laborer ... huh? Well, is he or isn't he ... that's right, he is! So there ... we can't afford any trouble. Hmm. Let me finish. This is the most cooperative, the friendliest, and the safest country in Asia for us. Huh? Would you let me finish, please? America has no intention of getting stuck in another quagmire. Our president and our people all feel the same. Now look, let's drop the subject ... just send him there ... um. All right. I'll take full responsibility ... okay, I'll call right away ... right ... right, that's how we'll do it. Good-bye."

The Labyrinth

A young foreign-affairs policeman led a tall, heavyset foreigner to a neighborhood of tiny illegal shacks made of wooden crates and sheet metal. No clearly delineated streets or byways here—everything was laid out in capricious disorder. They made their way through the area for a while, as if meandering through a labyrinth. "Boy, what a great place for a game of hide-and-seek!" said the foreigner with a laugh as he walked behind the policeman.

"That's what I was thinking too." The policeman detected a dubious tone in the man's comment, even though he'd laughed when he said it. He wondered if the foreigner was mocking him for not being able to find Jiang Ah-fa's house, a clear dereliction of duty for a policeman. He was stung by the injustice of it all. The man was probably unaware that foreign-affairs police only assisted the local police in incidents in which foreigners were involved. He regretted bringing him here straight away instead of first checking in with the locals. Now even he had to find his way through all this confusion.

He bent down to look for numbers above one doorway after another. The foreigner was a head taller than any of the shacks, so all he could see was a mass of rooftops thrown together with sheet metal and plastic covers, held down by old tires and bricks. Some of the roofs also sported an array of wooden crates, chicken coops, and the like. When the policeman turned and saw the bewildered look on the foreigner's face as he surveyed the roof-top landscape, he said, "Their new homes are nearly finished—those apartments by the river. Once these people move over there, they'll put up a high-rise here." Pleased with himself over his quick reaction, at the same time he was uneasy about lying. If the man hadn't insisted on coming to see Jiang Ah-fa's family, he'd never have brought a foreigner to this kind of place. He was attentive to his companion's responses, but all he heard was the occasional "mm-hm" so common in American-style conversations, pregnant with ambiguities and dubious connotations, the sound a listener made to show he was paying attention. Meanwhile, his efforts to determine what was on the foreigner's mind distracted him from his painstaking search for house numbers. They had continued for several paces without exchanging a word when they met a little girl standing in the lane with a baby strapped to her back. The policeman asked her a question and was dumbfounded the moment she opened her mouth. The foreigner uttered a muffled "Oh, my God!" The little girl, it turned out, was a mute.

They walked off, the mute peppering their retreating backs with a stream of incoherent grunts accompanied by a flurry of hand motions.

The Rainstorm
The rain, which had stopped briefly, began to fall again, beating a resounding tattoo on the myriad materials that served as rooftops and stretching the young policeman's anxieties to the limit. Just as he was about to tell the foreigner to return to the local precinct in the midst of embarrassment and indecision—he saw that the house number directly ahead was 21-7.

"Here it is!"

"Well, I'll be damned," the foreigner blurted out spiritedly.

Just then the rainfall turned into a downpour, so, without a thought for the niceties that ought to accompany a visit by civilized people, they burst in on Ah-gui and her daughter, who abruptly looked up from a pickle barrel and were face-to-face with this uninvited foreigner. Despite the kindly, embarrassed look on the man's face, when he and his escort barged in on them, the mother and daughter knew at once that something bad was about to happen, and a shadow of terror settled upon them.

The rain beat down hard on the sheet-metal roof, producing such a clamor that the policeman had to shout as he translated what the foreigner was saying. Since Ah-gui did not understand Mandarin, all she saw was the policeman energetically opening and closing his mouth, which, compounded by his gestures, caused her to look even more apprehensively toward her daughter, Ah-zhu, hoping she'd tell her what was going on. When she saw her daughter tighten her lips, with a look of alarm and anguish, she asked in a terrified voice "Ah-zhu, what's wrong?"

"Ma …" Opening her tightly pursed lips to speak, the daughter burst into tears.

"What's wrong? Tell me quickly!"

"Pa … Papa's been run down by a car …"

"Oh! Papa …" Where? Where is he?" Ah-gui's face contorted. "Where is he?" This was followed by a stream of incoherent babbling.

The policeman tried to comfort her by saying in halting Taiwanese, "Don't worry, it's not that bad." Then reverting to Mandarin, he said to the girl, "Tell your mother not to be upset, and don't you cry either. They've already rushed your father to the ER." The foreigner stood there looking remorseful. He said something, which he asked the policeman to convey to them.

"This American says they'll take full responsibility, and he urges your mother to stop crying." The foreign man walked up and put his hand on Ah-zhu's head, nodding repeatedly to make his point, hoping she'd understand.

At that moment, the little mute girl with the baby strapped to her back burst through the doorway, sopping wet. Unaware of what was going on, the moment she entered to discover the two men she'd encountered only moments before, her eyes widened and she began making loud grunting noises, accompanied by hand gestures. All the while, Ah-gui continued to moan almost witlessly. "What are we going to do? Oh, what will we do?" When the little mute realized that a pall of grief had settled over the room, her grunts quickly subsided and she walked softly over to Ah-zhu.

"Is she your sister?" the surprised policeman asked.

Ah-zhu nodded.

Feeling ill at ease, he said anxiously, "Hurry up and untie the scarf—the baby's soaking wet." Then he turned to the perplexed foreigner. "It's her kid sister."

"Oh, my God!" the foreigner softly muttered for the second time.

In the Rain
Ah-zhu covered her head with a sheet of transparent plastic and rushed out of the neighborhood of squat houses, heading toward her younger brothers' school.

The heavy rainfall soaked one side of Ah-zhu's back, where her clothes stuck to her body. Had she arranged the plastic more carefully on her way out of the house, she wouldn't have gotten so wet, but she was preoccupied with her thoughts: *If Papa can't work, there'll be no money for the family, and Mama will have to sell me out.* "Ah-zhu, if you don't behave yourself," her mother had sometimes said to scare her, I'll sell you off." But this time would be different.

She wasn't frightened, not now. She kept telling herself that in a new family, she'd be a well-behaved, obedient daughter, accepting any and all hardships that came her way. Her new parents would have no cause to mistreat her and would let her return home to see her brothers and sisters once in a while. By then she might even have a little money saved up to buy toy guns for her brothers and a ball and a doll for her sisters.

But even though the prospect did not frighten her, the more she thought, the faster her tears fell. Before she knew it, she was standing in front of her brothers' school.

Civics Class
During the morning civics class, not a single student's voice emerged from the classroom, only the sounds of a few loud, shrill-voiced teachers, which could be heard even from a distance. The old principal, hands clasped behind his back, moved stealthily down the hallway outside the classrooms like a shadow.

The third-grade White Horse homeroom teacher was at the podium leveling a pointer at Jiang Ah-ji, who was standing in the corner to her left.

"The semester is almost over, but Jiang Ah-ji still hasn't paid his fees," she said to the class before turning to face him. "Jiang Ah-ji!" He jerked his head up to look at her. "You have to stand there every day during civics class," she said. "Aren't you ashamed of yourself?" He quickly lowered his head. "Lin Xiunan paid his today, so that leaves only you standing there. How do you feel about that?" The children all turned to look at Lin Xiunan, who first raised his head and smiled smugly, then dropped it bashfully. "So, Jiang Ah-ji, when can you pay it?" Walking to the end of the podium platform, she drew closer to Ah-ji and tapped him lightly on the shoulder with her pointer. "Well?" He looked up to give her some kind of answer, but the instant he saw the look in her eyes, he lowered his head again. The teacher tapped him once more. "Ah-ji, when are you going to pay?"

"To—tomorrow," he answered softly.

The Taste of Apples

"What?" the teacher exclaimed loudly. "Just when will this 'tomorrow' of yours ever come?" Everyone in the class giggled. "I don't put any stock in what you say anymore. I'm not asking you to pay tomorrow, next Monday will be fine. Don't get the idea that all you have to do is stand there all semester to get by without paying. If you don't come up with the money, I have other means. Remember now, you must have it by next Monday! Do you understand?" Ah-ji nodded. "Good, I'm glad you do."

Bowing his head very low, Ah-ji ran toward his seat without looking up.

"Hey, you!" the teacher shouted. He stopped in his tracks amid his classmates' desks and turned back to look at her. His classmates were giggling. "What are you doing? Just *what* do you think you're doing? Come back here. Since you haven't paid yet, you have to keep standing. If you can pay tomorrow, you won't have to stand anymore. Otherwise, it would be unfair to Lin Xiunan, wouldn't it?" Again the children turned back to look at Lin Xiunan, who felt both proud and sheepish. He lowered his head, not knowing what else to do.

The matter concerning Jiang Ah-ji had just about run its course, so the teacher returned to the podium and asked the students seated below, "Little friends, what moral lesson are we learning in civics class this week?" She scanned the seats in front of her briefly and saw that every hand was raised. "That's fine. You can put your hands down. Let's say it together."

"Co—op—er—a—tion!" they shouted in unison.

"Right, cooperation. Take Jiang Ah-ji, for example: everyone has come up with the fees except him. Can we call that cooperation?"

"NO!" Once again, the class responded loudly.

Ah-ji, who had just breathed a sigh of relief, grew tense again as he heard the teacher say his name. He thought of himself as an uncooperative child. The very mention of the fee brought up the image of his father staring down at him. Then he thought longingly of the rural elementary school down south. He couldn't figure out why, when they were in the south, his father had kept telling his mother how good things were up north. Down south, if they were late in paying their fees, his teacher, Yang Jinzhi, wouldn't punish him by making him stand in the corner.

When Ah-zhu reached the White Horse classroom, the first thing she saw was Ah-ji standing in the corner. Racing up to the window, she called out with undisguised trepidation: "Ah-ji!" His heart skipped a beat when he saw his sister and dropped his head low. The momentarily startled teacher ran out of the room as all the children turned to look outside, those at the rear standing up to do so.

"Is Ah-ji your brother?"

Ah-zhu nodded and then said, "Our papa was run down by an American's car."

"Oh! How bad is it?"

The classroom was all astir.

"I don't know," she said, beginning to cry.

"All right, now, try not to feel too sad." The teacher turned to go inside as the students clambered back to their seats.

"Jiang Ah-ji, hurry up and go with your sister to see your father."

The news was no worse for him than having to stand in the corner. He bowed deeply to the teacher, then walked slowly back to his seat to gather his stuff and put it in his book bag.

From that moment until he walked out of the classroom with Ah-zhu, the eyes of all the children in the room followed his every move.

"Where's Ah-song's classroom?" Ah-zhu asked him.

"Over there," he said, pointing to the door at the end of the hallway.

On the Overpass

The rain still had not let up, so Ah-zhu squatted down and arranged a plastic cover over Ah-song. "Why can't you do this yourself!" As she thought again about being sold into adoption, she drew back one of her hands and wiped the tears that were spilling down her face. "Don't feel bad. I'll come home to see you sometimes." Actually, neither Ah-ji nor Ah-song displayed the slightest trace of sadness; they were in a daze, and Ah-zhu's words served only to confuse them more. "Let's go. Hurry now, Mama's waiting for us." Ah-zhu took Ah-song by the hand, Ah-ji walked beside her, and the three of them passed through the front gate of the school together.

When they reached the nearby intersection, they watched cars pass by in both directions, waiting for a chance to dart across. The shrill sound of a whistle came from the bus shelter across the street.

"Ah-ji, we can't cross, there's a policeman over there. We'll use the overpass."

Ah-ji walked on ahead and lightheartedly jumped up onto the steps. Ah-song cried out anxiously, "Hey, wait up."

"You're the one who's walking so slow, why should I wait for you?"

Ah-zhu looked up at Ah-ji, who had turned back to face them, the sky above him serving as a backdrop. "Ah-ji, wait for your brother," she said. Then she looked down again. "Hurry up," she urged Ah-song. Ah-ji's waiting for you."

While Ah-ji waited for them to catch up, he looked down at the cars passing below. Then he turned back to look at his sister and Ah-song, who were five or six steps behind him.

"Sister," Ah-ji said with a tone of sadness creeping into his voice. "I don't want to go to school anymore." Ah-zhu stopped and gazed up at him while Ah-song continued up the steps.

"Ah-ji," she said, her head sagging in deep thought as she started walking again behind Ah-song. "What would Papa and Mama think if they heard you say that?" She grabbed the silent Ah-ji, and together they continued across the overpass.

"We can't afford the fees."

"Wait till Papa has some money, then we can pay it."

"But the semester is almost over.""

"That's all right," Ah-zhu comforted him. "Wait till I've been adopted, and I'll give you the money."

"Is somebody going to adopt you?" he asked in amazement.

'Uh-huh." Even though she answered him firmly, tears coursed down her cheeks faster than she could wipe them dry.

"Does Mommy want to adopt you out?"

"I'm afraid this time it's for real. Papa was run down by an American's car."

Ah-ji did not understand or imagine what that had to do with their future. As a matter of fact, his attention was caught by the fact that Ah-song wasn't there beside them. "Hey! Where's Ah-song?" They jerked their heads around and spotted the boy squatting down next to one of the railings in the middle of the overpass, watching the cars pass beneath him.

"Ah-song!" Ah-zhu yelled.

"Ah-song really makes me mad. He does this every day on our way to school. He even throws pebbles down on the cars!" Seeing that Ah-song was ignoring her, Ah-zhu ran over angrily.

The sight of Ah-zhu dragging Ah-song over toward him made Ah-ji laugh.

"I'm going to tell Mama when we get home that Ah-ji says you do that every day."

"He does too—he started it!" Ah-song said as he glared at his brother.

"Who said so?" Ah-ji was still laughing.

"Come on, let's go. Mama's probably worried sick. It's taking us all day just to cross an overpass."

"Piggyback," Ah-song said when he reached the head of the steps leading down.

Without a word, Ah-zhu squatted down to let Ah-song climb onto her back.

In the Sedan
Having learned that her husband had lost a lot of blood and was undergoing emergency surgery, Ah-gui cried helplessly and muttered reproachfully, "I told him that jobs are the same everywhere, but he wouldn't listen. He kept saying we should go up north and try our luck there. Now look at the luck we've found! My God! Just what kind of luck have we found?"

She was still crying as they approached the street, though she wasn't aware that they'd reached it—she simply followed Ah-zhu wherever she led.

The policeman and the foreigner signaled to them from a big black sedan.

"Mama, there's the American. Ah-ji, take the others over there," said Ah-zhu.

When the foreigner saw them walking toward him, he jumped into the driver's seat and started the engine. The policeman climbed into the passenger seat. As she walked up next to the car, Ah-gui began crying even louder, more than likely intending to make this American aware that he had brought her family to ruin.

The policeman stuck his head out the window. "Get in," he said.

Ah-gui simply stood there and sobbed while Ah-zhu stared at the closed door, not knowing what to do. While everyone stood around indecisively, Ah-ji reached out and grabbed the door handle. Nothing happened, so, with his left foot against the car as leverage, he used both hands and pulled with all his might. Still nothing. Just then the foreigner, realizing that they hadn't yet opened the door, turned halfway around in his seat with a little hiccup of surprise, reached over, and opened it from the inside, nearly sending Ah-ji sprawling backward.

Ah-gui and the children could never have managed to seat themselves if the policeman hadn't told them all where to sit. Fortunately, even with her lack of experience and her apprehensions, Ah-gui bumped her head only slightly as she climbed into the car and was merely startled by it all. The unexpected opulence of the interior combined to bring her crying to an abrupt halt.

Before they had driven far, Ah-gui realized she'd stopped crying the minute she was seated, making her mournful cries of a moment earlier seem a bit contrived. She recommenced babbling and sobbing and soon abandoned herself to loud wails.

The policeman, unable to endure her doleful crying, turned and said, "There, there, Mrs. Jiang. Don't cry so hard. Who knows, maybe Mr. Jiang was only slightly hurt. But if you cry too hard, you might make him worse—he might even die! Now, stop crying." At first, he was feeling pretty bad himself, but this little speech of his nearly made even him laugh. He quickly tuned back and faced forward, biting down hard on his lip.

Ah-gui was crying out of a genuine sense of grief, to be sure, and not understanding clearly what the policeman had said, she figured they must all be in sympathy with her, so she cried even more bitterly, mumbling as she did, "How are the five children and I going to live? How will we live now?"

The policeman wanted to try something else to console her, but as he turned around and saw her crying so hard she was shaking, the words stuck in his throat. He could think of nothing to say that might stop her crying. Viewed from a different angle, he realized that for an impoverished woman to give rein to her grief this way wasn't necessarily bad for her emotional health. As this thought formed in his head, he was struck by his own callousness.

Ah-zhu, holding the baby, was pressed up close to her mother, though her thoughts were only on what might happen after her adoption. Ah-ji, Ah-song, and the mute girl were all squatting on the back seat, gazing at scenery out the back window and giggling. For them, their father's accident had been left far behind one of the curves in the road

As the car followed a gently winding mountain road, the three children on the back seat pressed up against the side window to see the scenery outside. They watched the houses at the foot of the mountain grow smaller. Ah-ji and Ah-song kept pointing to things, excitedly telling each other in soft voices to look here and there. Even the little mute girl was exuberant, but when she opened her mouth, she only made loud grunts. "Ai ya! Ba, ba, ba ..."

The White House
A clean, white, medium-sized hospital stood on the scenic mountaintop. Although the parking lot was filled with cars, there was no one outside. There were white cars and ambulances, and a short white fence surrounding a patch of Korean grass made dazzling by the recent rainfall.

Ah-gui was still crying bitterly as the car drove into the parking lot.

"All right," the policeman said to her, "all right. We're here now, so you'd better stop crying."

Facing the cold white hospital and the absence of any people around, Ah-gui thought about her husband inside and knew she'd have her answer soon. Was he dead? Crippled? Or what? Suddenly, she could no longer restrain the emotions she should have been able to control. Covering her face with her hands, she let herself be led along by Ah-zhu, wails of grief sticking in her throat like an animal's death rattle, as she tried to choke back her tears.

When they followed the foreigner into the hospital, her grief that had surged unchecked was contained by the stern atmosphere inside. Having regained control of herself, Ah-gui looked around at her children, who seemed frightened by the strange, new environment. Gathering them together, she squatted in front of the mute girl. Using gestures, she pointed to her own mouth, then to the mute's mouth, indicating she wanted her to quiet down. The girl nodded, then grunted loudly, quickly realizing she'd goofed from the angry glare in Ah-gui's eyes. She backed away instinctively, but Ah-gui pulled her up close and made hand motions of sewing the girl's mouth shut. The frightened girl shook her head vigorously.

The policeman walked over from the reception desk and told Ah-gui, "Mr. Jiang is in no danger—two broken legs, that's all. He'll be out of surgery soon."

From his expression and tone of voice, plus the few words she understood, Ah-gui had a rough idea what he was saying. She glanced at the reception desk as the foreigner, a comforting smile on his face, walked up with a foreign nurse. He began talking feverishly, bending at the waist to make hand motions first against his left leg, then his right, and then he nodded. At that moment, to everyone's surprise, the mute girl, seeming to comprehend what he was saying, walked up to him, patted his leg, and began grunting and gesturing. He smiled and nodded.

The foreign nurse took them into an empty ward to wait for Jiang Ah-fa. Knowing that her husband was in no immediate danger, Ah-gui felt considerably relieved and, like her children, began to scrutinize everything she could see inside and everyone walking around. Being sick in a place like this might not be so bad, she was thinking. After the foreigner and policeman had left the ward, Ah-zhu asked Ah-gui, "Mama, Papa's going to stay here, isn't he?"

The Taste of Apples

"I don't know."

"How long will he stay?" Ah-zhu asked with growing interest.

"You little imp, what are you so happy about?" She was nearly laughing herself.

Ah-zhu could tell that her mother wasn't really angry, so she said bravely, "I have to go to the bathroom."

To her surprise, her mother said with a laugh, "Me, too. I've held back since this morning. This is awful! Where do we pee in here?"

"I don't know."

"This is just awful!" As she was bemoaning the situation, Ah-ji and Ah-song ran into the room. "Where the hell have you two been?"

"We went to pee," Ah-song answered.

"Where is it?" she asked impatiently.

"Over there," Ah-ji pointed casually. "Go out here, turn, then turn again, and there it is."

"You little brat, aren't you afraid of anything? Where do you think you are? What's the idea of running all over the place? Now, where is it? Take me there."

"This way." Ah-ji gleefully threw open the door and started out.

"Wait a minute. Slow down … and stop shouting."

Ah-ji and Ah-song took Ah-gui and the girls to the toilet. Then they ran back to the empty room.

"Hey, everything in the place is white," Ah-song noted with amazement.

"It's an American hospital."

"Their clothes are white, so are their hats and shoes."

"So is the room." Ah-ji looked around. "The sheets are white, the blankets, even the bed. So are the windows and the walls …"

Ah-song grew anxious, since his brother had covered everything in sight, everything worth mentioning. He rolled his eyes as he thought hard, then blurted out, "The place where we peed was white too."

"Besides, there's the …" His thought was interrupted by the return of their mother and sisters. Ah-gui began scolding the moment she walked through the door. "You little imp, someone would think you were having a baby instead of taking a pee, you were in there so damned long. There was some American guy in there who kept saying 'Noh noh' or something like that when we walked in. What the hell does 'Noh noh' mean? He had me so nervous, I damn near died." She then changed her tone of voice and asked, "How did you pee?"

"I sat on it. Aren't you supposed to?"

"You sat on it?" Only after she saw Ah-zhu nod did she say with a sense of relief, "Me too." Then she noticed a bulge around Ah-zhu's chest. She reached out. "What's this?"

Unable to back away quickly enough, Ah-zhu let her mother reach under her blouse. "It's great toilet paper," she said awkwardly.

"Ai, what an imp you are." She pulled a wad of clean white toilet paper out from under Ah-zhu's blouse and straightened it a bit. "Really!" she exclaimed. "What if someone found out about this?" She turned her back to the children and put the neatly folded toilet paper together with the pile she'd taken. Seeing that it gave her too much of a paunch, she took the baby from Ah-zhu and held it low to cover the bulge. Then she said, "What's wrong with this kid today? She's sleeping like a corpse." She looked herself over and straightened her clothes.

Just then the policeman walked in unannounced. Ah-zhu and Ah-gui were so rattled even he noticed it. He quickly tried to comfort them: "Don't be frightened, please don't be. He's not in any danger. You can see him in a few minutes. Take it easy." He'd barely finished when the foreigner and a nurse rushed in, looked things over, and said something to the policeman, who translated. "Everyone out of the room for a moment."

Ah-gui led the children out into the corridor, after which two male attendants entered and wheeled out the empty bed. Before long, a bed carrying the unconscious Jiang Ah-fa was rolled past them into the room. The sight was enough to cause Ah-gui and Ah-zhu to weep softly. Ah-ji, Ah-song, and their sister stood in the doorway staring dumbly into the room, watching the nurses' bustling activity. The children simply could not believe this was their father. Except for his closed eyes and his nose and mouth, he was swathed in bandages.

Unable to shake his suspicions, Ah-song gently tugged on Ah-ji's sleeve and asked in a soft voice, "Brother, is that white thing our Papa?" Then he just stood there, eyes open, mouth agape.

The Winged Angel
By now there was no one in the room but members of the Jiang family, including Ah-fa himself, who was still under the anesthesia. Ah-gui was again seized by anguish, but this time it was not caused by imaginary fears. She felt genuinely disconsolate for the head of the family, upon whose existence they all depended. Both his legs were broken, his head and arms had been injured, and it was quite possible that he would become a cripple. What were they to do? What would she do? She mumbled as she sobbed, looking into Ah-fa's face and hoping he'd come to. Ah-zhu was holding the baby and crying, thinking of all the hardships she could expect as an adopted daughter. She lost the bravery she'd had that morning when these thoughts had first occurred to her as she'd walked with Ah-ji. She was so frightened she nearly wailed out loud. With their mother and sister feeling so distressed, the other three children didn't dare run about or cause a commotion. They quietly glanced around, and even when they wanted to ask something, after thoughtful consideration, they held back.

After a while, a nurse in a nun's habit walked in, looked at the patient and then at Ah-gui and the children. "Has he come to yet?" she asked.

With the exception of the mute girl, they were astounded; they simply could not believe their ears. Sensing from their facial expressions why they were so shocked, the nun smiled. "I can speak Taiwanese. I'm a Catholic sister. I was working at Saint Mary's Hospital, but in accordance with the wishes of the Lord, I've been temporarily assigned to the American Hospital to take care of Mr. Jiang." She glanced around the room at Ah-gui and the children. "Is your whole family here?"

Ah-gui could only nod. If she hadn't been so upset, the sight of a woman who didn't look anything like her yet spoke her language with such fluency would surely have seemed comical. The children were staring in amazement, smiles adorning their faces. They were reminded of the winged angels they'd seen on greeting cards. Somehow or other, the appearance of this nun suddenly had everyone in the family sensing that their world had grown larger—which was why Ah-gui felt compelled to try to make the woman appreciate her predicament. But how? After giving it some thought, the old tried-and-tested method seemed the best: having been grief-stricken from the beginning, she quickly reverted to her previous state before the arrival of the nun, looking at Jiang Ah-fa's face, purposelessly touching his hands, sobbing, and muttering "What'll we do? Oh, what'll we do? Here we are, seven of us, what are we going to do for food and clothes? ... Ai! What's going to happen to us? Why didn't the car hit me instead? Why did it have to hit you?" She grew visibly sadder as she went along, and all the nun's attempts to calm her were in vain; in fact, her admonitions provided an added stimulus to cry. The nun was well aware of the effect this kind of situation had on a woman like Ah-gui: faced with harsh reality, her ability to go on would quickly be fortified. And so, she slipped away as Ah-gui cried.

Ah-gui was still crying. "This is terrible. What'll we do? What'll we do now?"

"Mama, she's gone," Ah-zhu said tearfully.

Ah-gui looked around, then stared at Ah-zhu with eyes red from crying and said with irritation,

"So what? What does her leaving have to do with us?" Seeing Ah-zhu lower her head, she continued, "Now you've all seen how your Papa was crippled in an accident, so from now on, I expect you all to shape up and behave yourselves."

Ah-zhu's thoughts turned once again to her adoption. She was surprised to see her mother so angry just because she'd told her that the nun was gone. She'd had the best of intentions, thinking that her mother had been crying for the nun's benefit. It wasn't fair. These thoughts produced a steady flow of tears from Ah-zhu's seemingly inexhaustible supply.

"Ah-ji! Ah-song!" Seeing the state Ah-zhu was in, Ah-gui felt she'd been too harsh with her, so she turned her attention to the boys. "The same goes for you two. Your Papa can't work anymore, so you'll have to work in his place."

For reasons unknown to him, Ah-ji was so tickled by this that he had to lower his head and bite down on his lip to keep his mother from noticing. Ah-song, who stood off to the side, heard his mother's threat that he'd have to work in his father's place and unexpectedly tuned serious, answering obediently "Yes."

Ah-ji could hold back no longer and began to giggle. Even Ah-gui's angry outburst of "What's this? That's just great. You can drop dead, you crazy child! Hurry up and drop dead" had no effect on his laughing, which would stop only when it had run its natural course.

Blessed are the Believers
The combination of the anesthesia wearing off and Ah-ji's laughter brought Jiang Ah-fa around. He moaned softly, bringing an abrupt change to the room's atmosphere. Ah-gui placed her hand on his chest. "Don't move," she said, "especially your legs."

Ah-fa lay there, straining to raise his head to look down. "What's wrong with my legs?"

"They're broken."

When he heard this, Ah-fa let his head drop weakly back onto the pillow, and he heaved a sigh. "I thought I was dead for sure." He grew silent as he looked up at the ceiling, his eyes still glazed over, then asked, "How about the kids?"

"They're all here, right beside you."

"Papa," Ah-zhu called out softly, followed by Ah-ji and Ah-song, and even though the mute made no sound, she quietly lined up with the others beside the bed, across from their mother. As Ah-gui watched Ah-fa cast a silent glance at each of his children, she was moved to tears. The whole family seemed to have turned into idiots, standing dumbly by, unable to say a thing. And the longer the situation persisted, the worse everyone felt, as each of them desperately hoped that someone would break the ice and say something. Just then, the baby in Ah-zhu's arms began to bawl.

"Give her to me," Ah-gui said, so Ah-zhu walked around the bed and handed her over. "This little imp seems to know something's happened to you. She hasn't cried all day, ever since this morning. She's got to be hungry." So saying, she exposed a breast and began to nurse the baby. The sounds of the suckling infant were the only ones heard in the stilled room.

Thoughts of his own injuries and of these people around him made Ah-fa feel miserable. He wasn't absolutely convinced he was still alive. *Why didn't I die? Why not just get it over with? How am I going to go on living like this? ...*

"Where am I?" he asked with a start, as if the question had just then popped into his head.

"An American hospital."

"Huh? An American hospital? Where ... where's the money coming from?"

"I don't know. We were brought here by an American and a policeman," Ah-gui said.

"Where are they now?"

"They said they'd be back in a minute."

Ah-fa didn't say another word, just lay there looking as if he had a great many things on his mind. His face grew tight one moment, loosened up the next, which led Ah-gui to assume that, to some degree at least, he was reproaching himself.

"How are we going to manage over the long days ahead?" As she uttered these words, her nose began to ache and tears started to fall. "I told you," she continued with a note of resentment creeping into her voice, "but you wouldn't listen. I said that if it was work you wanted, you could find it anywhere. But you didn't believe me. You said women don't understand, and that we should try our luck in a big city. Finding work isn't the same as opening a business—what kind of luck is there to try? No, there's luck, all right. And we've just found ours, haven't we?"

"Mama, that's enough," Ah-zhu cried out anxiously, when she saw her father's face turning livid with anger, though he didn't say a word. She knew that if her mother kept it up much longer, he'd explode with rage, after which nothing could calm him down. Ah-zhu had witnessed such scenes many times—this was how their arguments always started. Ah-gui herself was aware of that, but whenever matters reached this stage, she was powerless to avoid the inevitable. This time, at least, she stopped her complaint in the nick of time, and in the silence that followed, the only sound was Ah-fa's labored breathing. Remembering the nurse's instructions to press the buzzer by the head of the bed if she needed anything, Ah-gui pressed it, and almost immediately, the courteous, friendly nun rushed in.

"Ah, he's awake," she said when she saw Ah-fa. She walked up to his bedside, put her hand on his forehead, and asked, "How do you feel?"

Like the others before him, he was shocked to hear a foreigner speaking the local language.

"Good. He doesn't have a fever." She took a thermometer out of her pocket, shook it a few times, and looked at it. "Put this under your tongue." She stuck it into Ah-fa's mouth, then glanced around the room, taking in the others. "Still scared?" she asked with a smile.

"What difference does it make if we're scared or not?" Ah-gui replied. "We're worried."

"Do you believe in God?" Seeing that Ah-gui had nothing to say, she went on, "Blessed are the believers."

The American and the policeman walked in at that moment, carrying bags of things. They exchanged greetings with the nun, and the affairs of God were put aside for the moment.

They laid out the items one at a time. "Here are some sandwiches, and some milk, and here are some cans of cola, and here … here's some canned fruit. Then we have some apples," the policeman identified each object on the table. "This is your lunch."

The children eyed the bags, absorbed in what they had produced. The nun took the thermometer out of Ah-fa's mouth. "Good," she said after reading it. "No fever." Then she went to the foot of the bed to make an entry on the chart. The foreigner and the policeman walked up to Ah-fa and smiled. Bewildered, he returned their smiles.

"This is Colonel Gray. It was his car that hit you," the policeman said.

Colonel Gray reached out and grabbed Ah-fa's hand, a stream of unintelligible sounds pouring from his mouth. From his facial expression, Ah-fa could tell that the man was apologetic.

The policeman acted as interpreter. "He says he's terribly, terribly sorry and begs your forgiveness. He says he's prepared to assume all responsibility, and he'd like to become a friend of your family."

Like Ah-gui, Ah-fa did not understand Mandarin, but he'd figured out that it was Gray's car that had hit him, so he said accusingly, accompanied by moans, "Oh, so it was you! You should have been more careful. I saw your car coming a long way away, so I moved over to let you pass—I never expected you'd come right at me. Aiya! When you smashed into me, you also smashed my family to pieces ..." Wanting very much to know what Ah-fa was saying, Colonel Gray looked over at the policeman, who returned his look and shook his head. Eventually, it was the nun standing behind them who conveyed Ah-fa's words to Gray.

"You will be compensated by Colonel Gray's insurance company. Beyond that, because of a sense of moral obligation on his part and his official capacity, his office will assume full responsibility so you will not suffer financially because of Mr. Jiang's incapacitation. Additionally, he hopes you will permit him to send your mute daughter to a special school in the United States." Everyone quickly turned to face the girl, throwing a scare into her. If Gray hadn't just then rubbed her head, she'd probably have been shaking like a leaf. Ah-gui and Ah-fa exchanged a look. The nun quickly added, "No hurry—we can talk more about this later. But for now, here's twenty thousand." Gray handed her an envelope, which she placed on Ah-fa's chest. "You can use this to live on for the time being. There will be more later."

Twenty thousand! This nearly made their heads swim, but since the money was right there in front of them, something had to be said. But what, what should they say? All this indecision gave them the uneasy feeling that they'd done something wrong, offended someone.

The policeman, who had been standing off to the side, broke the silence.

"This has been a stroke of good luck for you," he said, "being run down by an American. If it had been anyone else, you'd probably still be lying in the road, covered with a straw mat."

Ah-zhu bent down near Ah-fa's ear and told him what the policeman had said. Through tears of emotion, Ah-fa said, "Thank you, thank you! I'm sorry, I'm so sorry."

The Taste of Apples
They ate sandwiches and drank cola as they chatted happily. The Jiang household had never been as harmonious as it was at that moment.

"Ah-gui, when you go home, don't tell anyone how much money we got."

"What makes you think I'd do that?" Then she turned to the children. "Now all you kids heard your father, didn't you? Anyone shoots off his mouth, I'll sew it shut."

"I wouldn't dare."

"Me either."

"Papa, I want to keep those soda cans," Ah-ji said.

"Me, too," said Ah-song.

"I don't want any of you kids losing those pretty soda cans," Ah-gui warned sternly. "I'll flay the skin off the bones of anyone who loses them."

"We know," they shouted gleefully.

Ah-fa was experiencing something unusual, a feeling devoid of cares or worries. It was written all over his face, and that made him seem like someone else to his wife; she hadn't dreamed that this man for whom she'd borne five children was capable of such an attractive expression. Seeing that he wasn't looking at her, she moved her head back a little to gaze at him. *Just look at him. When has he ever looked as pleasant as he does today? Today he really looks presentable.*

Ah-fa stole a glance at Ah-gui as he drank his milk. He was wondering why she hadn't started in with her grumbling. He was even hoping she'd repeat that sentence, "You said let's go up north and try our luck, now see what you've run into!" *When she brings it up, I'll fire back, "Well, if this isn't luck, I'd like to know what it is!" Ha-ha, I'd sure take the wind out of her sails with that.* Ah-fa took another look at her at the very moment her eyes were on him. Knowing smiles spread across both faces.

The happy atmosphere the family was enjoying was interrupted, but not unpleasantly, when Gray brought the foreman and the workers' representative, Chen Huotu, to call on the injured man.

They entered the room without a single consoling word, merely laughed and joked as usual, and said things like, "Wow! What a life you'll have from now on, Ah-fa, nothing but lying in bed, eating and shitting. As for the rest of us, nothing's changed. We're still working like beasts. Who could have it better than you? Ha ha ha."

"Heh heh, we'll have to rely on you from now on," the foreman exclaimed.

Ah-fa and Ah-gui were puzzled.

"Hey, Huotu, what are you two talking about? You're getting me confused."

"Don't put on an act. You think we don't know? That American guy told us all about it. They're even going to send your mute daughter to a special school in the US. Not only that ..."

"Who said?" Ah-gui asked.

"Everyone at the job, more than a hundred of us, we all know all about it."

"It's only right. Otherwise, how would we know if one of our brothers was being taken advantage of? Isn't that right?"

"Right. That's true. This Mr. Gray, he's a nice guy," Ah-fa said.

"Hey, Ah-fa!" Huotu blurted out, then asked slyly, "Did you do it on purpose? Ha ha ha."

"Damn you, Huotu, how can you say that? Damn you …" there was nothing Ah-fa could do; not knowing whether to laugh or cry, he simply cursed Huotu, with the trace of a smile on his face. By then, everyone was laughing.

"Huotu, if you think it's so great, why don't you give it a try?" Ah-gui teased him.

"Me? I could never be as lucky as you. Look here. With a pointy chin like this, where would I find that kind of luck?" Everyone laughed again.

Because their jobs were waiting, the foreman and Huotu counted that as a sympathy call and departed.

"Damn it, what's a guy supposed to so with a bunch of goof-offs like that?" Ah-fa's legs began to ache. "Ow, my legs hurt!"

"Call the nurse."

"Hold on, she was just in here. We don't want to put them to too much trouble." He saw the children looking longingly at the apples, so he said, "If you want one of those, go ahead—one each." The children quickly reached out and took them. "And give one to your mother."

"No, I don't, I don't …" But Ah-ji had already put one into his mother's hand. "Why don't you have one too?"

"My legs hurt too much. I don't feel like eating."

"Shall I call the nurse?"

"I already said you don't have to—weren't you listening?" Ah-fa said irritably.

Everyone was holding apples, turning them over and over, not quite knowing how to eat it. "Go ahead, eat them," Ah-fa said.

"How?" Ah-zhu asked bashfully.

"Like they do on TV," Ah-ji said, as he took a bite to show them.

While everyone was watching Ah-ji, Ah-fa said, "One apple costs as much as four catties of rice—and you don't even know how to eat them."

Following this remark, the children and Ah-gui all bit into their apples. The silence of the room was broken by the crisp sound of apples being bitten into, gingerly, one after another. After their first bites, they didn't know what to say, although they felt that the apples weren't quite as sweet as they had imagined. They were actually a little tart and pulpy, and when chewed they were frothy and not quite real. But they were reminded of their father's comment that one apple cost as much as four catties of rice, and with that the flavor was enhanced. When they took their second bites, they spiritedly bit off big chunks, filling the sickroom with a chorus of loud munching.

Ah-fa succumbed to the temptation.

"Ah-zhu," he said, "hand me one of those."

3

Rice Diary

Sung Tse-lai
(translated by Ian Rowen)

May 4 afternoon. Weather: Heavy Rain. Place: Under the cottonwood tree.
The weather had been strange for a while. Sometimes it was sunny and scorching inside the community of Daniunan, so hot it could peel off a man's skin. The air would fill with moisture and mosquitoes. Other times, a cold and damp wind suddenly rustled through the trees, and the northwest rains fell and flooded the village roads. Yes, you'd never have a chance to guess what the weather these days would bring—there is a saying that spring weather is as mercurial as a moody stepmother, and by July the temperature would hit infernal heights. And now it's that time squeezed between spring and the flames.

Rain had fallen for days. Alongside the wet asphalt roads, the fields sprouted fresh leaves.

The crops and assorted nameless weeds shook alike in the afternoon rain. Around two or three o'clock, chickens clucked and pecked at food scraps on the road. Then, suddenly there was a break in the big black clouds. The rain stopped, and a ray of light shone through. The sun was still yet to be seen, but at least the greens and reds of Daniunan's new tile walls were more visible. All the villagers were hunched over sorting, raking, and drying their freshly cut rice.

Toward the back of the village was a road junction with a shop selling miscellaneous goods. There were several big, intertwined cottonwood trees in front of the shop. Such trees were fewer and farther between since village renewal began in Daniunan. The village head required that the area be cleaned up and anything remaining from the olden days had best be removed. Only two or three whistling pines remained on the village road. Behind the buildings, the devilishly thorny bamboo had been cut away and replaced with planted coconut palms and willow trees. This made the cottonwood trees even more rare and special. During this season, with the flowers in full bloom, all the people drying their rice at this end of the village would come to take a rest at the foot of the trees, watch their harvest, play games, nap, stretch, and chat as the moist wind rustled the leaves and pollen-rich flowers above.

Bān-hok, forty-years old and with a flat nose, sat on a chair.[1] He lowered his head to look at two black ants crawling over fallen leaves. He wrinkled his nose and tightened his brow over his high cheekbones and black teeth. He looked to be in rather poor shape.

Years earlier, he was a big man in the village. He had acquired some Landrace pigs from the Farmers Association and was much sought after by farmers with sows. At that time, anyone passing by the village would know of him. There was even a riddle about it: *Who gets dressed up all in black and goes to the next village to find a wife?*

When the children of Daniunan heard this line, they right away guessed it was about Bān-hok's exclusive offering. Things were different now. Artificial insemination had become popular, and pig breeding took a little more technique. Bān-hok became just another ordinary farmer. Maybe because people still remembered his history, he tried to use it to maintain some dignity and status in Daniunan.

Now, looking at the ants climbing toward a grain of sprouted rice, he thought about something that made him furrow his brow even more tightly.

"It's been damp and cloudy for days. The rain won't stop," he said to Sin-thuân.

Sin-thuân was part of the cottonwood tree crowd, which always had less food than people. Sin-thuân was worrying about the fact that his pregnant wife would go into labor soon.

"Hey, Bān-hok, will the Farmers Association guarantee rice prices this year?"

"I've heard they will. They'll buy 970 kilos per hectare, and pay 689 a kilo," Bān-hok turned sideways toward him and said, "I still have three plots yet to harvest. I'm worried they'll start sprouting."

"What a mess. And the weather doesn't look likely to clear. Life is so hard for people these days. The Farmers Association is not going to accept these sprouted grains. It's going to be quite a scene."

"Yeah."

They laughed and frowned and shook their heads.

A few moments later, the village loudspeaker rang out: "Dear Farmers, it's rained for several days. There is no place to dry rice. To respond to the requests made by some of you, we're opening the village activity center. If you have nowhere else to dry your rice, you may send it over!"

It was the scratchy voice of the village head. Bān-hok listened distractedly and was further overcome with confusion when he saw Bigmouth Yang resting by the stone mortar.

Her real name was Tan Yuanyang, and she was a 40-something-year-old woman now on her second husband. The first had passed away, of course. Her hair was held up in a messy bun and her wrinkled face was caked with red make-up powder. Her lips, well...this is not charitable, but they looked like they belonged to a mamasan in a Taiwanese opera. Actually her lips weren't all that big really, but she liked to use them to start trouble. Whenever she opened her mouth, it sounded like cymbals crashing, or so people said. She and Bān-hok were neighbors who faced each other across a narrow alley over which they were fighting. It had already been months, and now they were taking the case to court. First, Bigmouth Yang spread rumors that Bān-hok was greedy and corrupt, which earned her some sympathy. Recently though, Bān-hok turned her late husband's son and his wife against her and directed them to fight with their stepfather over the property. This civil conflict within her own family had caught Yang on the back foot, and she found herself nearly taken down. Previously, Bān-hok had been willing to maintain some kind of peace, but now he couldn't stop himself. That piece of land was worth at least 50 or 60 thousand. These days, with the rice germinating early, and too many people farming, crop prices would definitely drop. Price guarantees might not work out either, and costs were going up on everything else too. If he could acquire this piece of land, why not? Sure, it would have been easy to split the disputed property. But in this downturn, with so much craziness and thievery all around—well, maybe he was a thief, too. Still, why not catch as catch can?

As he thought about this, he couldn't help but crack a sly smile as he gazed at Yang. Suddenly a big splash of rain fell on the top of her head—the water had been knocked down by birds perched overhead in the tree branches. She craned her neck up to see where the water came from, and then turned her head and found Bān-hok looking right at her.

"What are you looking at?"

Yang normally would pay a scrawny pig farmer like this no mind. Still, she was prone to say meaningless things like this, and they would sound fierce coming from her lips. Her tone of voice struck Bān-hok, her arch enemy.

"What are you looking at?" Bān-hok replied, knowing he was on the verge of victory in his battle with her. How could he lose to someone like this?

"You're disgusting, staring at a woman like that!" Yang blurted back. "You're a pig!"

Bān-hok's pride was hit hard by these words. He looked shocked. His face tightened like a drying kumquat. He stammered, "You... you... Whatever you say, that land will eventually be mine, in spirit, in law, and in deed!"

As soon as he thought about that land, he regained his calm. His scrawny body trembled from the agitation. He spoke this even though he knew nothing of the spirit of the law.

"Only a gravesite will be all yours," Yang cackled back. She raised her voice and said, "You're dreaming."

"I have proof." He took a moment to regain his composure. Then he said sternly, "Your daughter-in-law agrees."

"What daughter-in-law?" said Yang, gnashing her teeth. She stood up, spread her legs, put one hand on her hip and waved the other one in the air as she said, "I don't have a daughter-in-law like that, nor such a disrespectful son. No matter what, they have to look after me while I'm still around. Nowadays, they not only don't take care of me, they even want to steal their stepfather's property. What a world! That lousy girl, I can't forgive her. Even if I die, I'll come back as a ghost and get her!"

"Come on." Bān-hok felt satisfied seeing her get so riled up. He turned and said, "You've been fighting with the village folk for ages, and you've never been in the right. These days, you're fighting even with your daughter-in-law, and you're still not right."

"You monster!" Yang stomped her feet so strongly that the cottonwood tree flowers shook. "You're speaking on her behalf? How much money will she give you? You must be having an affair. You bred pigs, you pig god, and now you're having an affair with my daughter-in-law. When my son finds out, he'll flay you alive."

"You're just making stuff up now. Damn it!" Bān-hok was startled. His face turned bright red. He didn't realize Yang's words could be so cutting. The shameful and baseless accusation sent shivers through him. All he could say was, "I... I... I... An affair with your daughter-in-law? You vicious loose-tongued woman, I'll kill you!"

After he was finished speaking, Bān-hok took a swing at her.

In the olden days, the people of Daniunan practiced martial arts. In his own youth, Bān-hok studied the staff but gave up after getting into pigs. Then he got married and got busy with all sorts of things. The villagers had a joke about this: *Practice martial arts when young; practice domestic arts when married.*

This probably explains how he got so scrawny.

Bigmouth Yang's words left him emotionally exposed. It was only natural that he'd be angry—this was a major attack on his self-respect. Her vicious attack struck him straight in the heart.

"You dare?" Yang stood her ground, dug in her feet, and stuck out her ample bosom. "You dare touch this old lady? One kick from me, and you'll keel right over."

"Fine. You nasty woman! I'm going to smack you even if it kills me."

Bān-hok took a big step forward and smashed into her body.

Yang's feet were dug in but hadn't prepared for the intensity of Bān-hok's rage. She fell back onto the bench behind her and splayed out right on top of it. Ling, who had been snoring nearby, was startled out of his slumber. He shouted, "There's a fight! Fight!"

All the people drying their rice by the trees nearby ran over.

Yang got back on her feet, unwilling to show weakness. She grabbed a stool and swung its legs toward Bān-hok's belly. Bān-hok had studied martial arts and knew how to parry. He tried to block the stool legs with his hand and turn away from the line of attack. Alas, his body wasn't as nimble as it used to be. The stool hit him and knocked the wind out of him. Still, he managed to stay on his feet. He thrust himself forwards again toward Yang. He grabbed both the stool and Yang's hair, but she wouldn't drop her weapon. Both of them ended up on the floor, wrestling with each other.

"Fight! Fight!" yelled Ling, excitedly.

"Let's break it up," said Sin-thuân. He scolded Ling, "What are you yelling about? Let's stop this."

"Just watch the fight!" laughed Ling. "It beats watching someone just talk about Brother Pig."

At first, Yang still had the upper hand. She sat on top of Bān-hok's scrawny body and smashed his flat nose.

"Yeah, smash his jaw, too. Smash it flat!"

The bystanders laughed.

Bān-hok was feeble, but when he saw a bunch of people watching, he feared that he was losing whatever honor he had left. He fought back with all his might and screamed over and over again, "I'll beat you! I'll beat you!"

"Yes, fight back! Bān-hok still has his old strength. Watch your stance, watch your stance!"

Ling led the audience in egging the fight on.

Suddenly, Yang's expression changed, like she was struck by an electric shock. As soon as her movement slowed down, Bān-hok grabbed her hair and pulled her head down. Her body tumbled over and landed spread-eagled on the floor, exposing her thighs.

"Wow, she looks like that Marilyn Monroe on the TV!" exclaimed Ling.

"I'll beat you to death, you evil meddling woman," said Bān-hok, as he kicked her.

"Hey, Bān-hok, no more beating," said Sin-thuân, who saw Yang's eyes shut and realized matters were getting serious. "Yang just passed out."

Bān-hok looked startled and pulled himself together.

A short man who looked like a dark Shiba Inu dog leapt forward through the crowd of bystanders. It was Yang's second husband. As he picked up her crumpled body, people pointed at Bān-hok and said, "It was him! He hit your wife!"

Yang's husband looked furious. He thrust out his Shiba Inu hand and cursed, "Fuck all your ancestors! How dare you strike a weak lady? This isn't the end of this!"

As he stepped forward to hit Bān-hok, everyone urged him to stop.

"Don't. Go to the hospital. Yang is almost on her last breath."

"Fuck your ancestors," he said again. "Bān-hok, we're done here. Listen, I'm taking you to court."

He then carried Yang away.

The crowd chattered on. Bān-hok's face turned pale.

Sin-thuân turned toward the old Lim family estate by the front of the village and said, "Is that Lim Baiyi? Yes, that's Lame Yi, by the look of his limp."

Upon hearing this, everyone turned toward the village gate and saw a parked car and nearby a man with a large briefcase walking with a cane. Everyone fell silent and forgot for a moment about the fight, as if a god had just appeared.

Just who was this Lame Lim Baiyi?

May 5. Weather: Rainy.
In the morning, the people by the cottonwood trees spoke of Bigmouth Yang. They said she was in the hospital in serious condition.

After noon, Sin-thuân's wife gave birth to a boy weighing seven pounds, with a good appetite. Big news came later in the evening, around 8 p.m., when a bleak moon shone over Daniunan. Ling ran over to the shop by the cottonwood trees. He said that while he was fishing with electric shock devices, near the wooden plank bridge over the irrigation ditch, he saw the bare butt of a small bathing child. The smiling child's eyes emitted green fire. Ling said he saw the ghost of a child! Because Ling was short of breath from running so fast, everyone believed his story.

May 6. Weather: Rainy.
Around nine in the morning, the village head's eldest son was brought back. People said that he'd just bought a 150cc motorbike and rode it to the city, where he was caught by the traffic cops because he didn't have a license. He wasn't able to get a license because he was illiterate—how could he even take the test?

The police patrolled the area and put a message under cottonwood tree area. Anyone caught gambling could be arrested.

In the afternoon, the village conducted an environmental clean-up. Civil servants and teachers didn't have to participate in this volunteer effort. It was said that the government gave them this preferential treatment, and some of the folks in Daniunan were none too happy about this.

May 7. Weather: Rainy. Location: Barbershop.
The rain fell intermittently, at a slant. Clouds blanketed the whole sky. The air felt stifling. With no sun in sight, you'd have to look at a clock to know it was already noontime.

In the center of the village, next to the activity center, was a barbershop. Usually at this time of day, there'd be a dozen people, some barefoot and planning to rake their rice later, and others wearing boots fresh from the fields, sitting sluggishly and looking at the sky. One or two might be sitting in the hairdressing chair, carefully grooming their facial hair.

Daniunan was not a small village. With 500 or 600 households spread out over a large area, people's social lives were split into a few distinct areas. For example, the people staying toward the back of the village were usually a bit poorer. In front, by the temple, the households were wealthier and more powerful. In the center of the village, around the barbershop, maybe because of the changing times, the atmosphere was a bit more open. People who liked to add a little fun to their lives would gather here.

The boss of the barbershop, Lim Duo, was giving haircuts to two kids. He was short, with a big head and beard. If he came across people taller than him, he'd have to look up and turn his head like a spinning top. His own struggles were typical of those of the village. These days, it would be hard to keep a barbershop like his open, with just a few old guys and children around, and most of the other younger folks gone. With the population dropping, you could count the heads of hair left to cut. The hardest hair to cut was straight and strong, like that of Goldie, a guy who was in the shop complaining while Lim Duo was cutting the kids' hair. His hair would even dull the blades. Still, customers would come in and then you wouldn't see them for a month, so he took minor repairs as his duty and reminded customers to come back so they wouldn't forget. Especially these days with the city offering special services like massages, there was no guarantee people would come back here for a haircut anyway. Seeing these risks, Lim Duo bought some land and began farming it. If his barbershop went under, at least he'd have some extra earnings from his crops. Many people admired his astuteness.

You can't be rigid, you've got to adapt. That's what people in Daniunan said. Today though, his haircutting hands weren't doing what they were supposed to. He felt like his soul had left his body, and his hands were tense and trembling.

The Lim family had long been powerful in this town. Lim Duo's father was head of the local administration during the Japanese rule and was one of the wealthiest men around. But when Lim Duo was little, his father was lecherous. Soon after Retrocession, Lim Duo's father became even more debauched. Their paddy fell into disrepair and was eventually sold off. His shriveled father, covered in sores from years of venereal disease, had hammered a rusty nail into his own head just days earlier. He had come back from the verge of death, but upon being discharged from the hospital, his medical bill still had to be paid, and it would cost a pretty penny. Lim Duo had thought of using the earnings from the rice crop to cover the expense, but the weather looked like it wouldn't clear for a while yet, and he was worried. Of course, his dexterity would be affected.

"Damn you, father!" muttered Lim Duo to himself. Turning to Tenn Bák-sim, next to him, he said, "Kid's hair is hard to cut."

"Yes," said Tenn Bák-sim. "Kid's hair is definitely hard to cut. It's not meant to be cut—it's meant to be killed." Everyone in the shop laughed.

Tenn Bák-sim was about 30 years old. He had worked as a guard on a night express bus that ran between the north and south. His face had a knife scar. By now though, he'd mended his ways and returned to the village to farm. When he responded to Lim Duo's observation, he was really referring to massages.[2]

Lim Duo's heart sank when he heard about the massages. He'd heard that city folk were setting up barbershops in far-out villages. By day, they looked like places to cut hair. By night, pretty girls would come out to do massages. The old-style barbershops would all go out of business.

"What have you heard?" Lim Duo asked nervously. "Will our village get a massage parlor?"

"No," said Tenn Bák-sim, spitting out some betel nut juice. Looking out toward the wet bamboo grove outside, he continued, "But yesterday, Lame Yi came back to town."

At the sound of Lame Yi's name, the ears of everyone in the shop perked up. They sat up straight to listen.

"He wants to open a massage parlor?" Lim Duo asked.

"Hard to say," answered Tenn Bảk-sim, his eyebrows arching over his knife scar. "It's hard to know, but he brought a big briefcase, right?"

"Yes," said people in the shop.

"I think it's full of cash," said Tenn Bảk-sim.

"Oh." Everyone's eyes opened wide.

Kachun, a sullen man with a taste for women, laughed and said, "I hope he builds a massive massage parlor, and I can go sit in there and enjoy the air conditioning and not come back to Lim Duo's filthy barbershop."

"What is this silly talk?" said Goldie to Kachun. "You think you can do that? Massage is massage. It costs 400 for one go. Even for a wife, you wouldn't have enough for more than one or two visits."

Everyone in the shop laughed again.

Lim Duo felt immensely relieved. After all, the people of Daniunan weren't wealthy and probably didn't have enough money for massages. Still, knowing that Lame Yi was back in the village made him feel uneasy.

"I've heard that Lame Yi made a lot of money in the city," said Lim Duo. "He's made many deals."

"Yes," said Tenn Bảk-sim with the air of someone who'd roamed the city. "He built an enterprise, built buildings, bought land. Do you understand enterprise?"

"No," said the people of Daniunan.

"It's big business. He also ran many grain factories." Tenn Bảk-sim said, "Anyway, he's got enough money to buy up all the property in Daniunan."

"Wow." The barbershop crowd was impressed.

Suddenly, a kid ran out from a nearby room and shouted, "Grandfather's gone out, grandfather's gone out!" Everyone turned to look and realized that it was Lim Duo's son talking about Lim Duo's crazy father.

"Quick!" shouted Lim Duo, knocking over his barbering tools. "Help me stop him! Help me stop him!"

Everyone in the shop ran outside to the road to see Lim Duo's bald father, standing by the notice board at the activity center, with razor blades hanging around his neck.

May 8. Weather: Rainy.
As people were getting out of bed, the shrill sound of Redhead's prayer horn was heard around the cottonwood tree. It turned out that Ling had become ill after seeing the ghost, so he asked for Redhead's supernatural assistance to exorcise it. However, according to Redhead, what Ling had seen wasn't a ghost, but a god!

There was another joke going around the cottonwood tree after Sin-thuân's family took the baby for a walk outside. Everyone saw that the child didn't really look like Sin-thuân, but more like Bān-hok. This rumor troubled Sin-thuân.

At dusk, Goldie from the barbershop crowd sat on the bench, sad and slumped over. The thunder had roiled the skies all day, and two of the piglets he was rearing had been struck dead by lightning.

May 9. Weather: Rainy.
In the morning, Kachun paid no attention to weather omens and filled the well behind his house.

Daniunan's gamblers evaded the police ban by moving their operations to Bān-hok's old pig shed.

Nighttime: Quiet. Nothing much happened.

May 10. Weather: Rainy. Location: By the temple.
The rain fell more and more vigorously these days. Before, the big torrents would wait until the afternoon. Now they're unrelenting and don't seem to follow any schedule. Upon waking up, everyone would see the dense raindrops already falling. Villagers who wanted to use the early hours to dry their harvest could only sigh. They heard the cities were flooding too. To show his love for the people, the county magistrate was literally kneeling and praying to the gods to show their mercy and stop the disaster.

Of course, the people of Daniunan also prayed and burned incense at the temple. Still, even though the divination blocks indicated that the rain would stop, it showed little sign of letting up. There wasn't much else for everyone to do but stand guard over their covered rice piles.

In the front of the village, at an old tiled house by the main temple, there was all sorts of activity. Many people stood around the courtyard. At the corners, under the trees and roof eaves were piles of freshly cut rice set out to dry. Under a guava tree was a pile of rice ears, the top of which had already started sprouting. It looked like a bumper crop this year, except for the critical problem of drying it all.

This big family was under the control of Li Thih-tō. In the olden days, he was one of the "Three Oxen" of this village. The three oxen were the richest and most powerful families. They included Li Thih-tō, Wang the village head, and Lim Oo (Lim Baiyi's father). After the 37.5% rent reduction policy, Lim Oo moved his whole family to the city to do big business.[3] Village Head Wang divided his family's property among his offspring. The estate and status enjoyed by the Three Oxen waned, except for that of Li Thih-tō, who continued farming ever more vigorously as his family grew larger and his family property remained undivided. In an age when many rural folks were moving to the city, Li Thih-tō's approach was unusual.

The Three Oxen were legendary. How could they fall apart like this, wondered some of their admirers. Others scoffed at dynastic family politics that caused so much damage to their offspring. Isn't this a more civilized age?, they asked.

Naturally, Li Thih-tō knew that the times had changed. Still, he was resolute in his belief that his kids were useless if they wouldn't farm. Most days, he'd be sitting inside the temple, talking in serious tones with the regulars there about the news of the day, or listening to the radio. The children didn't dare to talk to him. He looked cold and stern, the last emperor of an older era.

At this moment, all the people around Li Thih-tō were his sons, their wives, and the temple regulars. Today, however, they weren't tending to their rice harvests.

Li Thih-tō was standing in the center of the courtyard, his body shaking with anger, his face bright red, white hair standing straight up, his arms extended. His left hand held the shirt collar of his eldest grandson. His right hand held a wire chicken cage. In front of him was a stack of firewood.

"I'm going to burn him! This rotten grandson can't be allowed to live! This disgraceful animal!" Li Thih-tō shouted. His daughters-in-law bowed their heads in fear.

The grandson was only 17 or 18 years old, a strapping lad with an ashen face. While studying in business school, he had a baby with a classmate. Her family had come knocking at their door. Li Thih-tō felt that this brought him shame. There was a saying that even the most dignified families could do disgraceful things. Such a saying seemed to be coming true for Li Thih-tō.

"I'll say it again to all of you," said Li Thih-tō as he turned around to face his sons and daughters-in law. "I never wanted him to study at that business school. You didn't listen. You said that society was changing and all that. Now this shameful thing has happened. Who will take responsibility? What is this change you were talking about? I, Li

Thih-tō, don't buy it. He should come back to farm. No matter what he does, he should farm."

Everyone was silent. The sky was dull white behind the green gleam of the rain-soaked guava tree.

Li Thih-tō saw that everyone was silent. He became even more furious. He roared like one possessed and held the cage to stuff his grandson inside. He shouted, "You bastard! I'll burn you to death! I'll kill you!" He took out a lighter and ignited the firewood.

Li Thih-tō's daughter-in-law snapped out of her shocked state and ran to stop him. "Father, it's not his fault! That girl will also take responsibility. He's a good kid. He's just a bit young and made a mistake." She knelt down as soon as she finished pleading.

Actually, Li Thih-tō wasn't sure if he was really angry. Sometimes he just took pride in performing. He'd vent his spleen whenever he felt like it. Even if he wasn't really angry, sometimes he still put on a show and then find himself in a fury. He thought he'd perform well in the role of General Zhang Fei in a stage production of the classic *Romance of the Three Kingdoms*—damn you all, I, Li Thih-tō, am his reincarnation! No wonder his son was as afraid of him as he were a tiger. He thought about this a lot.

He fired live rounds in his performances. They were getting realer and realer. So, as soon as he lit the fire, he pushed his caged grandson toward it.

This escalation worried the neighbors. Li Tshing-ian, who'd once run and lost in an election to serve as village representative, came over and said, "Thih-tō, he's your grandson. Forgive him for his foolishness. He's your family. You've raised him for years already."

"No. I won't forgive him." Li Thih-tō gritted his teeth. "The Li family is not like this. I won't have this kind of heir."

His anger peaked as he spoke. He put the cage aside and thrust his grandson's head toward the fire.

"Father!" His daughter-in-law rushed forward and kneeled in front to block him.

"Where are your manners?" Li Thih-tō craned his neck, spread his legs, and tilted his head as if he was acting in an opera. "Anyone who dares to speak like this is going to have the same fate as him."

"Father!" everyone shouted.

Li Thih-tō looked at his ashen-face grandson as he spoke. The grandson looked like he'd seen a ghost. His reaction just spurred on Li Thih-tō's performance.

"All of you, back off!"

"Father!" His eldest son Ong-kin stepped forward. Forty years old and hard-working, he'd always wanted to go to the city, but Li Thih-tō held him back. He was Li Thih-tō's favorite. Ong-kin said, "For better or worse, he's my son and your grandson. Don't treat him like this. There's nothing to be gained by burning him to death."

"Shut up," said Li Thih-tō. "He's getting what he deserves."

As soon as he was done speaking, he stirred up the firewood.

The scene upset Li Thih-tō's second eldest son, Kok-siânn, whom Li Thih-tō always considered a wastrel. Kok-siânn was frustrated by the posturing of the clique led by his father. He'd sometimes go gamble and play games by the cottonwood tree. He didn't care at all for his father's performances. After getting married, he wanted the family to divide its property and for him to go his own way.

He would tell people that his father was old, blind, and out of touch. He was the only son that dared to rebel like this.

"What are you doing with this fire?" Kok-siânn went over to pull his nephew away and said, "He's alive and you want to burn him to death. What kind of society is this? A death penalty requires a trial, and here you are playing judge and jury."

"What are you doing? Damn it. What are you doing?"

Li Thih-tō saw his second son coming over to block him. Li Thih-tō lost his actor's poise and yelled, "Are you rebelling?"

"Rebellion? Whatever. You'll pay if you commit murder." He pulled Li Thih-tō's hand off his nephew's collar and kicked the firewood aside.

"What are you doing?!"

Li Thih-tō lost his focus for a moment and then recovered his anger. This time his reaction was total. His body and spirit were taken over by a brutal rage. When his family saw the second brother step in, they mustered the courage to grab the grandson and tell him to run for his life.

"Damn you! How dare you go against me?" Li Thih-tō shouted himself hoarse as his grandson ran off. "Unfilial son!" He pointed and shrieked at Kok-siânn.

"Father, forgive me," said Kok-siânn. "I said before that our family should split up. If we'd done that, you wouldn't have any need to worry about this matter. We'd handle it ourselves. Father, you're old. You should just let us look after you."

"What are you saying? Divide the family property? It's still too early. With all I've got, no one would want to do that."

"Father, life is difficult these days. This year's rice harvest is all germinating. The price won't be high. If we split and go our separate ways and look after our own families, everyone will be better off."

"Unfilial son! What are you saying? What germination? I won't let that happen! I'll sell at a good price. You'll see. You dare to go against me? How can I not teach you a lesson today?"

Li Thih-tō stepped forward, still filled with anger, and hit his son. His relatives stepped in to stop him. One said, "Father, cool your anger! Calm down! Don't lower yourself to Kok-siânn's level! It's not right to divide the family."

Originally, Li Thih-tō had some faint inkling that he was out of line, but hearing the rest of them reaffirm his criticism of Kok-siânn caused him to regain his blind confidence and poured oil on the flames of his anger. He hurried back to the living room, pulled out a garden knife from behind the door, and came back to kill Kok-siânn. Everyone jumped aside when they saw him wielding the knife.

"You disrespectful son. I will stab you!"

Li Thih-tō chased after Kok-siânn.

After a while, Li Thih-tō fell short of breath and came back to the hall to take a rest. He couldn't stand being disobeyed like this. He thought that no matter what, he'd been in charge for decades and knew what was right. Farming was right. Ong-kin and those sons were all in their 30s and 40s. What could they do besides farm? Farming could fill their bellies. The times may change, but rice would grow all the same. As for dividing the family, it was too early to speak of that. He was still gasping for air and felt gloomy about the rice germination issue. On top of that was Kok-siânn's aggressive attitude. He couldn't keep himself from shouting, "I'm Thih-tō! I'm Thih-tō!"

Soon someone came in carrying a leather bag.

"Oh!" Li Thih-tō quickly rose to his feet and said, "Take a seat."

The person said, "I come on behalf of Lim Baiyi."

"Ah, one of Lim Oo's people. My apologies. It's an honor to receive you."

They sat and spoke about the piles of rice in the courtyard.

May 11. Weather: Rainy.
Last night the rain fell hard. A chicken coop built by someone from outside town had flooded. In the early morning, seven or eight village women each paid 10 NT to buy one of the freshly slaughtered chicken.

Bigmouth Yang was back from the hospital, her face pale and body covered in ointments. She cursed Bān-hok's bad behavior to anyone who would listen and rallied people to support her cause. She talked like she was running for office against him.

Villagers figured that the police were unlikely to patrol on a rainy night, so they gathered on the roof of the barbershop and gambled and drank and had the most fun they'd had in ages.

May 12. Weather: Cloudy with rain.
The ghost that Ling saw was the talk of the town today. Redhead said it was a god, so they went to ask Brother Rat for a divination. He determined it had to do with the temple turtle, who would reincarnate in Daniunan to serve as Governor-General and resolve the flooding problem. Someone pointed out that there were no more Governor-Generals in today's administrative system. Brother Rat said that the Governor-General was simply the provincial chairman.

Brother Rat's fantastic claims were heard even in the neighboring villages. They also became an object of ridicule for Daniunan's civil servants and teachers.

Today, all the junior high and high school students were working hard. It was said that the day for exams in the city was approaching.

May 13. Weather: Overcast. Location: Near the cottonwood trees.
At dusk came a few short spells of thunder and lightning. They ended quickly, and the downfall diminished into a pitter-patter dropping from the eaves. A beam of light came through a break in the clouds in the western sky, like a ray of hope. Everyone was excited. Like early birds waking up from fear and trembling, they stuck their necks out and looked at a sun that hadn't been seen for nearly half a month. Faces lit up with joy. They hoped that there would be demand for their rice. Even better news came from a team of rice cutters at Liau Tshiū-tiong's place.

Rice Diary

Liau's family lived in the middle of the village. Because of the location, it was natural that he'd be part of the cottonwood crowd. His half-mud brick house was left over from the Japanese occupation period. It was renovated now and finally had new roof tiles. Given the village renewal and beautification projects, many outsiders might mistake it for a totally modern house. Liau had built a low fence around his property within which to store items and raise pigs. Garlic hung from the eaves and cobwebs covered the mud wall, refracting the light cast from the dry well in the front of the courtyard. Normally it looked dry and musty, except it was the rainy season and the whole world was covered in water.

At dusk, in the light of the setting sun, a flock of birds perched and chirped on a power line by the courtyard. Bees buzzed around the walls and then disappeared into their nearby hiding spots.

The rice cutters washed their hands and feet and moved a bench and an eight-sided table out from the hall. They took off their damp shirts, sat down, and smoked some Longlife cigarettes.

"Finally, we see some sun," said Liau Tshiū-tiong, shaking his head as he took out a bunch of cigarettes, booze, and betel nuts from the kitchen. He was slender and had a sharp face. He often had a flash of fear on his face when he looked at people.

"Guess it's your good luck. Maybe tomorrow will be a hot and sunny day and your rice will be saved," said one of the cutters, Hok-ah. He was just saying this to console him. The cutters knew that out of everyone in Daniunan, Liau Tshiū-tiong's rice was in the worst shape. He planted it two weeks late, so the grains were still green. Now that they were flooded, they had to be cut, even though they weren't even 40% mature. Such consoling words showed that Hok-ah was a kind person.

The sky was resplendent in colors, layered with dark blue clouds fringed with gold. The sun rested on fluffy clouds. It almost looked as if it was smiling like a plump and happy baby.

Liau Tshiū-tiong put his goods on the low bench and said, "Have some. Don't be shy. The food will be ready soon." He nodded his head again and said, "You all enjoy this here, and then go home drunk. My Shaoxing wine is superb."

The cutters smiled and took some betel nut and cigarettes.

"Tshiū-tiong, didn't you say you were going to get some military pension? Any news?"

The person asking the question was the foreman of the cutting crew. He was the one who paid all the laborers and arranged their room and board.

"Soon," said Liau.

"Last month around the tree, didn't you say you got it? But now still nothing?" The foreman pressed.

Liau Tshiū-tiong was well known in Daniunan for his ambitions, dreams, and schemes. In his youth, for whatever reason, his harvest would always be a bit less than his neighbors. He was never concerned enough to find out why. He'd just tell them that how that little bit didn't matter much and how he'd grow that much more than they would in the following year. Two years earlier, he ran for village head on behalf of the cottonwood crowd. He lost, but he didn't take it as a setback. He said, "Even if I won, I wouldn't have taken the job. Next year, I'll run for town representative! You'll see!" Even now, his ambitions were just getting higher and more imaginative. For example, Liau was sure he was going to get a military pension. During the Japanese period, he'd gone to fight in the Pacific. He was filled with ambition at that time, too. He was always hungry in the Taiwanese countryside, so he went to serve as a soldier, where he'd get paid 200 a month, which would make him rich in a year or two. Alas, Japan's fortunes turned toward the end of the war, and they didn't have enough money to pay him. Instead of giving him 200 a month, they paid him 30 and said they would send the rest to Taiwan. After the war, when he and other soldiers returned home, they discovered that the money never made it. The military kept it in their own accounts. Now, there was a group trying to sue for compensation and they sent a letter to Liau, who acted like he had just won the lottery after receiving it. His dreams were driven by the promise of the payout, which might be as large as 50,000 NT. It wasn't long before he spoke of it under the cottonwood trees.

"You all know who's the richest guy in town?" he asked.

"Lim Oo," said Bān-hok. "If it's not him, it's the village head and Li Thih-tō."

"No," said Liau, cutting him off.

"No?" Everyone was startled.

"Next month, there will be someone even richer than them."

"Who?" said Ling. He didn't believe it.

"I'm not going to say who it is." Liau's face lit up. He continued, "But you can guess. Did anyone in Daniunan go to Southeast Asia?"[4]

"Oh." Bān-hok thought about it and said, "Shuibo, the guy at the end of the village, but he's dead now. Li Gu's two sons, too. They apparently died in Borneo. That just leaves you."

"Yes, just me."

"Fuck off." Ling had no time for such games. "You're lucky to be alive, but what does going to Southeast Asia have to do with money?"

"I'm going to get 500 thousand!" Liau raised his head high and looked at Ling with disdain. Soon, the whole village heard about it.

The cutting crew heard about it too.

But everyone knew that Liau always started talking big when he was down on his luck. The cutters had reason to be concerned because their fees ran into the thousands. What would happen if he couldn't pay up?

Liau could guess why the foreman was asking the question but didn't think it was worth worrying about. After all, the flooding was everywhere.

If he couldn't pay, the others around the cottonwoods probably couldn't either. Why were the cutters only worried about him, especially when he was going to get a big military payout soon? He regained his confidence.

He walked over to the other side and said, "Hok-ah, what do you think about my crop this season? It's done well, right? If the rain hadn't come early, how would you rate it?"

"100%!" Hok-ah bit his lip and, as usual, gave an unduly kind answer.

"That's right!" Liau took the chance to tell the whole crew, "Next year it'll be 120%. You'll see!" They all burst out laughing.

A bit later, the sky began turning dark. A white fog overtook the sunlight. A few stars twinkled. Everything on the ground looked as if it had just been salvaged from the water. The sounds of drinking continued reverberating through Liau's courtyard.

After everyone had a few drinks in them, the eight-sided table was covered by spent candles and chopsticks. Liau reclined and started thinking about the olden days. "Tell me, how did people deal with the troubles of the past?" Liau raised his glass and asked everyone.

"When? You're asking about which time?" They didn't follow.

"30 years ago, Java, Bali."

"Oh." The crew realized he was talking about the war in the Pacific again. "What about it?"

"Every afternoon it poured there." Liau looked at Hok-ah and Ling like he was looking at his wife. He shook his head and said, "They have rice, too!"

"They have rice, too?" The crew looked like it was the first they'd heard of this.

"While fleeing from battle, we ate brown rice, too." Liau scowled as he said, "Their rice isn't as tasty as ours. Still, we never had a month and half without sun."

"That's the tropics!" said Hok-ah, based on what little he knew of it. "The sun is always out there."

"That's right," nodded Liau. His ardor had returned. "Those are the tropics. Plants and fruits grow easily there. There's always something to eat. The rivers are filled with fish. You never go to bed hungry."

"Wow." The crew raised their eyebrows and laughed incredulously.

"Fuck!" Liau turned to the crew boss and said, "When the war ended, a lot of men stayed and married local women. If I hadn't come back to Daniunan, and stayed there, I'd be an overseas Chinese. You know what that means?"

Some of the crew nodded, and others shook their head.

"It means that I'd be rich." Liau continued, "Richer than Lim Oo!"

The food on the table got more and more elaborate. Liau may have been poor, but he was generous. The crew got more and more enthusiastic as more food came out. The deputy foreman, Lim A-píng, stood up and said, "Speaking of Lim Oo, I have good news. We're relatives. Yesterday I came back to see my grandfather, and heard he's going to do some big business."

"What business?"

"I heard he's going to buy up a lot of our rice."

"Oh!"

Liau and the crew were excited at the thought.

May 14. Weather: Rainy
In the morning, a car arrived in the village and parked in front of the temple. It was soon followed by several large buses. These were carrying some villagers coming back from the northern cities to worship at the temple. The organizer was Fire Lion, who'd moved to the city after opening a martial-arts studio in the temple. He'd gone to the city to

expand his martial-arts business and made a lot of money. He'd even acted in some *wuxia* films.

Bigmouth Yang and Bān-hok went to court. Yang thought she could speak for herself and therefore didn't need a lawyer. Bān-hok thought differently; he hired a famous lawyer from the city and treated the judge to a restaurant meal.

At night, the cottonwood crowd gathered around the town shop and watched a new puppet show on TV. Too bad it was in Mandarin and they could only follow a fraction of it.

May 15. Weather: Rainy.
There was big news at the temple today. Brother Rat had been jumping about all day, possessed by the spirits. This was because last time he'd said that the ghost child that Ling saw was the temple turtle, which would be reincarnated as the provincial chairman and resolve the flooding problems. But some people said that the provincial chairman was too high an official to help a village as small as Daniunan. To find the truth of the matter, Brother Rat did another divination. First he said that the turtle would be reincarnated as the head of the irrigation agency, and then he said that it might become a provincial representative.

Which would it be? No one knew for sure. Still, the people were happy to hear that a god was on its way to help them.

May 16. Weather: First sun. Location: Village road.
By the middle of the month, the weather had gradually turned. The clouds thinned, and the rain went from big droplets to small drizzles. The TV reported that the rain might finally stop. By this time, most of the rice had been cut. The green bamboo rods in the fields looked wet and refreshed. At the same time, the freshly harvested rice stalks were wet and moldy. Everyone knew that nothing could be done about it, so they put their harvest in the paddies to be used as fertilizer for the next season. Fortunately, Daniunan had modernized enough by now that

they didn't need to use the dried stalks as cooking fuel. At least there was no loss, in that respect.

But a different kind of loss became clearer today on the village road.

At noon, the sun shone brightly enough to dry up much of the water pooled around the village. People smiled as some of the rice that had been harvested early finally dried out. After the sun started to set behind the temple, some of the villagers came out to the activity center and the roadside. They carried bamboo and stood against the electric poles or leaned against the wall as a fan circulated over the piles of rice, which were then lifted and dumped into a funnel.

This was a way to process poor-quality rice. This was important to the village because this rice would become animal feed for ducks and geese. Too much poor-quality rice was bad for the people, but too little was bad for the poultry. During a typical harvest season, people would let some of the decent rice also get blown in with the discards for the poultry.

This time was different though. People were less generous. They didn't want a single grain of good rice to get blown into the feed batch. Starting at the front of the village, the first farmer to get his rice processed was Li Tâi-se, with his Kaohsiung #1 rice, followed by Lim Hōng-bé, and then on to the cottonwoods, the barber shop, and so on. The roads were lit up and bustling with people. Everyone wanted to process their rice today in case the weather turned rainy again later.

Two power poles away from the cottonwood trees, Lim Hōng-bé and her husband were busy fanning the leaves away from their harvest. They were newlyweds who had earlier followed the crowd and moved to the city. Lim Hōng-bé had studied tailoring, and her husband made sheet metal, but because such crafts were not very profitable, they moved back to Daniunan, where they met and got hitched. It was rare to see returning villagers get married like this, and it seemed to give a new lease on life to the place. People said that the times had changed, that the village had turned a corner.

They also felt that the countryside was on the upswing, so they did their part and planted some crops.

CLACK-CLACK-CLACK. Lim Hōng-bé rhythmically fanned the leaves away and consolidated the good rice into a pile. Her husband raked it to one side. It was their first time doing this, so they looked more excited than most people, almost like they were welcoming a first child.

As they fanned and raked, their joy turned to gloom as they realized most of their rice was spoilt.

At some point, Yang and Auntie Tshiu-song came by. Yang's temper had gotten even sharper after going to court. Seeing the couple's rice lit up under the electric pole, she exclaimed, "Whoa! So much broken rice! What a calamity!"

She picked up a handful of rice to inspect and turned to face Lim Hōng-bé. The young couple froze. They knew their rice had been flooded but didn't think the situation was so dire. Upon hearing what Yang said, they thought it might be beyond repair. It was their first season growing rice. Of course, they were worried.

"Auntie Yang, it's not that bad, is it?" the husband asked nervously.

"You youngsters wouldn't know the difference. Go ask your parents and you'll find out. This season's sprouted rice will be hard to sell, and even more so this broken rice."

"Yang, don't scare the youngsters!" Tshiu-song quickly tried to console them, "Yang was exaggerating. Don't worry about it. All of us are in the same boat."

"Yes," Lim Hōng-bé said, sounding aggrieved. "I don't think we've done much worse than anyone else."

"Come on. Your rice is only 60% good. You've got a land tax, duties, cutters, and so on to pay. It won't be enough."

As Yang went on like this, Tshiu-song did her best to smooth out the situation.

By night, everyone heard that the earliest harvest in the village was only 60% good.

That same night, a large tricycle pulled up by Lim Baiyi's ancestral home.

May 17. Weather: Mostly sunny, with some clouds and rain.
The morning saw some showers, but then the sun came out strong. The villagers dried some rice and harvested some more.

Around noontime the sun was still intense, and the villagers danced with joy.

After lunch, Brother Rat did another ceremony at the temple. This divination concluded that the turtle would be reincarnated as a provincial representative. Everyone approved because the representative would be able to speak on behalf of the people. But then, the turtle had a surprising message. When Ling had come to light incense and pray to the turtle, he discovered that the turtle walked unstably. Upon inspection, it turned out to be lame. The cottonwood and barbershop crowds all ran over to see it. The temple was packed tightly with people.

Brother Rat did another divination but said nothing because this time, heaven's will was supposed to be kept top secret.

At night, the gamblers played cards in the straw piles behind the activity center. They talked so loudly that the police came. Tenn Bák-sim and Li Kok-yong were arrested and brought to the station to get their details taken down.

May 18. Weather: Sunny. Location: By the temple.
The weather cleared up. A high-pressure front was coming in from the sea, and a southern wind blew in from the Bashi Channel, flitting from

the sea to the fields and through the coconut palms of the village. People rested and slept in their homes, farm tents, and in the temple.

The rainy season was over.

At this time, the paddies of the south and central parts of Formosa were almost all harvested, while the rice in the north was still green. Rice merchants moved from place to place to buy from growers, trying to extract the best price within the parameters set by the government.

Now was the time for the people of Daniunan to sell the rice they'd grown over the last half a year.

Today, a large crowd surrounded Tshiu-song's rice piles, including folks from the cottonwood crowd like Bān-hok with the flat nose, Sin-thuân, Bigmouth Yang, Liau Tshiū-tiong, and so on. The barbershop crowd's Lim Duo, Tenn Ba̍k-sim, and Goldie were also there, as well as people from the temple crowd, like Li Thih-tō, Li Tshing-ian, and so on. They'd all come to see how Tshiu-song's rice would sell.

Unexpectedly, the purchaser was not Lim Baiyi, but a stranger from the north. He wore a large and flowery shirt with a dragon motif, and rubber shoes. He was fat with a dark complexion and a down-to-earth, trustworthy appearance.

Tshiu-song's rice was also harvested early. Not much had sprouted. It was among the best in the village. Her son had recently been working in the fishing industry and wanted to invest in a boat. Tshiu-song wanted to use the earnings from this rice to support his business, so she hoped to get a good price.

Everyone in the village stuck out their necks to watch the negotiation.

Tshiu-song opened up the sack of rice, which emitted a warm and moist rush of air. Only the bottom layers had sprouted.

"Hmm." The merchant grabbed a handful of rice and inspected it in his palm for a while before saying, "Ma'am, this rice is no good."

Rice Diary

"What?" Tshiu-song wrinkled her face in response. "It's fine. The top is good and fully grown. There's only a little damage in the bottom layer."

"I can't buy this.," said the merchant. He pointed his fingers and said, "Ma'am, at least 30% of this is bad. If I buy it, how am I supposed to sell it?"

The onlookers felt worried upon hearing this. Still, they knew that business was business, and that even if you had a piece of jade to sell, someone would try to bargain like it was a brick. How else does anyone make a profit? Everyone knew they were in a similar situation. If Tshiu-song couldn't sell her rice, what were they supposed to do? Liau Tshiū-tiong, watching from the sidelines, already had an ideal price in his mind. He hoped this wouldn't undercut it. So, he stepped forward to intervene.

"Boss, everyone eats rice. Everywhere has been flooded. Not just Daniunan, but elsewhere too. If you can't buy good rice here, you can't buy it anywhere. Tshiu-song has the best rice in town. If you don't buy hers, whose will you buy?"

Liau spoke with intensity, bearing himself the way he had after returning from the war. He was worried that the merchant would see that his own harvest didn't measure up. He emphasized every single syllable as he spoke. When he said, "If you don't buy hers, whose will you buy?" he pulled out a cigarette from his pocket and ended with a grunt.

The merchant smiled upon hearing this, but his dark face revealed little else. He also pulled out his cigarettes, nodded as if he was considering what Liau had to say. He offered a few smokes to onlookers and laughed.

"Let's consider this. Yes, this year's crop is indeed unfortunate. For one thing, there are many growers, and for another, there were floods. Naturally, the price can't be high. If you don't sell quick, the price may collapse even further, and no one will want it anyway. It's not just you farmers—we merchants are concerned too."

Rice merchants were worried? They all gasped. Still, what he was saying made some sense. If the commodity price also collapsed in the next few days, they might suffer losses too. There was no choice but to sell. Everyone pursed their lips. The situation frustrated Li Thih-tō the most. This year's harvest was supposed to determine whether he could divide his family's property. If the price dropped, and his offspring still wanted to go ahead and split, he'd have no leg to stand on. He thought for a moment before speaking up.

"Boss, name your price. How much do you want to at least not make a loss?"

"Yes, how much?" Everyone joined in.

"It's like this." The merchant extended the four fingers of his left hand and all five fingers on his right.

"540," said everyone, with disbelief.

"No." The merchant shook his head and said, "450."

"450." Everyone's eyes opened wide. "You're saying 100 catties for 450 NT?"[5]

"Yes, that's right."

"That's a crazy price!" Everyone shouted and muttered as if it was the end of the world.

"Boss." Tshiu-song spoke up, tugging nervously at her own shirt sleeve. She'd bought the floral print garment for 5 NT at a stall on the road. She said, "You're joking, right, boss? Before, when there were price guarantees, the price was 720! How can it drop so much?"

"There's no way. Times have changed. Everything depends on timing."

The villagers looked like roosters who'd just lost a fight and stood there dumbstruck. Lim Duo had an idea. Maybe it came from his barbering sensibility.

"What you say is true: the price will indeed fall, but that's a matter for later. We've just harvested. There's not much rice in the rest of Formosa.

Rice Diary

The price should be better. Your 450 is not enough. It's not fair. There's been inflation. What happens if someone has already bought out the rice wherever you go next?"

"Hmm." The trader thought for a while after being thrown off balance by Lim Duo's argument. His cigarette smoke drifted into his hair.

"Yes, yes." The villagers regained their confidence. "Boss, you're smart. You should buy now while you have the chance."

"You, you..." Flat-nosed Bān-hok began. "You said yourself it's all about timing."

Of course, Bigmouth Yang couldn't just keep silent while Bān-hok spoke. Sure, she was in court with him, but she also had to join hands with her neighbors on this. Standing next to Tshiu-song, she chimed in, "Tshiu-song, you have the best rice in the village. If someone is going to be so cheap with you, don't sell to him. See if he can do better somewhere else."

"Boss." Tshiu-song felt buoyed by her neighbors' support. Still, she was nervous. "500, okay? I'm just a woman who doesn't know much about business. I'll sell you my best rice for 500. It's hard and dry and good. Think about it."

"Okay." The trader drew deeply on his cigarette before tossing it and stamping it out with his feet. Finally, he said, "500 is too much. How about 480? If that works, I'll send my assistant to the temple in the afternoon, and you can work it out with him."

He turned away as he finished speaking. His shirt's golden print glinted in the light.

After he left, all the villagers scattered and carried the bad news with them. 480! 480! Everyone sighed and shuddered. Even the withered papaya trees by the temple seemed to shake. That afternoon, people saw Tshiu-song looking anxious around the temple, as the trader's assistant moved her rice sacks onto his tricycle. The villagers were both jealous of her and worried about their own situations.

More importantly, though, the rumors about Lim Baiyi grew louder and louder.

May 19. Weather: Sunny.
Fire Lion, who'd moved to the city to start a martial-arts studio, had started a brand called Golden Lion Firm Muscle Medicine, a remedy for bruises.[6] It sold all over the island and everyone in the village was proud of it.

The high schoolers were nervously preparing for their exams. The activity center was cleared of the rice piles and opened up for them to study late into the night.

The biggest news was about the temple turtle, whose condition had changed yet again. Brother Rat did another divination and found that it had already been reincarnated as a person who would rescue the village. People would receive its blessings soon.

The cottonwood crowd was delighted. Ling gathered a bunch of people to go burn incense at the temple. Yang told people the good news as she did her laundry. Soon, everyone in the village was exclaiming: "Daniunan has a savior, Daniunan has a savior!"

The teachers and officials were not impressed. They told their kids not to believe such superstition.

May 20. Weather: Clear. Location: Activity Center.
The sun was still high in the sky. The weather report predicted there would be a week of good weather. Everyone was happy for the good news. The rice had already dried and been stuffed into sacks. They waited for the merchants to come and negotiate.

BANG BANG POP. A string of firecrackers went off by the walls of the activity center.

Now, at seven o'clock in the evening, the sky turned dark but for the silver light of the Milky Way. Inside the activity center was a podium,

Rice Diary 113

a large cloth-covered table, with two flower vases on top, and many seats lit up by bright fluorescent lights. People filled the audience seats, while others stood by the walls as if they were getting ready to watch a performance.

This was not a performance, however. It was the village meeting. Apart from weddings and funerals, it was a rare occasion that would gather this many people. People usually couldn't be bothered to attend village meetings, but this one was full.

Today was the day that county officials came to inspect the disaster. In the morning, a bus had parked on the village road. The passengers emerged wearing suits and sporting combed, oiled hair. The villagers didn't think much about them first, because temple worshippers from out of town would sometimes show up like this too. However, everyone's attention was grabbed when the village loudspeakers announced the arrival of the county magistrate, officials, and experts. After all, everyone had worked hard to elect the magistrate. He was like a parent, so of course they would pay attention to him. Modern elections weren't easy. Educational qualifications were higher than they used to be. You couldn't bribe your way in with soap and MSG like you could before. Sure, some voters would take bribes, but even after they took them they wouldn't necessarily vote for that candidate. Everyone had their own opinions and points of view. They all voted for whoever they saw the most on TV and in the newspapers. Before, they might even hand all their ID cards over to someone who would stamp their ballots for them. During recent elections, they learned about the sacredness of voting by watching TV. Turnout had gone as high as 98%, and villages with the highest turnouts would get praised as model villages on TV. So, even though no one knew anything about this magistrate except that he was surnamed Hsieh, they all wanted to see him, especially if he was coming to inspect the disaster.

Given the circumstances, the people of Daniunan were excited.

Inside the venue, Li Thih-tō and his temple crowd sat in the front. From left to right were Li Tâi-se, Li Gaoshan, Li Tshing-ian, and another fellow surnamed Lin. They were all holding cigarettes and acting like they were waiting for something. These people were not to be underestimated. The temple crowd was measured and upright in their speech. This came from Li Thih-tō. They all knew the proper etiquette for weddings and ceremonies, which put them in good stead with the village head, whose son had recently married Li Thih-tō's daughter. From this angle, they were like the helpers of the village head, or even like the ruling party they heard about sometimes on TV.

Of course, Li Thih-tō and the rest of them understood little about the ruling party. Even Li Tshing-ian, who'd just run for village representative, had only the faintest idea.

Behind the temple was were the barbershop crew led by Lim Duo and Tenn Bȧk-sim. They were like the middle class of the village, not dominant but also not the poorest. They were relatively sober and objective. In the back were the folks of the cottonwood trees, including Bān-hok, Sin-thuân, and so on. They were the most uneducated and knew the least about modern politics. Still, they loved to talk even if they didn't quite understand what was going on and ended up making fools of themselves. They didn't show up to this event just for fun. When the fields were still flooded, the TV had spoken about them and even flashed a few seconds of a conversation between Tshiu-song and Bigmouth Yang. If only the show hadn't edited out so much of Yang's speech, everyone would know the truth. So, they came prepared to speak.

After the customary firecrackers went off, a group of people walked inside the doors, including a short, fat, rich-looking, bald, round-headed man wearing gold-rimmed glasses, who was followed by a group of men in suits and slicked hair. In the back was the barefoot, frog-eyed, short-necked village head, and some township office staff and village officials.

Li Thih-tō jumped up to clap and welcome them. He was followed by the people behind him.

Finally, the guests reached the podium and took their seats. The village head served as chairman of the meeting and sat in the center. On his right was the bald man. The men in suits sat on either side. The village head's secretary served as emcee. He stood to the side laughing and socializing with participants. The meeting had not yet begun. The emcee went to tell the attendees that the bald man was the magistrate.

Everyone started happily chattering.

"Magistrate." Li Tshing-ian went to give him a Longlife cigarette. He'd run for office and knew the drill. The magistrate nodded and warmly accepted the cigarette.

"Thank you." Li Tshing-ian felt acknowledged and quickly lit the cigarette. The cottonwood crowd saw this and clenched their teeth. They hated seeing the temple people behave this way. They were usually fierce and acted like everyone in town owed them money. But here meeting their betters, they shook their heads and wagged their tails like army dogs.

"What brings the magistrate to our humble village?" asked Li Thih-tō in an exceedingly polite tone.

"To see your rice," said the magistrate. "I've heard your loss has been severe."

"Yes." Li Thih-tō took the chance to press on, "It's terrible, terrible. If you have a moment to take a look at my home, you'll see." He put stress on the words, "*my home.*"

"Okay, okay." The magistrate turned to ask the village head about the possibility.

The bell rang and the secretary and staff announced the start of the meeting. The village head spoke for a while. Then, the magistrate stood up and spoke, "Ladies and gentlemen, I've come today to the village to see your township head." He turned to face the township staff, who all sat up straight at attention. He continued, "The township head has raised the issue of your village, which has done well and looks impressive. Under the village head, you have earned recognition as a model village. This is not an easy achievement to make."

As the magistrate spoke, his gold-rimmed glassed slipped down his nose, amusing the villagers. "But this flood has really been unfortunate." Now he was getting to the point. "Today we come to resolve the problem for everyone. Before we discuss a solution, I've asked an agricultural expert to explain the current policy."

No one expected the magistrate to be so considerate. Everyone clapped and spoke to each other before the expert stood up. He wore a white dress shirt and finely cut trousers. His hair was radiant and his skin fine and fair. He looked intelligent. He began his speech by saluting all the attendees, and then he spoke about the pricing plan for the rice. He started by surveying the price of rice over the span of Chinese history, illustrated with examples from Emperor Qin Shihuang's conquering of the six kingdoms over two thousand years prior. The villagers didn't have any grasp of classical Chinese and followed very little of this. They smoked and remained silent until the county finance official spoke about rice production in a much more modern register which regained their attention. He asked for everyone to share their suggestions so that they all could learn from each other. The villagers became increasingly animated.

"The rice has sprouted. It's not okay. We hope the county can speak to their superiors on our behalf and help us sell it." The first to speak was Li Tâi-se, from the temple crowd.

"I think the land tax should be lowered," said Li Tshing-ian.

"The government can help with a subsidy," said another.

The cottonwood crowd saw the temple people talking so much and couldn't help but join in.

"Yes, yes, land taxes and duties should all be waived."

The expert couldn't suppress his smile. "You must be joking to suggest waiving taxes. Don't you know that our government relies on your land tax?"

Lim Duo stood up and said, "If you can't waive the land tax, then take it in rice this year. Everyone's rice has sprouted. We've all suffered. To take it as is would not be asking too much."

The expert said he'd pass this suggestion on to the provincial grain bureau.

Another official said, "To improve the well-being of the farmers, it would be best to increase the amount of rice that gets sold, to reduce imports, and to encourage exports of surplus."

The expert said he'd also pass this suggestion to the bureau.

Everyone started talking and the whole room was filled with noise.

At this point, Liau Tshiū-tiong stood up from the corner where he'd been stewing in silence. It was just yesterday that he'd used the air blower to divide the good and bad rice and discovered that nearly half of his yield was nothing but empty husks. He was not happy. He said to the room, "You all have a lot of theories, but you don't need to talk so much. I think the most important thing now is the price. During past times of inflation, we could sell for over 600. Everything is even more inflated now, and we can only sell for 480. That's a huge loss. How are we supposed to survive?"

"That's right!" Bān-hok stood up on behalf of the cottonwood crowd. "Damn it, we work day and night in the fields, hungry as ghosts, and now no one wants our rice, and still you tell us to grow more. What are you talking about?"

"Yes, that makes sense," an official said. "We have to think of some way to increase the price. Even if it can't all be sold to the government, at least they should increase the amount that they'll guarantee! Right now, 970kg per hectare is practically nothing."

"Yes, so purchasing is the most important thing." Liau stepped forward, tapped his head, and came to light a cigarette for the magistrate. He said, "Magistrate, I have a suggestion. Let's build a storehouse. Every village puts forward 100 people. It will only take a month or two to build. We can do it. What do you think?"

"Damn it, a storehouse? Damn." Kachun shook his head and shouted. He wanted to say that two years prior, the Farmers Association said they would build a warehouse, but there was still no sign of it. He lost his nerve when he tried to speak in front of the magistrate and ended up just waving his arms around.

The meeting began descending into chaos.

The emcee read the mood and shouted, "Silence!" Everyone took their seats. The officials and experts looked on with pained expressions.

"From now on, people who want to speak shall raise their hands," said the village head.

"I have an opinion." In the far back, Sin-thuân raised his hand and stood up. "I think the government should put up some money to bail us out."

"Yes. A financial bailout," said someone nearby.

The official heard this and then stood up.

"This is not possible. The county government has no money!"

"What do you mean, no money?" A civil servant stood up and said, "Didn't you say that you use our land tax to fund your budgets? How can you have no money? Plus you have other sources of revenue."

"Too many villages are flooded."

"That's not the issue," said Sin-thuân, interrupting the official. "Dani-unan is in the worst shape. You can budget a bailout for us."

"This...This..."

"Damn it," Sin-thuân continued. "When it's time for our rice to be taxed, we line right up and kindly send it to the Farmers Association. If it's less hard or dry than they like, they refuse it and we suffer the loss. And now that there's a disaster, there's no support at all."

The scene got noisy again.

"Please understand our difficulty!" The officials could do little but plead.

"Understand what?" Liau drew on the memory of his vigor from thirty years prior, from his time in Java and Bali, and said, "You should understand our shriveled bellies."

The meeting went on like this for a while with no resolution. Finally, someone at the entrance, shrouded by backlighting, spoke up. Everyone turned to see his silhouette. He looked fat. He said that fighting would not solve anything, and that people should face facts and come to terms with prices. He said that in a day or two a group of merchants would arrive and that Lim Baiyi would start buying rice.

May 21. Weather: Sunny.
The Farmers Association sent a notice that Daniunan residents could get seeds to grow Meinung melons and pear melons. This would be a good fruit crop for the period between the two seasons for growing rice.

Lim Duo prepared to build a small wooden structure by the barbershop. He'd planned to sell pesticides, but the villagers warned him that his father would think it was soda and drink it. Lim Duo changed his mind upon hearing such comments. Someone suggested he sell animal feed instead. Even if his father ate that, the worst that could happen is that he'd turn into a fat pig, which wouldn't be worth worrying about.

The temple always had something going on. Brother Rat did divination at night and said that a supernatural force had moved toward the village entrance and would soon rescue everyone. To show that the gods were really speaking through him, he grabbed a knife and cut his back till it was bloody. The cottonwood crowd was impressed.

May 22. Weather: Sunny. Location: By the cottonwood trees.
After the village meeting, everyone in Daniunan had one of three attitudes in facing the problem. The first was like the black-faced temple god. This camp believed what the officials said and thought the government was helpless. Another camp was like the spirit of Guandi, the god of war, who fought to overcome obstacles. They said that the village had long suffered at the city's expense, and they cursed the bureaus for encouraging them to grow more rice and ignoring their problems. Another camp was more like the Maitreya Buddha, willing to laugh it off and keep an optimistic attitude.

No matter what attitude they had, they hoped that a miracle would happen and the price of rice would shoot up.

Who knew that today their prayers would be answered?

There was a dilapidated bamboo house by the cottonwood trees. Such a bamboo house was a rare sight now in the modernizing countryside. Sure, there were some in the city, but those were used for cafes or tourist visits. In the village, bamboo was for the poor. This dark and dank little house belonged to Li Bóng-sing, who, needless to say, belonged to the cottonwood crowd.

In the brilliant morning light, his family diligently separated the good from the bad rice for further drying because they worried that it wasn't all quite ready yet. Some of the cottonwood crowd dropped by to sit at his place.

Li Bóng-sing's son, Li Kim-hô, had returned from the city where he worked in a steel factory. Li Kim-hô was a hardworking kid. He moved out because he couldn't make a living farming and sent back money every month. He was 27, able to toil, and unmarried. Other people in the tree crowd had relatives like Li Kim-hô who also worked in steel factories.

People talked and laughed under the eaves.

"Kim-hô, you shouldn't have come back. You should have kept working in the factory. Now you're just here eating your father's rice." Sin-thuân was talking to him like an elder instructing a youngster.

"Uncle Sin-thuân, don't be like that." Kim-hô put the rake down and held out his right hand. He said to everyone, "The boss said I could take a few days off to rest."

"Oh." Everyone looked and saw that Kim-hô's right hand only had one finger left, the rest were nubs shriveled like the dead leaves of winter.

They'd heard that his hand had been injured by machinery. Before, he had three fingers left, and now there was only one. The tree crowd was a sympathetic bunch and couldn't hide their shock.

"Kim-hô, you're so unfortunate!" Bān-hok said to the people next to him, "How do these horrible things keep happening to you?"

"Fuck!" Kim-hô laughed bitterly and waved his hand, "This hand is almost finished. Just one little finger left. If only my dad had given me a few extra."

Everyone laughed at his self-deprecation and waited for his father's reaction.

"I told him to stop working in that factory," said Li Bóng-sing. "He never listened. There was no use in saying it. Now he has to eat with his left hand. I won't let him go back. If we can get a decent price on the rice, I'm keeping him here to farm."

Everyone could do little but laugh. "Hey, Kim-hô, how much compensation did the factory give you?" Of course, it would be Liau who would ask something no one else would think of.

"Huh? Why are you asking me this?" said Kim-hô.

"Tell us!"

Everyone knew that there'd be some kind of payout for such accidents, and sometimes it was a lot of money. If you got hit by a car, or if a building collapsed, or if your kids were injured by a schoolteacher, you could make a legal request for compensation.

Kim-hô tried to refuse an answer but couldn't help himself. He unfurled all the fingers on his left hand and said "50 thousand!"

"50 thousand?" They had never heard of so much money.

"Break a finger and get 50 thousand." Liau couldn't help but be envious. "So, for five fingers, you can get 250 thousand. What a good price!"

Liau tapped his head and spoke as if he were the one who'd severed his fingers.

His eyes lit up. "Hey, if any of you want to pay me 250 thousand, I'll give you all five fingers."

As he spoke, he stuck out his left hand, put his right hand on top of it, and gestured as if he was cutting it off.

"Shut the fuck up!" Ling was furious. "Even if you cut your head off for free, I wouldn't take it." He ran his finger across his neck like he was slitting it. Everyone laughed even louder.

At that moment, a motorized cargo tricycle pulled up behind the courtyard. It sputtered and parked.

A man wearing a gauzy white shirt and his three bare-chested sons hopped out. The man was tall and strong, middle-aged with jowls. He wore wooden clogs and grey Bermuda shorts over his veiny legs. He looked like he'd been doing business with farmers for quite some time.

"Hey, Bóng-sing, the rice buyer has come," said Bān-hok.

The folks around the tree stood up and went over the bamboo house to check him out.

"Hi boss, have a seat." It was Liau who arrived first, agile as ever, to welcome him.

"Thanks." The businessman relaxed and took a seat.

"Boss, where are you from? We've been waiting for you forever," said Liau.

"Yes, you sure took your time!"

"Lim Baiyi sent me." The trader passed his pack of cigarettes around. "Lim Baiyi, from that old estate in the front of the village."

"Lame Yi. Yes, we know." Liau lit a cigarette and drew from it as he spoke. "We saw him come back a few days ago. Then at the village meeting, someone said he was going to start purchasing."

"That's right. That's was me who said that," said the trader. "We want to buy a lot. Today we'll first look at Bóng-sing's and the others in the back of the village."

"Bóng-sing, he says he wants to buy yours first."

"What a jackpot," said Ling.

"How much?" Everyone wanted to know.

"550," said the trader.

"Wow, 550 per 100 catties! What a good price!"

Everyone hooted and hollered so loudly that the house almost tumbled down.

May 23. Weather: Sunny.
Many people weren't sure if they wanted to grow cucumbers and melons. All it would take is a heavy wind or rain to ruin the crop. As for Li Thih-tō, he thought that it rained so hard in May that the next two months would be nice and sunny.

Today everyone was talking about the temple prophecy. The turtle divination and Lame Yi's return corresponded strongly, especially because the deity was supposed to arrive around Lin's estate. Everyone thought Lame Yi must have returned to rescue the village. From the cottonwood trees, to the bamboo house, to every corner in the village, everyone was talking about it.

The teachers and officials still weren't impressed. What day and age was this? How could people still believe in such tall tales?

May 24. Weather: Bright and sunny. Location: Temple.
The sun baked the whole village, and there was not a cloud in the sky to cover it. The tree limbs drooped listlessly. The ducks and geese as well as the cats and dogs didn't dare to go outside. They stayed under the pomegranate trees or the eaves, stuck out their tongues and stayed motionless to beat the heat.

The square in front of the temple was bustling with carts and people and rice, all set up in an area that had been cleared to hold performances before the village roads were paved. The square had a few pits where wooden poles could be planted. Blue canvas hung through the air, waves of canopies casting shade. The whole temple square was a market!

It turned out that because Lim Baiyi offered such a good price for the rice, and because he was willing to pay 500 even if it was immature or sprouted, so everyone wanted to sell to him. The whole village was elated and gathered at Lin's old estate to sell. He stood there, holding his cane, standing by two persimmon trees, smiling, and pouring tea for anyone who arrived.

Wow, this Lame Yi had good manners, everyone thought.

Lim sent his representatives to go from house to house to buy rice. The process was as slow as an ox pulling a broken cart. Finally, they reached agreements for everyone to send their rice to the square in front of the temple, where a canopy would be set up.

Sure enough, Lim Baiyi showed his face more after starting the purchases. Not long after Retrocession, when the Japanese primary school became a Republic of China school, all the kids of the town played here —the temple kids, the barber shop kids, the cottonwood kids—and Lim

Baiyi was no exception. The Lim family had a big plot of land that was going to be reformed through the 37.5% Rent Reduction Act. Lim Oo sold the land and went to the city to pursue new opportunities. Like father, like son, Lim Baiyi didn't like to study. He was ugly, his right leg was unusually short, and people liked to ride piggyback on him just for kicks. But he had a sharp and crafty mind, with many tricks up his sleeve. Maybe it came from being lame.

Lim Baiyi was different nowadays. He stood by the scale, wearing a white dress shirt with a checkered print, and a paisley tie. His suit jacket was hanging on a pole beside him. His silver sunglasses glinted in the light. He looked very sharp and civilized, a far cry from his time as a child.

He'd set the terms for the rice. He said the farmers would get 30% in cash up front. Because it was inconvenient to withdraw the rest of the money from the bank now, the farmers could pick up the balance at his place after he completed the entire purchase. The farmers were happy to get some money in their pockets right away.

The sun continued beating down as fiercely as before. The flowers by the temple drooped and closed in the heat.

The barbershop crowd had arrived even before the sun rose. They lined up to weigh their rice, which took a while. After it got hot, Lim Duo, Tenn Bȧk-sim, and Goldie sat by the cars and fanned themselves with their hats.

"Finally, our fortunes are turning," said Goldie. "I thought it was hopeless. Thankfully, Lame Yi is here."

"It can be hard to know when the good times will really come." Lim Duo was in good spirits. "Now I'll have money to pay for my dad's medical expenses."

"Your dad's really scary. One day he's hitting his head with a nail. Another day he's got a razor hanging from his neck. Why doesn't he think to hang money from his waistbelt?"

"I don't get it either." said Lim Duo.

"Who knows. Maybe he's practicing Qi Gong?" said Kachun. "The TV has people playing with knives on their throats like they can perform miracles."

"What are you talking about?" said Goldie. "You have no idea, and still you talk, talk, talk."

Everyone laughed.

"Damn it!" Tenn Bák-sim yelled suddenly.

"What?" asked Goldie. Everyone looked over.

"I forgot. If even sprouted rice can get such a good price, this isn't just a miracle for the town, but a blessing bestowed by my ancestors." Tenn Bák-sim spoke in the tone he would have used when he worked as a bus guard. "I'm going to open a massage parlor."

"What? What are you opening?" asked Goldie.

"I said I'm going to open a massage parlor."

"Open a parlor?" Lim Duo was suspicious. "Where?"

"In Daniunan." Tenn Bák-sim flashed his blackened teeth. "Here."

"Really? Here?" Lim Duo was shocked.

"Yes, why would I joke?"

"Who knew you were that kind of person?" Lim Duo's surprise turned to dismay. "Some friend!"

"What?" Tenn Bák-sim seemed possessed by the idea. "I'll give all the villagers 20 percent off."

"Ha," sneered Kachun. "Twenty percent. For me too?"

"Of course."

"Twenty percent for me, for Goldie, too."

"Calm down," said Goldie.

"Are you serious about doing this?" Lim Duo asked seriously.

"Yes."

"Fine, go ahead. I'm not worried." Lim Duo was mad.

"Hey, Lim Duo, it's your turn for the rice," said someone.

Lim Duo jumped up and got on the tractor and pulled the rice under the awning. Several helpers came over to lower the rice. Lim Duo had had been Lim Baiyi's classmate in primary school. Of course, he'd bullied him then about his short leg. It was strange to see him so well-off now. Lim Duo felt a bit embarrassed, like he was a dog who'd bitten a man, and now that man was coming to feed him.

Am I, Lim Duo, a dog and not a man? The thought made him laugh. Maybe it was just the effect of being around a rich person.

"Hey, Lim Duo, long time no see!" Lim Baiyi came forward and extended his hand to shake.

"Good to see you!"

Lim Duo stuck out his filthy hand and smiled.

"How's the rice this year?" Lim Baiyi fished a cigarette out of his pocket. "Not bad, right?"

"It's sprouted," said Lim Duo, who suddenly regretted opening his mouth. "Well, maybe 10 or 20 percent."

"You're lucky!" Lim Baiyi sounded like a skilled businessman.

Lim Duo felt a little bewildered by Lim Baiyi's attitude. He was a discerning person and wanted to ask what Lim Baiyi meant.

"You want all this rice?" Lim Duo pointed to a nearby pile.

"It's not much." Lim Baiyi drew on his cigarette. "I've bought a lot elsewhere. Every year."

"You must make a lot of money."

"Sometimes I lose money. But for the sake of our village's prosperity, I hope I don't lose too much this year." Lim Baiyi smiled as he spoke, like a businessman in the city might.

"Will you come back next year?" Lim Duo felt some affection for him. After all, they grew up in the same village.

"Let's see. If your price is not too high, then I'll be back."

The rice was being piled up as he spoke. Lim Duo went to the accountants to take his 30 percent payment in cash. They were three pretty ladies calculating all the prices. Apparently, they were all Lim Baiyi's concubines.

Wow. Lame Yi really had it good!

May 25. Weather: Intense sun.
The villagers guessed about whether or not to grow melons. Some said that last year's harvest was big, and that south and central Taiwan had made a fortune on them. So this year, a lot of people would want to grow melons too, and the price might drop. Some opted instead to grow lettuce or cabbage, while others thought that even those were unreliable. Usually during the selling period, there'd be rotting vegetables and traders would always bargain the price down ruthlessly. By the end, only a few hundred catties would move. Every day the news reports would say that prices were rising, with a catty of lettuce going as high as 20 NT, but no one really wanted lettuce from rural farmers.

Still, no matter what, the villagers would choose to grow something extra. This season's rice harvest was so bad that they needed to make up for it with melons or vegetables.

The 4-H Club and the KMT Public Service Station held a dance party in the township. Everyone there danced happily under the moon and stars, but none of them were from Daniunan. After all, how would old people know how to dance? All the dancers were youngsters from the city.

The cottonwood crowd quarreled loudly into the night. Bān-hok and Sin-thuân were certain that the spirit Brother Rat spoke of was Lame Yi. Why? Well, the turtle had a bad leg, like Lame Yi. Moreover, his purchases helped save the village. They felt that he played the role of the irrigation head or provincial representative. The other side, including Ling and Liau Tshiū-tiong, agreed that the divined spirit was definitely Lame Yi. However, they thought that the irrigation head or provincial representative were in insufficiently high offices because the village would certainly face more problems. They thought that he must be the minister of agriculture and forestry, or the head of the grain bureau.

There's no need to look at the cottonwood crowd through the eyes of officials and teachers. These were dignified and decent people who were just trying their best to figure things out.

May 26. Weather: Very Sunny. Location: Near the Farmers Association.
News of Lim Baiyi's purchase rocked the town. People from nearby villages, which had also been flooded, poured in to see the grand occasion. They couldn't believe such a good price could be had. There was no need to doubt it, of course. As soon as they came to town and saw the scene at the temple, they knew Daniunan indeed got lucky. No wonder the Feng Shui masters had said that Daniunan was an auspicious place.

It looked like a savior had indeed arrived.

However, not everyone sold their rice to Lim Baiyi. For example, Li Gaoshan sold his rice to a relative who traded. A few others did as well. Yes, the price was lower than what Lim Baiyi was paying, but there were other advantages. The payment would be settled in full, on the spot. Those least likely to sell to Lim Baiyi were the civil servants and teachers. For one thing, they got their salaries from the government and weren't reliant on earnings from rice, which were just a sideline. For another, they were smarter and paid more attention to the price of rice. For example, Tan Bûn-tī, a schoolteacher who had three kids who studied economics and finance in technical school; Li Thài-pîng, who worked in the township office and whose son worked in the county finance department; Liau Daqing, who worked in the Farmers Association; the secretary Li Qiran; and the township representative Ke Baijin...well, there's no need to go on.

Yes, about 30 percent of the village didn't sell to Lim Baiyi. And their reasons were revealed by Bigmouth Yang.

It so happened that Bigmouth Yang and Bān-hok's case had gone all the way to the High Court. Yang received a subpoena, but she was illiterate. All she knew was that something important had arrived, so she went to the home of Tan Bûn-tī for help. She spent a lot of time with his wife when they were young. While standing in their hallway and seeing a pile of rice in the bathroom, she asked a bunch of questions.

"You don't get it, do you?" Teacher Tan said, "Think about it. Why would Lim Baiyi be so generous? He's up to something."

Yang pressed him.

"Yes. He's going to use the name of the farmers, and the whole Farmers Association to sell what he can at the guaranteed price of 690 NT per 100 catties. As for the rest, he'll dump it on the city market for 550 or so, because it's the first rice of the season. He'll make a lot."

"Oh," She nodded, though she didn't totally follow. She did know that the teacher wouldn't lie.

After hearing this, whenever she saw anyone, she'd say, "Damn Lim Baiyi. He's taking all our money!"

Word got around, and because Yang was the first to have exposed other people's folly, she went around feeling as clairvoyant as the goddess

Rice Diary

Matsu. She around saying "Damn Lim Baiyi! He's taking all our money" even more enthusiastically and seemed to have forgotten all about her court case with Bān-hok.

Today was the third day for the Farmers Association to purchase at guaranteed prices and levy land taxes, but no one seemed to notice after Lim Baiyi swept through and bought everything up. No one wanted to sell to the Farmers Association at the guaranteed price because the association demanded higher quality and it was a hassle. And, it wouldn't be enough anyway because the Association guaranteed only a purchase of 970 kilos per hectare. So, the farmers gave up the rights to their quotas and sold it all to Lim Baiyi. As for the land tax, in the past, they could pay in cash, but the grain bureau wanted to control quantities, so they required payment in rice and the villagers had to comply. The tractors were busy all over the roads to collect. Daniunan was late to be levied. Nearby villagers had already paid up, and now the tractors were all lined up outside the bureau warehouse's, starting from where the scales were and running all the way out into the road, stretching one or two kilometers.

Today, Tan Bûn-tī and Li Thài-pîng showed up.

The weather was stifling. Everyone hid under their hats and sweated profusely. Families delivered food so they could stay in line. They ate rice and drank soup and then sweated out all the moisture they took in.

Two days earlier, they heard that the Farmers Association had gotten stricter about rice quality and would refuse anything that had sprouted. The Farmers Association was also understaffed and it would take a while to weigh everything.

Damn it. Everything was at a snail's pace. People cursed as they waited.

Teacher Tan and Li Thài-pîng requested leave from work for this day. They didn't farm a large area. Between the land tax and the quota, they had only 500 or 600 catties to sell. They brought it all on a pushcart. They waited on the road, under their hats, in the sweltering sun. Everyone hoped to get this over with quickly and go home to rest. Alas, there were too many people. They could only look from afar toward the Farmers Association, watching the ground moisture evaporate and rise up its high walls, which shimmered like an unreachable heaven.

"Bûn-tī, it's been forever. Why isn't there any movement?" asked Li Thài-pîng.

"No doubt it's the Farmers Association messing around," said Teacher Tan. "They're first taking care of the people they know."

"It's still like that this year?"

"Of course. It's hard to change these habits. And even without the Farmers Association, who knows how we'd be."

"Ha. I won't grow any rice next season. I'll just raise some pigs and won't have to work so hard. I don't have that much land anyway. You know, ever since we harvested, we've been worried about pricing, sprouting, taxes. What's the point?" They continued eating as they spoke, until they saw a vehicle coming down the road. They put their bowls down and flagged the car to stop.

"It's so fast," said Tan.

"Hey, what's the hurry!" said Li Thài-pîng to the driver.

"How can't I hurry?" The driver asked, drenched in sweat. "I've waited two whole days! I started early yesterday, too." He pointed toward the mosquito nets and pillows in his car.

Li Thài-pîng laughed and said, "Bûn-tī, let's not bother with this. Let's just sell it all to Lim Baiyi. It's easier."

"I've heard the market price has dropped anyway. I hadn't wanted to sell to him, but with these kinds of conditions, there doesn't seem much other choice."

That night, they went to sell to Lame Yi. They also sold him the taxable portion, thinking that the Farmers Association wouldn't accept it anyway and hoping they could just pay the Farmers Association in cash and save the hassle. Their earlier doubts about Lame Yi dissipated.

May 27. Weather: Sunny with some clouds, and showers in the mountains.
Although people didn't all agree that growing melons was the best choice, they were all clear about the need to earn extra money. Teacher Tan didn't want to farm, so he rented his land to Liau Tshiū-tiong. Their arrangement was as follows: Liau would pay for pesticides, labor, transport, fertilizers, and weeding, and they'd split the profits equally. Liau planned to grow crops on eight plots and figured he'd make a fortune. The whole village laughed at his willingness to work himself to death.

The Farmers Association was promoting rural development, which included a new agricultural initiative to mechanize the farming in Daniunan. By the temple, they displayed a sleek, new reaping machine that could cut six rows at a time. The villagers were intrigued and sent Ling to inspect. Everyone wanted one. Lim Duo asked how much it cost. The Farmers Association said 200 thousand! Everyone's eyes went wide. Ling nearly fell out of his seat. No one said a word after that.

May 28. Weather: Cloudy.
In the morning, Brother Rat held a temple meeting with all the important people in town. Speaking on behalf of the turtle, Brother Rat said he wanted to stage a puppet show and requested the temple roof be repaired. The village head said that such a decision would require a village meeting.

Nothing much happened in the evening.

May 29. Weather: Cloudy.
Nothing much happened.

Jun 1. Weather: Sunny. Location: Lim Baiyi's Estate.
A few days of rest and quiet were very precious for the people of Daniunan. After such a brief period, everyone would be busy again farming the melons.

Today, just as the sun rose over the thin layer of clouds to the east, everyone jumped out of bed and went to their usual spots, be it the cottonwoods, the barbershop, or the temple, as if they were taking positions in a stage play.

But they weren't out and about to receive guests or to farm. Today was the day Lame Yi was supposed to settle his accounts, and everyone was eager to receive their piles of cash.

As the 8 o'clock morning sun lit up the glazed tiles of Lim Baiyi's estate, people gathered around the locked gate. Soon someone opened the gate and a clamor ensued.

Li Thih-tō never had any difficulty making money. As the patriarch of the largest clan, he lined up the whole crowd and stood in front as if he was leading a platoon. Everyone knew he'd sold the most rice so they just let him go right ahead.

The Lim family estate was pretty much empty except for two persimmon trees. Full of fruit, their large branches covered the courtyard. Large side houses and pigsties just stood there, dilapidated and abandoned. No one understand why they'd just let this place go to waste like this. The main hall had opened, and the household attendants told the visitors to have a seat, take a rest, have a smoke, and drink some tea.

"What a scene, like a fire truck descending on a fire." Li Tshing-ian, who'd run and lost an election for township representative, said, "Lim Baiyi's going to have to bring all his cash on a truck."

"We're going to make a lot of money!" said Li Thih-tō. "I'm not going to divide my family!"

"Forty thousand! Forty thousand," said Kachun, with excitement.

"I'm going to open up a massage parlor," said Tenn Bȧk-sim.

"I'm not going to sue Bān-hok anymore," said a piercing female voice. It was Bigmouth Yang, of course.

As for others, like Li Kim-hô who was missing four of his fingers, and Teacher Tan and Li Thài-pîng, they sat around chatting with everyone.

It was as if everyone was waiting to pick up a prize from the lottery.

Amidst the hubbub, as the sun rose higher in the sky and the time drew closer to 9 o'clock, the morning glory plants continued growing along the side house, and the chickens continued pecking around the property. Still, Lim Baiyi was nowhere to be seen.

People started whispering to each other.

Li Thih-tō lost his patience. He went to the front to speak on behalf of the temple crowd and ask members of Lin's family what was going on.

Just then, a businessman in a gauzy white shirt and Bermuda shorts appeared.

Li Bóng-sing recognized him as the man who bought his rice, and went right over to him and asked, "Boss, please settle my 5000 catties first."

The businessman looked calmly at everyone. Was he really going to settle all the accounts? He didn't have a bag of cash.

"Hello gentlemen," he said. He extended his hands as if he were about to deliver a speech or an explanation or something.

Everyone immediately quieted down and sat at attention, as if they were at a township meeting.

"My apologies to make everyone wait. Actually, I'm also waiting, like you," he said.

Why? Why was he also waiting? Everyone was confused.

"Mr. Lim had said that today would be the day to settle payments. He said you were all in immediate need of cash."

"Yes, that's right."

"So, yesterday, he went to the city to withdraw money."

"Is he coming or not?" Li Thih-tō asked loudly. The village chief's son had also arrived by now, on his father's behalf.

"There's no need to rush. He will be able to get the money," said the businessman.

"When?" asked the village head's son.

"Now, of course. But yesterday before leaving, he said that if he's not back by ten o'clock today, that means he's been held up in the bank, and he won't be able to pay you until tomorrow."

"What?" Everyone was getting upset.

"It's almost ten already," said someone from the cottonwood crowd.

"If you want to get rich, sometimes you have to wait," said someone from the temple.

"If I don't get my money, I'm going to have to sell my shirt," said someone from the barber shop.

The officials and teachers, with their higher level of education, just clasped their hands and watched quietly.

The sun started wilting the morning glory as the air temperature rose. The chickens retreated to the grass after eating their fills. The businessman wiped his brow and passed around more cigarettes and tea. The temperature kept rising. Bān-hok and Sin-thuân grabbed some extra cigarettes while no one was looking and went to smoke near the persimmon trees. Other people looked for shade against the walls.

The sun reached the middle of the sky and beamed down over the entire village. Still, there was no trace of Lim Baiyi.

Gradually, people stopped chatting and turned morose.

"Hey, everyone, let's stop waiting. It's almost 11 already. If he doesn't settle today, we'll just come back tomorrow. Let's just go make our lunches," said the village head's son.

Everyone heard him and then started heading out, disgruntled.

Li Thih-tō was the most reluctant to leave. Still, all he could do was tell the village head's son that if Lim Baiyi came back, he better announce it on the loudspeakers. Only then did he leave, though he lingered, like a man who couldn't bear to be parted from a lover.

At night, more people than usual gathered in front of the temple because the Lim estate could be seen from there.

Jun 2. Weather: Sunny. Location: Lim Baiyi's estate.

The chickens clucked around the low fence. A waning moon shone through the coconut palms, suspending both the newly built and shabby homes together in the cool light.

These quiet moments were the most comfortable of all for the Formosan countryside. The villagers of Daniunan slept soundly, deep in dreamland.

In the stillness, the sound of a lash echoed through the village. An ox and a hat-wearing farmer appeared. Ah, it was a hardworking man already out to farm.

They passed through and the road fell silent again.

Lim Baiyi's estate was also quiet in the early morning. The persimmon trees stretched out over the walls, but the gate stayed shut. Several stars twinkled over the roof of the main house.

Flickers were visible just under the roof.

Were they fireflies? The tips of incense sticks left by Redhead the night before?

They were neither! Neither?

Ah, it was a group of people. A group of farmers smoking cigarettes.

The eastern clouds dissipated as the sun rose over the village and cast light on the faces of the farmers by the estate. They waited through most of the night. Some still slept in the grass, while others raised their heads and looked up toward the sky.

Soon, more people streamed in silently.

The sun rose higher and shined on the roof like the day before. The chickens and geese were out and about.

"Hey, Lim Duo! How was it staying up all night?" asked Tenn Bȧk-sim. He wiped the morning dew off his mustache.

"What?" asked Lim Duo. Ever since Tenn Bȧk-sim said he wanted to open a massage parlor, Lim Duo wouldn't speak to him. He pointed to the bags under his eyes.

"I just meant to ask if you'd seen Lim Baiyi." Tenn Bȧk-sim fished out a cigarette from his pocket to offer Lim Duo.

"Haven't seen him. I didn't come till very late night. Ask Goldie. He's been here since yesterday evening."

Lim Duo saw the cigarette. He was going to wave it away but thought that would be a waste, so he took it reluctantly. He really didn't care for disloyal friends.

"Fuck you," said a half-asleep Tenn Bȧk-sim to Goldie. "You've been keeping watch all night like you're in a cemetery. Did you see anything or not?"

Goldie sighed when he heard their conversation. He was too exhausted to say anything, and he just waved his hand and nodded off to sleep again.

At eight o'clock, everyone who was supposed to be there was there. Even their relatives came to share in the happy scene, having heard of all the money that Lim Baiyi would deliver.

Finally, even the village head showed up. He stood in front and said, "Everyone line up in order of who came first. That way, we can keep this from becoming a mess."

The village head had authority and was to be obeyed. Everyone got in line.

"Make sure you take care of your money after you get it."

Li Thih-tō, with his superior family status, led the line-up, as if he was the deputy village head. "Everyone follow me in."

Before long, the village head waved his hand and everyone moved in formation. They were all rather excited and chattering away.

They entered the hall. The estate had been cleaned up a bit, and there was more furniture, including two long benches at the entrance, a drinking water dispenser on each side, and lots of cigarettes and betel nut.

The village head then entered the hall. Soon, the businessman came out with a bunch of random people from outside the village. Li Thih-tō went right up to him and asked, "Hey, yesterday you said Lim Baiyi would be back. Is he?"

The businessman frowned a bit but said politely to everyone, "Don't be shy. Take some betel nut and cigarettes." He pointed with his hands as he spoke, like he was the conductor of a funeral band.

"Boss, we're not here to socialize. We need our money."

Liau Tshiū-tiong, in the back of the line, was also tired of waiting. He hadn't sold a lot of rice, but he had the cottonwood crowd to represent.

"Don't worry," said the merchant.

"There's no way Lim Baiyi can't come back today. He's a respected man of the town. His word is to be trusted," said Liau.

"This is all a bit much. I slept all night just outside the gate," said Goldie.

"My apologies!" said the merchant. "He's not back yet."

"What?" Li Thih-tō's eyes opened wide. "Not back yet?"

"That's right," said the merchant, in a soft tone of voice. "Many apologies."

"You've lied to us again!" said Lim Duo. "Don't stand there and try to fob us off with a few nice words. When is he coming back?"

"Nine o'clock," said the merchant.

"Nine again," said Liau. "Yesterday, it was nine. Today, it's nine. Tomorrow, it will be nine again."

"Fuck! What nerve!" Everyone yelled.

"Calm down, everyone," said the village head. He raised his hands up, "There's a saying that good things come to those who wait. I know you've waited all night. I, the village head, am here now to help."

Everyone quieted down upon hearing the village head speak. Then, a voice rang out in back.

"He's here! He's here!"

Everyone turned their heads to see.

A big, brand-new truck parked by the entrance. Two people got out, the driver and a tall man with neat white hair, a stylish suit jacket, and a well-groomed, noble-looking face. On seeing this kind of person, even a local heavyweight like Li Thih-tō would cower like a frightened mouse.

"Oh, it's the Lim patriarch."

Everyone in town knew that that was Lim Oo, the father of Lim Baiyi. He looked to be in good shape.

"Ah, it's Thih-tō and the village head!" Lim Oo walked over to the entrance and put his hand out. They hadn't seen each other in 30 years.

"Long time no see!" Thih-tō and the head looked happy to see him again.

None of the villagers were clear about what was going on, but they were sure that Lim Oo's arrival meant that they'd get their money.

"Mr. Lin, your son Lim Baiyi said that he'd bring our money today. We've all been waiting," said Liau Tshiū-tiong, as polite as could be.

"I know." Lim Oo smiled gently. "That's why I've come today."

"Oh, it's you who is delivering the money," said Lim Duo.

"No, no, no." Lim Oo shook his head. "I need to apologize for our poor manners. Perhaps the villagers here aren't aware about how things have changed outside. Withdrawing money is not so easy. Baiyi does really big business. Tens of millions of dollars. He's very busy, so withdrawing money may take another day or two."

"Another day or two?"

Everyone looked hugely disappointed, but they stayed silent in front of Lim Oo and spoke at most in whispers.

"Mr. Lim!" A voice rang through the crowd. "If it's another day or two, it's okay. You have status here; everyone will believe you. But you need to let us know when and where. We have a valid basis for our concerns. Things can't keep going on like this."

Everyone turned to see that it was Teacher Tan. Unsurprisingly, it was an educated person who would speak like this.

"Of course." Lim Oo raised his hand and extended two fingers. "After two days, I'll have Baiyi and my daughters-in-law deliver the money to your homes personally, okay?"

"Wow, home delivery. We won't need to wait here again. Okay!" The people were placated.

"Everyone, Mr. Lim is a man of status. His word is to be believed. He will follow through," said the village head. "He's said this now. You can all rest easy."

"Mr. Lin, your word is your bond," said Li Thih-tō with some theatrical flair.

"Of course, of course." Lim Oo smiled wide.

The people left with nothing but smiles.

June 3. Weather: Mostly clear, with some clouds.

Today, the people growing melons and vegetables were all out turning the soil. The fields were full of hardworking farmers. Li Thih-tō planted melons on two plots of land, even if he wasn't sure how they would turn out.

Teacher Tan, a civil servant, prepared to send his son to America to study finance. He used his land as collateral for a bank loan to pay for it. None of his neighbors knew what good going to America would do, although they did hear that people who went to America were all very impressive.

At night, many people want to the temple square to watch the stars. Li Thài-pîng played an old song on his flute, "The Foggy Harbor." As the plaintive notes rang through the air, everyone felt that the tune sounded ominous.

June 4. Weather: Sunny. Location: Village road, home of the village head, and the Lim estate.

With modern pesticides sprayed all over the place, the bugs that people typically used to predict the weather were all dead. Still, the farmers of Daniunan knew that a profusion of ants and dragonflies meant rain. If the moon was surrounded by a halo, that meant wind was coming. If there was fog at night, it meant a sunny day ahead. And sometimes a bright, sunny day would start with morning fog, too.

Sure enough, this morning had a thick fog covering the homes and fields of the village. You couldn't see more than three meters in front of you.

It was in this thick fog that matters finally came to a head.

Around 6 o'clock when the sun rose through the fog, no one could see a trace of anyone else. All they could sense were the sounds of oxen being whipped.

A voice called out. "It's all over! We're screwed!"

The voice rang loud and clear through the otherwise quiet village roads, startling everyone who heard it.

Everyone who heard the sound went toward the cottonwood tree, where the voice came from, and found Liau Tshiū-tiong there with a moist face.

"Hey, Tshiū-tiong, what's the matter?" Tshiu-song and her husband parked their bicycles and asked. "What's over?"

"Tshiu-song, you won't believe it. Last night I went to the neighboring village. They said Lim Baiyi also hadn't paid them. They sold their rice to him two days after we did. Some of them went to his residence in the city and found a seal on the door."

"A seal?" asked Tshiu-song.

"Yes, it must be by order of the court."

"Oh my. This must mean there's a lien on it."

"Yes! Lim Baiyi is bankrupt!" said Liau.

Tshiu-song's legs started shaking. The drops of mist shrouding her face hardened like hail and rolled down her nape, sending chills down her spine.

Soon, one after the other, people appeared in the foggy village streets.

As the sun nibbled away at the fog, the coconut palms began to peek out and cast gloomy shadows on the tiled roofs below.

The weather looked like something you'd see in Africa.

As the late morning grew hotter, people poured toward the village head's office. They'd heard the news through Liau Tshiū-tiong, stopped working their fields, and raced over in an uproar.

"Village head." Li Thih-tō stood in front of his desk, impatiently. "We can't wait anymore. Let's go find him. No more games. We've been waiting and waiting. What's going on?"

"Lim Oo keeps his word." The village head was also flustered. He anxiously rolled up his pant legs. His face was caked with dirt from the field he'd just raced back from. "He's a high-status person with a reputation to protect."

"Who cares. We need our money." It was Lim Duo. "Another village had bad news. How can we not go deal with this? Lim Oo said he'd hand deliver the cash. I bet he's lying."

"Let's go!"

The villagers all shouted.

"Okay, but don't show disrespect to Lim Oo," said the village head.

The walls of the Lim estate towered against the burning sun, baking the ground around them like the bottom of a cooking pot.

Everyone was waiting at the gate, staring intently. Lim Oo's reputation did still carry some weight.

"Whatever!" Ling didn't care about hurting his foot. He kicked open the gate and people streamed into the main hall. Strangely, no one was there. Everything inside had been cleared out.

"We've been cheated!" shouted Li Thih-tō.

His voice electrified the crowd. It was like they were waking up from a bad dream only to fall into a worse one. They were stunned, as if a typhoon had just ripped through the hall.

"What are you saying?" Li Tshing-ian broke through the crowd, speaking with the same level of disbelief as when he'd lost the election. "We've been cheated!"

"Lim Oo dared to cheat us?" Bān-hok flared his nose as his voice cracked.

"Damn it! We're ruined! Ruined!" Tenn Bȧk-sim said, paralyzed in anger.

Everyone was shaken. They ran up and down the whole village like dogs in a graveyard, looking for traces of anyone from the Lim family.

"Village head, you've got to think of a solution."

Tan Bûn-tī and Li Thài-pîng, the civil servants, were at his office. They had anticipated the situation and were a bit calmer than the rest.

"You need to calm everyone," said Li Thài-pîng.

"Yes, yes." The village head looked harried as he stood on the steps outside. He said loudly, "Don't panic! It's not like a thief has taken your things. Everyone calm down and stay hopeful."

A group of people stood outside and looked at him with rage.

"Thih-tō!" The village head recovered his authority. "Go at once to the city with Teacher Tan. Find Lim Oo. Even if you can't find him, go figure out what's going on. Hurry!"

June 5. Weather: Sunny with occasional afternoon clouds.
The cucumber and vegetable plots needed weeding, but no one was in the mood to do it. Everyone just did a cursory job and went home. The women sat outside and watched the sky and muttered to themselves, "Damn it, damn Lim Oo, damn Lim Baiyi, what a cheat, may he be struck by lightning!"

It was the beginning of the summer vacation. Many of the village kids were returning from universities and vocational schools. They had an inkling of what was going on but tried to stay out of it.

Brother Rat did another divination. He said that the village savior still hadn't shown up. Lim Baiyi was a fraud. By now, many people didn't believe him anymore, anyway. Ling cursed him to his face, "Fuck you. If you do another divination, I'll break your legs."

June 6. Weather: Sunny. Location: Tan Bûn-tī's house.
At noon, smoke rose over the homes of the village, covering the scenery like a cartoon. It was lunchtime, but no one was sitting around the dining table. Normally, all these people lived to eat, whether the food was good or bad. Today, they had no appetite.

Instead, barefoot and nervous, they went over to Teacher Tan's house.

Teacher Tan had been busy after returning from the city where he looked for Lim Oo. Indeed, things were as the neighboring villagers had said. Lim Oo's house was sealed. He reported this upon his return. Being the person with the most up-to-date knowledge, he was tasked to handle the matter.

People started surrounding his small house in the early morning. After the village renewal program was implemented, the village wasn't as tight as it used to be. Walls separated all the houses, letting each family go their own way. People designed their houses differently. Tan Bûn-tī taught at school while raising his kids and farming the land he inherited from his parents. His house was small, with red walls, an asphalt courtyard, and some chickens and ducks. It was neat and orderly, more so than the typically messy properties nearby. In this respect, teachers and officials stood on opposite sides from the farmers, and sometimes fought over cleanliness and noise. But ultimately, this was like a married couple quarreling—the squabble never lasted long, and when push came to shove, they would undoubtedly stand together.

So of course, Tan Bûn-tī would do his utmost to fight it out with Lim Oo and settle the issue for the whole village.

Folks filled Tan Bûn-tī's tiny parlor, eating betel nut, wiping away their sweat, and plotting strategy.

They were consumed by a mix of anxiety and indignation.

The temple crowd had always advocated that people follow proper etiquette. They were men of principle. They prepared a proposal.

"Teacher Tan, we should take him to court," said Li Tshing-ian, his face covered in sweat.

"Yes. Sue him. Our loss is too great. There's no way Lim Oo can win," said Li Thih-tō in his booming actor's voice.

"Damn him. He's no gentleman, destroying the good name of his ancestors. I'll sue him," said Li Tâi-se, rolling his sleeves up.

"I heard that people in the other village are also suing him," said Li Tshing-ian. "Lim Baiyi can't go on like this."

The temple crowd had prepared a rational plan of action and wanted to pursue legal remedies. They believed that if they had right on their side, that they would triumph, that the world was fair. After all, it was said that even the president of the United States was taken down after breaking the law.

The barbershop folks agreed with the temple crowd, although the detail-oriented Lim Duo wanted to be a bit more specific. "Sue him? For breaking which law?"

"Fraud!" Li Tâi-se spat as he answered. "Defrauding all of us of our rice. He's worse than an animal."

"Yes, fraud," said Li Tshing-ian. "We'll ask the court to return us our rice."

The temple crowd spoke with a sense of righteousness.

"We can't sue for that," said Teacher Tan, shaking his head calmly. "He didn't commit fraud."

"Why not? Didn't he take our rice?" said Li Tâi-se. His sleeves were already undone.

"There's no evidence. We didn't ask him for documentation," said Teacher Tan. "We were too trusting. There are no receipts. We had a verbal agreement that each hundred catties would be 500 NT, and the amounts we sold him was also on our word. A verbal agreement doesn't provide grounds for a lawsuit."

"But it's the truth!" Li Tâi-se glared.

"Okay then, think about it. We don't have any evidence. You go to court to sue for your ten thousand catties of rice, but Lim Baiyi says he only took one thousand from you. What will you do? If you say that it's 550 per catty, and he says it was 300, what will you do? He could say that the settlement was supposed to take three months. You still have no proof. We basically just gave him all the rice," said Teacher Tan.

Li Tâi-se looked like an ox who'd just been struck speechless by the sound of thunder. "But... but..."

Everyone realized the situation was serious.

Their whole lives, they never knew anything about the law, but still they believed in it like a Catholic believes the Bible. They didn't realize that the law might have such requirements. They figured that hiring a lawyer would be enough.

They sweated even more profusely in the silence.

"Okay." Bān-hok had a clever idea and spoke on behalf of the cottonwood crowd. "We'll go capture him and refuse to let him leave until he pays us back."

"Yes, let's capture Lim Baiyi and have Lim Oo come to negotiate," said Ling. "The tree folks can go get him and cage him like a monkey under the tree. If he refuses to pay up, we won't let him out."

"No, no, no," said Tan Bûn-tī, shaking his head. "That's kidnapping. It's a crime."

Everyone got frightened at the thought of committing a crime.

The weather was as hot and sticky as before. Still, they stayed tightly packed.

"OK then, sue him for robbery," said Kachun, excitedly tapping his feet. "Robbery is punishable by the death penalty! He'll be terrified."

"Shut the fuck up," said Tenn Ba̍k-sim. "Sue who? If you can't sue for fraud, how can you sue for robbery? He didn't rob you. You gave him all your rice."

Everyone chuckled bitterly about Kachun before falling back into quiet despair.

"Teacher Tan, what can we do?" Tshiu-song wept.

"Let's relax a minute. There's still something we can do." said Teacher Tan.

"Oh? What is it?" asked Ling.

"We go and beg him."

"Beg him? No way," said Liau Tshiū-tiong, indignantly. "I wouldn't ask him if my life depended on it. He cheated us out of our rice and now we're supposed to beg for it for it back?"

"Yes, this is the only way left," said Tan Bûn-tī.

"Really?"

Everyone was in a state of delirium and sorrow.

"Yes, let's join hands," said Tan Bûn-tī. "Anyone who is related to Lim Baiyi needs to help out. We'll go ask him to show consideration for his village and return what he can."

"Really? Really?"

The villagers were shaken. They opened their mouths. No words came out.

June 7. Weather: Sunny with showers in the afternoon.
The school examination day had arrived. All the children of the village had studied diligently, and now there was no use in accompanying them to the testing sites. They could go north or south on their own. Li Tâi-se was in a foul mood and said to his son, "Don't think that if you don't test into school, you can come back here to farm. If you hand me a hoe, I'll beat you to death with it."

Bigmouth Yang's second legal appeal had hit a snag because her injuries weren't entirely due to Bān-hok. Some were from a chronic ailment.

Fire Lion had heard that Daniunan had been cheated and rushed back to the village to offer help, but his fists were of no use for handling legal matters.

That evening, the temple crowd heard a revelation about Lim Baiyi's whereabouts. Around noontime in the city, Li Thih-tō, Li Tshing-ian, and Lim Oo's relatives found Lim Baiyi's wife and raised the issue with her. She said that Baiyi may not be able to pay the rice money for three reasons: One, Lim Baiyi's city enterprise had shut down; two, Lim urgently needed money for another project; and three, as far as Lim Baiyi was concerned, Daniunan was just another insignificant little village.

Li Thih-tō implored her to consider that he had relatives in the village and should return the money. She just smiled. Smiled beautifully.

She should be a movie star!

June 8. Weather: Sunny.
In the early morning, Ling ran toward the temple in a mood of despair. He wanted to see the turtle, which had once given hope to some people. But the turtle was gone!

Damn it! The turtle had already been captured and boiled into soup, someone said to him and smiled.

Brother Rat wouldn't dare show his face again.

This evening, the cottonwood crowd had their own news about Lim Baiyi. Liau and Bān-hok went to the city and looked for him in the busiest part. They saw that Lim Baiyi had taken his wives out to shop. Liau and Bān-hok sprung to action and surrounded them. Liau warned him that they would beat him if he didn't pay up. Lim Baiyi was unperturbed. He said he'd sue anyone that laid a finger on him. Some youngsters snickered nearby and said that they'd beat back anyone who hit Lame Yi. The cottonwood crew was scared.

Tshiu-song fell ill with anxiety. Everyone went to see her jaundiced face.

June 9. Weather: Sunny with some clouds. Location: Lim family estate.
The sun suddenly slipped behind the clouds. The weather bureau had reported that a cold front was moving northwards. Still, it was hot and muggy.

In the front of the village at the Lim family estate, people started filling in. Their sleeves were rolled up. Sweat poured down their brows. Some people even stuck their tongues out like dogs.

A layer of clouds condensed in the sky and darkened as it extended, like sticky ink preparing to rain down a cataclysm.

It's so muggy, everyone muttered.

"Fuck! There's no money and no rice! Why should we stay polite?" Someone came through the crowd. It was Ling. He snatched a hatchet and waved his arms, "There's no need to see Lim Oo's face again!"

"Yeah, if we don't get our money, let's take some stuff at least," said Kachun.

"Are you nuts?" Tenn Bák-sim vented his anger on Kachun. "They've moved all their stuff out!"

"If there's nothing here, we can just take apart the whole house. Whoever takes down the pillars first will make some money," shouted Ling to everyone.

"Yes, tear down the house! If there's an issue, I'll handle it!" said Li Thih-tō, directing everyone.

"Tear it down!"

The door came down first with a pop. Sin-thuân's pigsty had just fallen apart, so he wanted to take the door for it. He crouched down and grabbed it.

"I'll chop the trees," said Bān-hok, who needed firewood. He had brought an axe. He wasn't strong enough to do it on his own, so he called on Liau for help. Liau had already entered the rear of the courtyard where he spotted a marble table.

"Handle the tree yourself for now. I'll be there in a minute to help."

Li Thih-tō had bigger plans. Earlier, he'd eyed the glazed roof tiles. If he could move them to his house, he'd be the envy of the village. He directed his children and grandchildren to remove them.

Everyone else took their positions.

Through the commotion, the village head and two policeman rushed over. The policemen blew their whistle and interrupted everyone's work.

"What are you doing?" The stern Officer Lim was angry. "You're damaging private property."

"This is illegal!" said the more personable Officer Ouyang. "This is robbery."

"Officers! We've doing nothing wrong. We're just taking Lim Oo's stuff to offset our losses," said Bān-hok, who didn't want to let go of the persimmon trees.

"I know, but we have to follow the law. You can't just take other people's stuff as you please. Who's in charge here?" said Officer Ouyang.

This question made people realize the matter was serious, because whoever was in charge might be taken by the police.

"I am," said Li Thih-tō, standing up. "Me."

"Okay." Officer Lim got ready. "Mr. Li, I'm very sorry, but I have to take you in."

"Take me where?" asked Li Thih-tō.

"The police station," said Officer Lim.

"Officer Lin, slow down," said Lim Duo, who felt the situation was not right. "You know that taking other people's stuff is wrong. Why don't you go arrest Lim Oo and his son? He took all our rice. You've done nothing. Here we are just taking down a few tiles and you're going to arrest us. What's this about?"

"That's right. Damn it. Take a single dollar and you get the death penalty, steal millions and get off scot free. Some law this is," said Liau.

Everyone got agitated.

The policeman saw the mood and released Thih-tō.

The village head came to mediate.

But the policemen insisted that the villagers had to leave, and later, Officer Lim and Officer Ouyang returned to guard the door, their batons in hand.

The sky opened up and heavy rain poured down.

June 10. Weather: Northwesterly rains.
The weather began to shift. The rain started falling before dawn, and the village looked orderly and beautiful. Watching the rain, people thought back to the floods from the month before. From that time until now, everything seemed as if it were a dream.

This morning in the rain, a young couple carrying bags waited for a bus by the roadside. Everyone went to see. It was Lim Hōng-bé and her husband. They were going back to the city to work, having given up farming. Their parents came to send them off. Rain fell and pooled around their pants.

Around noontime, Sin-thuân carried his newborn to see a folk doctor. Because he had no money, he hadn't fed expensive milk formula to the infant. He instead gave the baby rice flour, which swelled up his stomach.

The most interesting case was that of Ling. Having seen that ghost in the ditch a month earlier, he now rarely went out to try to stun fish. Still, in order to keep eating three meals a day, he now walked the canals at all hours. He said that if he came across the ghost, he'd electrocute it and sell it to for display at an exhibition.

As for news of Lim Baiyi…well, there was none.

June 11. Weather: Clear with occasional rain.
Liau Tshiū-tiong's continued his run of bad luck. In the morning, various creditors came to collect from him. The rice cutters were the fiercest. Liau received them with a smile but couldn't pay more than half of what he owed them. Everyone cursed Lame Yi. Still, Liau was totally humiliated.

Bigmouth Yang was the busiest. She had to win her appeal or else she'd owe compensation to Bān-hok and go hungry. Meanwhile, she was making frequent visits to see Tshiu-song and make sure that she wouldn't kill herself.

The most foolish of all was Kachun, who got dumber by the day. He would walk on the road, even when it rained, and mutter mindlessly about the world. He was really going insane.

No one played recorded prayers at the temple anymore. Brother Rat didn't dare live inside it again for fear of losing his life.

June 20. Weather: Light rain. Location: Under the cottonwood tree, and by the Lim family estate.
Rain fell as the sun went down. Bright rays lit up the western sky. Light showers fell on big houses and ramshackle sheds alike.

A group of children ran barefoot through the rain, shouting "It's raining and sunny at the same time!"

It was the moment just after the end of the workday.

Many people gathered under the cottonwood trees. They were still wallowing in misery about the rice issue. If they said anything, the pain would bubble to the surface, so they stayed quiet, like sullen children.

"Damn it!" Ling suddenly appeared, his thin body hunched over, hands turned down, rocking to and fro. His eyes had bags and were bloodshot from not getting enough sleep due to the late-night fishing. He said, "I can work like a horse, or fish my rice out of the sea, but what I won't accept is getting cheated. I'm... I'm glorious Ling!"

"You're nuts. Go get some sleep!" Bān-hok hopped up and kicked him. "You're upset? We are too."

They were both sick of this silence. They really should have gone faraway to shout at the gods or have a good cry or a good laugh.

They walked back and forth together. They gave the tree a shove, raining water and flowers down on their heads and the ground.

"Yes," said Sin-thuân. An idea struck him when he sat back down under the tree. "Why don't we write a letter to the grain bureau or the provincial chairman and tell them of our disaster."

"You're dreaming," said Bān-hok. "These big officials aren't your relatives. They've got a lot to attend to. They don't care about your private affairs. Even if they knew, what would they do? If a court can't handle it, how would they?"

"Yes, if your dad was an official, we could write to him. But your dad's in hell. Write to the King of Hell, why don't you."

Everyone chuckled and made fun of Sin-thuân's idea.

Just then, a *suona* horn was heard coming from the front of the village, like the sound of a birthday party crossing a desolate landscape.

"Hey, there must be a puppet show at the temple," said Ling. "I didn't hear Brother Rat mention anything. And we didn't know to prepare any offerings."

"It's probably Bighead Kan's show," said Sin-thuân. "He puts on a good show, and sets up quickly too."

As they were thinking about it, they saw Goldie ride over on a bicycle. Ling went to ask him what was going on.

"Your mama's show," Goldie retorted. "Someone died and you don't even know. Lim Duo's father put another nail in his head and this time there's no saving him. His soul is being sent off tomorrow."

"Oh, I think I did hear that someone in the middle of the village had died."

"Come on, let's go to the funeral."

Some of the tree crowd stood up and set forth like a small army.

"Goldie, hold on. Something's not quite right," said Ling. "Lim Duo lives at the barbershop in the center of the village, not in the front. Why is the sound coming from the front?"

"You silly person. Lim Duo is holding the funeral at Lim Oo's estate. He says that Lim Oo should take responsibility for his father's death."

"Wow," said Ling.

"Yes." The cottonwood crowd got upset when they heard the mention of Lim Oo. They said, "If you're going to die, better die at Lim Oo's place."

They headed over to the funeral site. All they could see was the white canvas covering the courtyard. Around the persimmon tree stood a temporary kitchen for cooking vegetables, a resting place for relative and friends, and another place for guests to sit. Outside the coverings were wreaths, flowers, lanterns, and the like. It looked like a 4-H Club event except there was a red coffin. The sons and grandsons were crying loudly. Cymbals clanged and the *huqin* lute was played.

The tree crowd approached, not all at once, and saw the Taoist priest reciting prayers and the sons and grandsons kneeling. They saw the eight-sided table full of flowers and fruit, and a pig with a pineapple in its mouth as an offering, like a maiden awaiting marriage. They felt relieved when they saw that the offerings were abundant.

Bān-hok and Sin-thuân were the fastest. They ran to the kitchen in the back, ate some meat, and then came out to console Lim Duo in the resting area for relatives and friends.

The tent was full of Lim Duo's relatives. Tenn Bȧk-sim, Kachun, and other barber shop regulars were also here together.

Lim Duo's face was downcast, filled with grief. He said to everyone, "I didn't know this day would come so soon."

"Yes, life and death are matters left to fate," said someone to him.

"As he died, he said, 'After I'm a spirit, I'll come back to protect you.'" Lim Duo turned to everyone and said, "You heard how lucid he was, not crazy at all, but how could... how could..." He covered his face with his hands. "How could so many unthinkable things happen?"

"When it happened, we all rushed him to the hospital, but I hadn't paid off the debts from last time and they wouldn't take him in. Guess what he said when he saw this?"

No one said a word.

"He said, 'I can't be helped. You've been cheated out of your rice. You have no money. Don't waste any more of it.'" Lim Duo took a deep breath to calm himself. Still, he couldn't help but yell, "Look, even he heard that Daniunan was cheated!"

Everyone went to comfort him.

"So you have to do your best," said Lim Duo to the spirit of the dead. "Go on the right path, to a better world, to a paradise of bliss."

His voice was overcome with sorrow, and he fell silent.

Bān-hok and Sin-thuân felt uncomfortable watching this.

"Come on! Lim Duo is lucky to send off his dad's spirit in a big place like this. As for us, we've gotten no reward at all."

"Come on, Bān-hok. If your spirit could live on in here, would you want to die?"

"No!" he said immediately, and then thought for a moment. "I don't want to die yet. But if I could leave this estate for my kids to inherit, I'd go right ahead and die on the spot."

They laughed for a while and then fell into an even darker mood.

June 13. Weather: Thunderstorms in the afternoon.
No one could forget what Lim Baiyi had done. While eating and sleeping, they'd still talk about it, but it all amounted to nothing. They didn't go

together in groups to the city anymore. Sometimes when one of them went on their own to buy things, they'd drop by Lim Oo's residence, even if they knew it was useless. They'd still go and look, like children visiting an amusement park.

The exams were over. Some people told their children to go to work rather than stay at home and eat up all the food.

A troupe selling kidney medicine came to perform at the temple square. The lights flashed through the evening, and performers took their clothes off and danced and sang. They didn't sell much. After all, the people of Daniunan had empty pockets. Still, they clapped their hands and showed support.

June 14. Weather: Sunny with occasional clouds.
The loudspeakers announced that a village lifestyle instruction team would come. Everyone should clean up the surroundings so as to better receive their lesson. Most of the visitors were students from the city. They tried to explain why hygiene was important. They criticized the hall and kitchen in Li Tâi-se's home. It all sounded so lofty. Li Tâi-se was furious and told them to get the hell out. He even sent a dog after them.

There was no more gambling going on. Among the many reasons for stopping, the main one was that no one had any money.

June 15. Weather: Sunny.
The rain ended again today. Sunshine draped the clean fields, but it wasn't hot at all. Everyone went to their vegetable and melon plots to weed. Their hands moved like bird beaks pecking through the soil. Small green shoots popped out of the ground.

Shocking news came around noontime. Li Thih-tō was finally going to divide his family's property. His descendants were beaming. A lot of people said that, from this angle, Lim Baiyi's fraud had helped the Li family, or at least the youngsters.

Toward dusk, an advertising company came from the city and put up a beautiful poster to promote a song and dance troupe. As soon as it went up, someone tore it down. No one was in the mood.

June 16. Weather: Sunny.
Unexpectedly good news came today. Apparently, the county government had a conscience and spoke with the provincial government on the village's behalf. The land tax could be discounted in cash and paid later in rice if necessary. It looked as if someone did care about the farmers, after all. The people of Daniunan felt touched.

Apart from this, someone saw something in the margins of the newspaper about a lot of sprouted rice from southern Chiayi that no one wanted. The price was 100 catties for 300 NT. This came as something of a relief. They said that if they still had their rice, they could only sell it for 300 anyway.

June 17. Weather: Sunny.
People from the neighboring villages came to light incense, pray, and hold a performance. Daniunan welcomed them. They said, wow, these people suffered like us, yet here they are, optimistic and moving on. Why shouldn't we learn from them?

June 18. Weather: Sunny with occasional clouds.
The melons and vegetables were growing well, and everyone was busy adding fertilizer to them. Little by little, the new crops became the talk of the people at the tree, the barbershop, and the temple alike.

Lim Baiyi was mentioned less and less.

June 20. Weather: Sunny.
Nothing much happened.

June 21. Weather: Sunny with occasional clouds.
Nothing much happened.

....

....

....

June 30. Weather: Occasional afternoon rain.
There was a typhoon warning in the evening.

   It didn't strike Daniunan.

July 1. Weather: Heavy rain and wind.
The rain was heavy.

   It didn't affect the village much.

....

....

....

....

July 14. Weather: Sunny. Location: Temple square.
After several days of good weather, the sun shone like a jewel in the sky. It was hotter than usual and baked the asphalt. It was around this time that the town started recovering from its wounds.

   The TV reported that the temperature was as high as 38 degrees in the north.

   The villagers weren't afraid of the heat. They were used to being outdoors and toiling in the fields.

   The melons and vegetables had done well after all. Prices were high. The people would be saved.

At noon, as the sun beat down on the temple square, everyone came out from their homes. Some carried bamboo rods and others carried canvas. They set up massive tents. This time the production wasn't put on by merchants—the people were doing it themselves.

After noon, melon merchants came with their trucks.

The temple crowd had set up their station closest to the exit and put their produce on dirty planks covered with straw. Li Thih-tō smoked a cigarette and instructed his newly divided family. His had always been the loudest voice around, but his tone sounded humbler now.

Bān-hok and the other cottonwood tree folk were squeezed toward the drainage ditch. They hadn't cultivated much land. Some smaller merchants circled around here and bought at higher prices. One person stood out. It was Liau Tshiū-tiong, who'd planted eight plots, the most of any of the tree crowd. He stood by the tractor and shouted, "I said I'd make a fortune, and I made a fortune!" He wanted to convert his victory into respect and dignity.

The barbershop crowd was a bit nimbler. They set up by the road and bargained for hours.

"8 NT and 30 cents," said Goldie. He'd never been so insistent. "8 NT and 30 cents, or I don't sell." The merchants nodded politely and made their purchases carefully.

Suddenly, there was a clamor. It sounded like there was a landslide taking place inside the temple. Kachun ran over to tell everyone to come take a look.

Everyone went to the temple.

It turned out to be Brother Rat doing another divination, but it was not like before. This time, the ritual bell, talismans, and scriptures were strewn across the ground. Brother Rat was under the eight-sided table, his ragged head stuck between the legs and unable to get out.

No one knew what to make of this. How could his head be stuck in that little gap?

All anyone could see was him struggling and babbling. It didn't sound like any god, but more like Lame Yi. The leg even seemed to move like his, too.

"I know what's going on," said Ling, stepping to the front of the crowd. "The temple god has captured Lame Yi's spirit. He's possessing Brother Rat! The god is punishing him!"

"Really?" Everyone was curious.

"Definitely." Ling was certain. "Look. He's almost been strangled by the altar table legs."

"Oh!" All the people screamed.

"Quickly," said Lim Duo to Kachun. "Go get the axe to cut up the altar and save Brother Rat. Go!"

Kachun was stunned and motionless. Everyone laughed.

A group of temple birds perched on the roof and cawed. From their crisp and bright tone, it was clear that they also looked forward to a bright and sunny day.

Notes

1. Given the setting as well as the author's notable advocacy for Taiwanese Hoklo literature, I have chosen to render the names of most of the village residents according to the Taiwanese Romanization System adopted by the Ministry of Education in 2006, a somewhat controversial decision which was supported by Sung Tse-lai, who was then serving as a member of the ministry's National Languages Committee. I have made a few exceptions to improve readability, including using English names for those can be easily glossed (Brother Rat and Goldie), using Hanyu Pinyin for those that have frequently appear as single syllables following descriptive nicknames (Bigmouth Yang and Lame Yi), and removing diacritics from most of the surnames.
2. The word for kill, 殺 *sha,* is also part of the transliteration used here for massage, 馬殺雞 *mashaji.*
3. In 1949, as part of a "land-to-the-tiller" rural land reform and urban industrialization policy, the ROC government reduced the maximum rent payable by tenant farmers to landowners to 37.5% of the crop grown on arable land. This reduced both landowner profits and the value of the land, incentivizing landowners to sell their land to tenant farmers and then reinvest the profits in urban industry.
4. Liau Tshiū-tiong says the term 南洋 *Nanyang,* literally meaning southern seas. It usually refers to Southeast Asia, which had long been a frequent destination for migrants and traders from China and Taiwan.
5. A 斤 *jin* catty is 600g.
6. The Chinese name is 金獅固筋運功散 *Jinshi gujin yungong san.*

4

DIXSON'S IDIOMS

Huang Chong-kai
(translated by Brian Skerratt)

So after all it was spelled Dixson, not Dickson. No matter which Chinese characters were used to transliterate the name, it didn't mean your dick's son. I thought I was the only one misspelling it all these years, until I discovered it was Lai Shih-hsiung, the father of English language teaching in Taiwan, who spelled it Dixon, and so ever since, a lot of idiom dictionaries by various editors are all titled *Dixon's Idioms*. Nobody knew the "Dixon" guy who had first assembled those 470 phrases, but whoever he was, he had been quietly responsible for promoting American English around the world. His teaching materials had followed Hollywood movies and the US Army, gradually occupying every corner of the globe. Dixson didn't have a chance to see reprints of this book emblazoned with his name in so many places, nor could he have known that his name, along with other experts on the English language, would appear in the last few lines of the preface to *A New English Grammar* in Taiwan.

Lesson 1: to get on/off (a bus, boat, or airplane)
Before Lolita got on the boat, she looked back at the pier. At this time she wasn't called Lolita; she was still trying hard to be María. It occurred to her that her life had been a constant coming and going, departing one place, arriving at another, always searching for a home of her own. Only when she was old enough to understand the world's complexities did she realize that her papá was not just her papá, he was someone else's too, and that far away on the other side of the world, there was another daughter like her also waiting for her papá to come home. So the first time María left, at age seventeen, it was to find her father, and she arrived along with her conspicuous foreign accent in a seaside village in Galicia. From the moment she stepped out of the suffocating cabin and onto shore, it seemed that all the ropes, the waves, the heave-hos of the dockworkers—everything was coated in a film of oil, the sounds slipping into her ears. The people on the docks, the vehicles, and street vendors were all broadcasting an intelligible but strange language. Unsure which way to go, she began to wander through the town, clutching her bag.

They call it the Old World: every house has a history, every person a story. She came from the New World, too young to have stories, but she knew she was a beautiful girl, and there would be no shortage of men to talk to her, to take her places, to buy her a drink. She was mentally adjusting to the local accent, silently imitating its pronunciation, hoping to blend into the background.

It was only when she heard the cries of her first child, Julio, that she realized that some words came without study, inborn, and that one didn't need to be too careful about the pronunciation. Other words came out of one's mouth and then floated far away, like a towel that had blown off a clothesline and landed on the neighbor's roof where no one could reach it. Like with her husband, José. Thinking back, it was that one sentence, "Let's go find your papá," that had made her willing to go away with him. But this was a promise with an expiration date, and after a year he had had enough. He said he needed to work to support the family and couldn't be so far away from home; he said he'd given her a family, wasn't that enough? He said she should just give it up. María knew it didn't matter if she found her father. Their life together had ended when he left Cuba, and now he had another family to provide for, another María to dote on. In the town of only about ten thousand people, there were some who knew her father. Some said he'd moved with his family to the big city to the east, where there were supposed to be jobs. Some said he'd gone all the way to Cuba because at first, Cuba seemed like heaven on earth to him; it was only later that he discovered it was pretty much the same as here, except hotter. A fisherman won't turn into a farmer just because he has gone to a new continent. María thought that must be why he'd given his daughters the exact same name: with his limited imagination, he had constructed an identical family, with a wife he could ignore and two rebellious daughters. Maybe someday, when the time came, he would decide to go back home and hop on a boat, never to return, just as he had hopped on the boat to Cuba back then and made his way across the ocean, with no sense of why he was going.

By the time María gave birth to her second son, Josito, her speech and mannerisms were already indistinguishable from those of the locals. At some point, her time without a father exceeded the time when she'd had a father. One day, as she was passing the port where she'd arrived, a thought came to her like striking a match: her father might have just gone back to Cuba, so they'd simply passed each other by. José said she was crazy, smacked her and told her to stay put. The children were crying, the calls of sea birds circling above the port faintly reached them along with a hint of salt water that mingled with the moldy damp of their house. María sneezed. Her senses overwhelmed, she lay down beside the kitchen table, her swollen flesh gradually finding equilibrium with the cool floor. The children kept crying, accompanied by the smell of piss and shit.

No one was sure when María left home, or how she'd managed to disappear from the port. Apparently when José came home, stinking of booze, it was the smell pervading the house that sobered him up. The two children were naked from the waist down, their dirty diapers strewn everywhere. In just a few months, José, the fisherman and dockworker, snared another seventeen-year-old girl from out of town to fill María's place. And the new girl wasn't always blabbing on about finding her papá.

After a couple years, when María came back for her children, no one knew how she was able to sneak them out of the house, or how she was able to smuggle them onto an outbound ship. At that time, all anyone was talking about was Franco, the fall of Barcelona. No one in that dilapidated seaside town in the northwest thought those royal houses, political parties, or revolutions had anything to do with them. They just kept up their little port, eked out their living, just as they always had and always would. But the war eventually sucked in every person, including left-behind José. When the leftist workers' group he had joined was purged after the war, he was arrested, jailed, assigned to a labor reform unit laying the railroad, and then transferred somewhere else, even he didn't know where, to continue his incarceration. Just before his short life came to an end, he thought of that mulatta who had borne him two children. José would never know that she had returned to Cuba, or that after the war she had moved to New York. Nor did he know that in the early 1950s, when she had remarried to an American named Robert, that woman had given herself a new name, along with her new identity as an American citizen who taught others how to use the English language.

Lesson 2: to wait for
She brought her mother-in-law along to Taitung to visit her husband, and when they got back they both had come down with something. She guessed it was from the dirty communal teacups at Dawushan station, which they'd used to drink water during a stop on the way back. She lay feebly on the bed, her entire body burning hot, clearly aware that she was alone in the pitch-black room. Downstairs was the three kids' room, and on the first floor was the publishing office. The second and third floors were piled up with their publications and an assortment of books and journals. Everything was still, yet she felt her consciousness

spinning. The doctor had told her that he suspected a lung infection, that she would need to take medicine for some time before it would heal, and that she should pay more attention to hygiene, and make sure to sanitize her bowls and chopsticks.

Sometimes she was capable of actually believing what she told her three kids, that their father was studying in America, so he couldn't be there to see them grow up. Husband and wife could only see each other once a year, for fifteen minutes each time. Right when they felt they were really starting to talk, their time would be up. Each year at New Year, she would go to the gift store at the nearby Kujiang shopping arcade and pick out some imported cards and gifts and then deliver them to the children, just to give them the slightest feeling that their father was still in their lives, only too far away for them to see him. It was times like this, when she was sick and weak, that she really wished she had those deep-set eyes with heavy brows by her side to look after her, those large, warm hands to take hold of hers. They were a scholar's hands, with long, slender fingers suited for writing, with a thick callus on the knuckle that supported the pen. But all she could do was wait, wait with the tiniest of hopes for when those hands would hold her again.

Even if it was that hope that was tormenting her. Every so often, her mind would replay the long trek to Taitung: first by the Golden Horse highway bus, teetering past Pingtung, past Fangliao, then turning onto the mountain road toward Taitung. Pummeled by dust and wind the whole route, the bus would shake the passengers every which way, as if it were winnowing out the pebbles and sand that had blown in. Once everyone's hair, eyebrows, and clothes were coated in a layer of dust, they arrived in Taitung by the end of the day, where they would spend a night. The following morning, a little after seven o'clock, they boarded another bus which they got off before it entered a tunnel, waited for a third bus toward the Chenggong fishing harbor, which would take them to Taiyuan Prison in Qingxi. Wire mesh cut her husband's face into fragments, there was no possibility of touch. Each time she would try to use her fifteen minutes to memorize her husband's bearing, so that she could spend the return trip carefully comparing his present state to memories from their life together. It was an excruciating process of counting down, each visit bringing her one visit closer to the day when things would reset and life could start over.

Lesson 3: to pick out
María remembered how Robert would pick out some newspaper articles for her to read when he was first teaching her English. Later he would write condensed versions of novels, pulling out the main plot points and important characters along with the original dialogue, so that she could practice reading. Robert was exceptionally kind to her children. When she and the children sat in Robert's classroom, the English vocabulary words melted gradually into their lives like pieces of candy, lingering on their tongues, radiating gentle sweetness. During English class, María could forget the cramped second-floor apartment in the Bronx where she raised her two kids side by side with two other families, she could forget the alertness she maintained each day from the moment she stepped out her front door, careful not to wander into the Italian or Jewish neighborhoods, hurrying to arrive at the factory or hurrying back home. So, to María, this was all too good to be true. What had started as María cramming together with a bunch of Puerto Ricans to work at a textile mill on the outskirts of the city had led to her tagging along when her fellow workers went to English class. And just like that, she met Robert, five years her senior.

Robert was a conscientious man, always joking that since he had come back alive from the Pacific, he might as well make some kind of contribution to humanity. Since he was an English major who could only speak a little Spanish besides his native language, why not do something language related? After the war ended, Robert was demobilized and returned to New York. He found a post at the textile mill managing a bunch of immigrants from Central and South America. At that time, there was a wave of Puerto Rican immigrants who mostly spoke no English.

This meant they were limited to unskilled jobs, were difficult to manage, and were prone to incidents at work. Robert simply found a blackboard and started teaching English to the workers in his factory at night, and soon he found it gave him a sense of accomplishment. These weren't just faceless workers, but individuals with their own names, personalities, and points of view. Their relationship evolved from foreman and work crew to teacher and students.

Robert would read out new words letter by letter; often he would correct his own Spanish pronunciation in addition to correcting his students' English pronunciation. He picked out María from his first batch of students to serve as his class assistant, to pass out mimeographed notes, or divide the students into groups for conversation practice. Robert liked seeing the looks on his students' faces as they got the hang of it, as if English were another tool like the spinning machines or spindles they handled at work every day. They assimilated more and more into the local way of life. His assistant María's progress was particularly rapid, as she demanded of herself that even her pronunciation and grammar should be as close to his standard as possible.

This idyllic period for teacher and students didn't last long. Someone at the mill reported Robert to the boss, saying that teaching the foreigners English was making them harder to manage, that they were starting to talk back. There was an implication that Robert might be involved with the Communists; otherwise, why would he spend so much time teaching those Latins for no pay? Who knows what he was planning to organize them to do? The boss called Robert into his office and asked him to explain himself. Robert couldn't hold himself back, he blurted out something about how America was a great country because anyone could come here to pursue the American dream. America was a big melting pot, and New York was a smaller melting pot; we should help these immigrants get a foothold here, help them assimilate, so they could compete on a level playing field. The manager cut him off, saying, "I'm sure your intentions are good. If you want to waste your time helping some Puerto Ricans or Jews, I'm not going to stand in your way. I respect you. And anyway it's a free country, didn't the Founding Fathers say we're all created equal? The thing is if somebody gets up to any nonsense in my mill, he and I are gonna have a problem. I guess you know what you've gotta do next, Robbie?"

Robert left his job at the mill, and while he was still looking for another place to teach English to immigrants, he got started editing his teaching materials, planning to publish them as a book. He was full of hopeful visions for the future. As America's postwar power grew, surely more and more foreigners would have dealings with America, and the demand for English learning would be huge. He felt he had been picked out to undertake this project. It was as if he could already see his publications flowing across the globe, until someday every corner of the world would have his students.

Lesson 4: to take part in
All these years, she had been trying to find ways for her husband to take part in her life. A few days ago, she came home and switched on the light to discover one of the kids crying. She assumed he'd fallen or had a fight with one of his siblings. But when she asked what happened, he said when he'd come home from school she hadn't been there, and he didn't have a papa to call to. The other kids at school had mamas and papas to take care of them, but he was like an orphan, and it made him sad. She looked around and saw only a few desks with some piles of books waiting to be packed and shipped out. The house was so empty and dark, no wonder the poor kid didn't feel any warmth. She made a decision to quit her teaching position and focus on running the publishing business at home while she waited for her husband to return.

Each week her husband wrote a letter home. If the weekly letter didn't arrive, she would have all kinds of wild thoughts, worrying that something must have happened there on the inside. Over the span of so many years, his letters were pretty much all the same. A letter limited to two hundred words or less couldn't express much beyond simple greetings and health updates; there was no way to say anything particularly heartfelt. Opening each letter, she would see a blue stamp with a slogan like, "Be loyal to our leaders! Devote yourself to reconquering the mainland," or "Preventing leaks is everyone's responsibility!", or just the censor's "REVIEWED" stamp. It was a reminder that she must restrain herself, that anything they wrote would have additional readers. She did worry that her husband wasn't eating well, so she often sent cookies, raisins, medicine, canned food, and milk powder. Then the return letter would be stamped, "No perishable items accepted." A numbing fear enveloped her life, as it had since she stood by and watched as her husband was awakened from a nap, handcuffed, and thrown into a jeep without the chance even to put on a coat, never to return again. She was completely at a loss—even after going to court in Taipei, she still had no idea how her husband, who spent all day teaching and working on his books, could be implicated in a conspiracy to commit sedition. It was the local police who made her the angriest. They clearly knew nothing sinister was going on in their home because they came to inspect them every month. One time they even demanded a photograph of their oldest son, still in elementary school. She snapped, "Photograph? He was four years old when his papa went to jail, what on earth could he have known? Unless you're gathering photographs of every child in Kaohsiung, I'm not giving you that." Having said that in the heat of the moment, she spent the night in the dark silence of their home, waiting for a knock at the door.

The three kids might have been sensitive enough to realize that their family's situation was out of the ordinary; they strove to be as independent as possible in order to keep their mother from worrying. Because of her husband, she bought *The Count of Monte Cristo* for her children to read, so they would learn that good and evil were not always so easy to discern, just like how the protagonist is thrown in prison on trumped-up charges. From time to time, she would tell the kids about their father in America, flipping through the book of newspaper clippings he had put together for them to absorb some new knowledge and learn how to adopt a healthy lifestyle. It seemed like someone far away was showing his care by passing on these informative articles, taking part in their everyday lives.

Many matters at the publishing house needed to be decided by him, and he needed to write the copy for their newspaper advertisements. He was the only creative in-house, and it was thanks to his careful work expanding and revising the new edition of that best-selling grammar reference that the publisher could continue operating on a stable financial footing. At the same time, she couldn't ignore what he wrote about in his short stories. After she first read "Letter from Northern Kyushu" in the pages of *New Life*, she'd felt utterly despondent. Later, when he wrote to her excitedly about revising it, adding to it, and publishing it separately, she felt a hesitation in her heart. They'd been living apart for close to ten years, like she was his widow, and now to have to see her husband pouring out his heart to some other woman she'd never met—it was like each line was a slap across the face. Was she just a substitute, after all? What kind of life had they been leading together all these years? She managed to wait several weeks without writing back, until finally she broke down and wrote to him her feelings on the matter, and the censors could go ahead and read them too. Even when her husband wrote, "I hope you don't believe there was really ever such a person. You're the only one I've ever loved. This is just how works of literature get written. Please forgive me," she wasn't convinced. She read that short story backwards and forwards so many times, she could practically recite every line. It was truly hard to believe the Japanese woman the protagonist was in love with didn't exist—and the protagonist's life story was almost identical to her husband's own past.

Their three kids read papa's short story, and they asked why papa was writing about loving some Japanese woman instead of mama. She was at a loss for how to answer, as she felt the urge to cry surging up within her. She didn't know, she told them, she wasn't sure. He was so much smarter than she was, more creative, and now with him so far away, she didn't feel confident enough to say she understood what he was thinking. She told herself it was fiction, it was fake, but then she was paralyzed by another detail drawn from real life. (Weren't the songs the girl sings to the protagonist exactly the same songs he'd wanted me to sing to him?) She desperately wanted to grab her husband by the shoulders and demand that he give her an explanation why he'd written that story, why he had such deep affection for that Japanese woman, why he even wrote that he hoped that his child would one day study abroad in Japan and stay at her house, so their children could fall in love! If he went ahead and published this story, it would be announcing to the world, "My husband has never moved on from his first love," and as his wife, she seemed like just a stand-in.

Since then, all her husband's letters came with an apologetic tone, repeatedly mentioning that his story was fictional, that he absolutely was not pining over an old flame. He even said he was willing to rewrite it or give up on publishing it altogether. The whole thing irritated her: one moment she felt she shouldn't stifle her husband's creativity, the next she felt sorry for herself all over again. Then one day, her eldest son, who had just started middle school, asked her haltingly to explain the truth about where exactly his papa was. She took out the papers documenting her husband's conviction. They both cried. Somehow, it was crying this way which made her realize that it was silly to get so worked up over the past. Supposing it was all true, what difference did it make? This child in her arms, and her other two children, each the result of nine months of hard pregnancy, who could laugh and cry—that was real. She only needed to take good care of them, so their invisible father could continue to be part of their lives.

Lesson 5: to change one's mind
Chapter V: Verbs

Section 6: Mood

(3) Subjunctive mood

Subjunctive mood (also known as thought mood) is used to express unreal statements such as suppositions, hypotheses, and wishes.

Conditional Sentences

A. Present-unreal

Expresses conditional or imaginary statements that are not consistent with present (or future) actuality.

While he was revising this section, he realized that if it weren't for this grammatical mood, he might not be able to go on living. Each example sentence he jotted down suggested a time and place. They helped him to imagine buying a car that he could take on trips (If I had a car, I should be very happy), or that he was a bird, able to fly free (If I were a bird, I could fly). He could fire questions back at the people holding him down (What would you do if you were in my place?). Practicing these sentence forms was a way of preserving a space for his deepest wishes.

1. If I were rich enough, I would buy a car.

2. If I had a car, I should be happy.

3. If I were you, I wouldn't do that.

4. If I had wings, I would fly to you.

5. If you could come, it would be very nice.

6. If he came, I might see him.

7. If I saw him, I should tell him that.

8. If Tom were here now, he would help me.

9. If you fell into the river, you would be drowned.

10. If you had more time, would you study Japanese?

11. If it stopped raining, you could go out.

12. If the plane left at noon, it would reach Tokyo at four o'clock.

At times, when he was feeling hopeful, he would make plans to buy a car once he got out, like he wrote to his wife: "Each day when I go for my morning walk around the grounds, I look out at the beautiful scenery all around, and I think how I could buy a car to take you and the kids to the countryside to enjoy the view. Sometimes I could take just you, and we could find a quiet hilltop or riverbank, where I could win your heart again. How happy I would be! This is what I wish for—what do you think?" Waking up after a fitful night, he could still remember how, in his dreams, his wife had come to pick him up in a taxi, how they'd spent a night in Taitung before returning to Kaohsiung, happy as could be. He suddenly couldn't understand why he had to be in this place. Why exactly was he wasting his life away in this cell? Writing in a foreign language was the only way for him to achieve his dreams. In English, Japanese, and Chinese, the enormity of time could be whittled down to thin slivers. He wandered among three writing systems and four vernaculars. Sometimes he wondered, if there were no language, would it be possible to *kangaeru/think/sikao*? During days which are blank, allowing oneself to slip into blankness is dangerous, so he kept himself busy, trying to rekindle his youthful enthusiasm for reading, soaking up knowledge, writing English teaching materials, tutoring his classmates in Japanese and English. He thought about strategies for the publishing house. At nine, after lights out, he would sit against the wall, lost in disordered thought. The flight from Taiwan to Tokyo took four hours, while his wife and mother took nearly a day and several buses just to come from Kaohsiung to Taitung to see him. He had never been on a plane or traveled the road from Kaohsiung. He could only wait for this storm to pass from his life. And maybe if the rain stopped and the sky was clear, he would be able to go out again.

B. Past-unreal

Expresses conditional or imaginary statements that are at odds with past actuality.

Language holds history within it. He imagined an alternative life where, after the war, Taiwan had declared independence, founding a nation that was no longer a Japanese colony but had not fallen into the hands of the Chinese Nationalist Party either—a nation of the Taiwanese people. His life would have to be completely revised. On February 28th, on the way from the dormitory at the Teachers' College to see a movie at Zhongshan Hall, he would never have witnessed the crowds smashing pack after pack of cigarettes in front of the Taipei Monopoly Bureau. And after he returned to the dormitory, he wouldn't have heard a classmate saying that the citizens attempting to petition the Governor-General had been gunned down by guards. February 28th would have been a day when nothing happened, when he would have seen a movie, and later he would have graduated and become an ordinary English teacher. There would be no compulsory Mandarin, no suppression of Japanese. Everyone would speak whatever language they liked. He thought of a short story he'd read in a magazine about Japanese bombers dropping nuclear bombs on Washington, forcing America to surrender. America became a colony of Japan. That would make America's status about the same as Taiwan's. Maybe he would have gone to America to teach Japanese.

Or maybe the Chiang Kai-shek regime could have been rooted out by Mao, and Taiwan would have fallen under the influence of the Chinese Communist Party. Maybe then he would have to study Russian. Maybe he would have been a Russian teacher.

But stubborn reality prevented him from considering how these eventualities could be possible. Had any of those experts on English grammar whose works he consulted—Harold E. Palmer, A.A. Hornby, A.J. Thompson, Robert J. Dixson, Akao Yoshio, Ono Keijiro—worked in a tiny room like this one, inserting their own views as they drew on the works of other scholars, completing their books on grammar? He knew nothing about their lives, no more than they knew about his. Still, they had met in the English language, and thanks to those mechanical sentence structures, usage notes, and example sentences, it seemed like they had penetrated to the beating heart of the language. He knew that Harold E. Palmer, his greatest source of inspiration, had lived in Japan for fourteen years, serving as a foreign-language education consultant for the Ministry of Culture, where he laid the foundation for modern English pedagogy. He remembered how, during his sophomore year, he had to save up for a long time and make three trips to Rainbow Bridge Bookstore in Ximending before he bought a first edition of Palmer's *The New Method Grammar*. He had no idea that Palmer died the following year, in 1949. Nor did he knew that when Robert J. Dixson had moved with his new bride and two stepchildren to start a new life in Miami, Florida, deep in the American South, it was the same time that he had completed his reform on Green Island, starting his own new life.

After his reformatory experience, he stopped keeping a diary and avoided discussing politics with anyone. If the world went left or right, it was no business of his. All he wanted was to live his life. It was plenty for him if he could start a family, run his business, teach, and write. And that was exactly what he did: got married, had children, and worked in English language education, right up until the moment that Jeep engine awakened him from an afternoon nap, ripping him out of the home and life he had built single-handedly.

C. Future-unreal

Expresses conditional or imaginary statements that are at odds with future actuality.

Ex.: If I were to go abroad, I would go to Japan (but I cannot leave the country).

His first published work of fiction was the story of his first love. The first time he went to jail, he would look at the messages left behind on the walls of his solitary prison cell by previous inmates and think with sorrow about his college girlfriend, whom he was unable to marry. It was in another prison cell, years later, that he put his unabated longing and regret down into words. He mingled past with present, inventing an idealized Japanese girl, beautiful and virtuous, and imagining himself a high school teacher, who receives a letter after many years of silence. Twenty years vanished in a flash. From his position in a future that would have been unimaginable to his past self, he lived an alternative life through his protagonist, Tsai Ming-che (a fusion of his wife and son's names). But his wife thought it was all real, and so she spent half a year nursing hurt feelings, just because of that short story.

Maybe that was the magic of language. She was like someone studying a map too carefully, who starts to believe the lines and symbols all drawn to scale are the actual borders of a territory. The first half of his life had been spent forming a relationship to language, communicating, or failing to, by means of those words and sounds. There were sounds that let him know a person was someone he could get along with, and there were sounds that told him to stay away. It was one's soul that lay hidden beneath the words, in a way that transcended which side of a strait you were born on. His classmates mainly fell into four camps: there were those, like him, who hoped for an independent, democratic Taiwan; there were the ones they called "red taros," that is, Taiwanese communists; there were mainlanders affiliated with the Nationalists; and there were mainland communists. The four groups could agree on basically nothing and constantly argued, often coming to blows. Different groups would team up against each other, even to make false accusations to the authorities against their opponents. What he hated the most were the Nationalist mainlanders who liked to say, "If Taiwan's going to be fucking independent, then just let the commies have it." Even his students were never as asinine, back when he was a teacher. As he thought about it now, weren't they all equally oppressed, deprived of freedom? With nowhere to vent their frustration, they could only take it out on the people around them. This was certainly cause for despair.

In 1970, on the third day of the lunar new year, when the prison uprising failed, he keenly felt the limitations of language. A person could be inspired to devote himself, even sacrifice himself, for something he learned through language. At the same time, language could seem just like this prison; it could constrain what a person knew, what he had access to. He knew beforehand that a group of young, strong prisoners, who'd had military training, were planning an uprising. They were planning to take control of the prison with the help of the native Taiwanese among the prison guards. From then they would occupy a nearby radio station and broadcast Taiwan's cry for independence to the world. To him, their plan was a little unrealistic; he thought it would be better to use their weapons to occupy the neighboring towns and then disappear into the mountains, waging guerrilla warfare until other parts of the island rose up in sympathy, like a chain reaction.

After the insurrection failed, six accomplices who had escaped with guns were captured. He heard that five of them were put to death the same day, the sixth given a fifteen-year sentence. He, who had spent the entire time inside the prison, meanwhile, was somehow denounced as a ringleader and sentenced to a year of solitary confinement. Under a light bulb that stayed lit day and night, his back pressed against the cold, hard wall of his cramped cell, he belted out every song he could remember, over and over, letting the music and words soothe his lonely spirit. If his wife only knew his present state, would she still dwell so much on his fictional first love? But he couldn't tell her. The authorities felt he was a little too "active," with his teaching English and Japanese to his fellow prisoners; they'd been watching him for quite some time. As a result, the young prisoners who planned the insurrection were afraid to get too close to him, and once the insurrection failed, the mainlanders in the prison, who weren't fond of him anyway, took the opportunity to denounce him. It was a fictional charge, created purely out of words, but it was doing real harm to his body and his spirit. He could hear prisoners, communists who considered him an enemy, mocking him from outside his iron-barred window: "Serves you right. Just hurry up and die!" He could hear others, his language students, encouraging him. He wrote on the wall "Wait and Hope," the words of the falsely imprisoned Edmond from *The Count of Monte Cristo*, as his motto. In his solitude, he repeatedly thought of the characters from the two short stories he'd written, how they had been kept apart by language and nationality. So many sleepless nights, he flipped open his English-Chinese dictionary and began sorting and categorizing English vocabulary, reading softly to himself, his voice faintly reverberating off the cramped walls. In moments of despair, he was afraid that the future he was waiting for was an unreal one. He used language, but he was suspicious of it. He relied on language to support his family, but language always demanded its pound of flesh in return.

D. Future-uncertain

Expresses intense uncertainty about the future.

Ex.: If I should fail, what shall I do?

In principle, another two years remained on his sentence, but none of the inmates around him were released at the end of their sentences. Instead, they were transferred to the labor-reform teams on Green Island. He could guess that the same would happen to him. In late April of 1972, he was strung together with some other prisoners, just like rice balls tied on a string for the Dragon Boat Festival, and led on board the boat to Green Island. The sea at night was inky black, the faint moonlight falling in patches on the waves. In the suffocating cabin, the smell of oil and exhaust mingled with the prisoners' body odors. As he was tossed about by the waves, his thoughts turned to the letter his daughter, who had just started middle school, had written to him. "I'm starting to think you aren't in America at all, but in Taitung. If you're in America, why is the stationery you use made in Taiwan, and why does it say 'Qingxi Village, Taitung' on it? Also, why do we send our letters to P.O. Box 7908-2, Taitung? Why not 123 XYZ Rd., Some State, USA? Papa, please tell me your real address!" He wept silently in his solitary cell. All he could do was tell them the truth, in the hopes that they would forgive him once they were older. He only didn't know if he could last long enough to see them grow up.

Dixson's Idioms 183

His feelings on returning to Green Island were complicated. He couldn't help but recall his experiences at the reformatory ten years earlier and to compare with them the newly constructed prison he now saw before him. The original reformatory had become the headquarters for the entire prison colony, overseeing the habitual offenders and the work teams. The radiating, two-story structure surrounded by high concrete walls in front of the headquarters was the Green Island Prison. During one of his recreation-time walks, he ran into a mainlander who had offended the Chiang Kai-shek regime by translating a *Popeye* comic,[1] and chatted with another mainlander who had been arrested for organizing a study group of communist thought. Both had been oppressed because of language, so neither had very much to say.

He began to feel that within the same words, there were two layers, one directed out and one directed in. The deeper, inner level said something that only the speaker could understand, something located in between the abstract thought and its formation into words. That something was not English, or Japanese, or Taiwanese, or Chinese, or any language he was familiar with. There was no way to analyze it into any formulaic grammar or sentence structure. It was, rather, an utterance much closer to silence, something that could not be spoken, a language that even lacked sound. It was the layer in his letters to his wife that, when he mentioned coming home, actually meant that he felt he would never come home—a meaning that his wife never detected.

The four years he spent on Green Island were even harder than the eleven years before. For one thing, he had been transferred to the work team despite having already served his sentence, so now there was no knowing when he would be free. When his wife and mother came to see him, thinking they would have a reunion, to their surprise, they found they were allowed only to wave, from a distance, through the rain. Then there was the general amnesty after Chiang Kai-shek's death. He could hear parolees from the prison next door setting off celebratory firecrackers, while he could only go on repeating the process of labor and thought reform. Sometimes he recalled an old man from his work team of ten years before, in his seventies and completely illiterate. All day with the team, the old man just went off to the riverside to take care of a flock of ducks. He was the most relaxed of anyone in the team. When they asked him how he'd ended up there, through his thick accent they were able to determine that his eldest son had run back to China, so the authorities could only grab his old man to compensate. So here he was someone who had gotten some education, learned two foreign languages, and in prison he was worse off than an illiterate? To the old man, prison was nothing more than some walls, iron bars, and barbed wire. Sometimes he envied that blankness, with no words to jump out and express meaning or emotion. You could even reduce yourself to nothing more than a lamp, a wall, a tiny cell. Maybe that would be real peace, with none of the emotional highs and lows, none of the anxious waiting. Hope and despair would be nearly equivalent.

He wouldn't feel any pleasure being transferred to work at the commissary, with its laxer rules. He wouldn't feel that his talents were being appreciated just because he had been chosen to tutor the assistant prison superintendent's daughter in English, and much less would he feel disturbed by the young cadet who seemed to have it in for him. He would try to rein in his linguistic sensitivity, to ignore words' connotations, to forget as much as possible. In twenty years' time, he would have successfully erased his entire vocabulary. He would have completed what needed to be done.

E. *Future-possible*

Expresses things that may occur in the future (or present), but which are not certain

Ex.: If you work hard, you will succeed.

María's full name was María Dolores Iglesias Andújar, but after she married Robert J. Dixson, she became Lolita Dixson. Her two children also took her husband's name. The family was doing quite well in the

Dixson's Idioms 185

sunshine of their new home in Miami. The couple spent most of their time writing English textbooks, sometimes lending a hand to Lolita's friends and relatives escaping from Cuba. Lolita's elder son, Julio, was already old enough to serve as assistant editor, and he and Robert authored a Spanish workbook for English speakers. Robert died in 1963 at the age of only fifty-five, but he has been outlived by nearly all of his language textbooks, which continue to guide thousands of students every year into the world of the English language.

During the years immediately before and after Robert's death, world events made Lolita increasingly concerned about the future. First, the Cuban Missile Crisis ended without her even noticing. Then it was protests over black civil rights raging in the South. When she, along with so many others, read Dr. King's letter from Birmingham jail, it was as if her own mixed blood were beating against the barricades of racial division, crying out for justice. And when, on August 28 of the same year, Dr. King gave his "I Have a Dream" speech on the steps of the Lincoln Memorial, she, like so many others, felt herself stirred by that sonorous voice. She was convinced that the owner of that voice would certainly realize his vision of the promised land. Maybe she could use the entire text of the speech as supplementary teaching material, playing a recording to help her students' listening comprehension and asking them to memorize certain key lines.

Lolita, now fifty years old, found herself thinking about one line in particular: "With this faith, we will be able to work together, to pray together, to struggle together, to go to jail together, to stand up for freedom together, knowing that we will be free one day." This would be considered the "future-possible" tense. She hoped this future would be actual. Lolita continued to live in Miami until she passed away at age ninety-six. Her elder son Julio, sick with cancer, followed behind her the very next year. Lolita's granddaughter, Julie, graduated from the University of Florida and became a practicing lawyer in Miami. Julie's friends were unaware that the English teaching materials used by two to three generations of language learners had been penned by the Dixson family.

Lesson 39: to fix up
Dixson's first book on idioms was *Essential Idioms in English: Phrasal Verbs and Collocations* (1951), which ran to five editions. Both the *Handbook of English Words and Phrases* and *Overview of High School English Words and Phrases*, edited by Ko Chi-hua in Taiwan, made use of Dixson's work. At that time, there were quite a few reprints and translations of Dixson's idiom book in Taiwan. Lai Shih-hsiung studied it on his way to becoming a famous educator; his Ivy Publishing would put out a revised edition in the early 1990s.

I'll never forget those days when I was trapped in evening study hall, back in the last few years of the previous century. Each night, I would tune in at the same time to hear Lai Shih-hsiung teach English and explain grammar, vocabulary, and idioms in his resonant voice. Clutching the copy of *Ivy English Monthly* I had ordered through my school, I would take notes and write out practice exercises. Upon starting my first year of high school, everyone in my class was given a copy of *Dixson's Idioms*, published by Ivy, but the truth was, even in middle school, when the English teacher made us memorize phrases, they came out of *Dixson's Idioms*. She had just graduated from the Department of English at National Taiwan Normal University, and she took her teaching seriously, at least with the more advanced students. She gave out a lot of supplemental handouts and encouraged us to open our mouths and read out in a loud voice; she told us not to worry if our pronunciation wasn't perfect, but to try to speak as much English as possible during class. Unfortunately, countryside kids like us were mostly pretty shy. When the teacher would ask if there were any questions, she would be met with a blanket of silence. If she called on someone, made him stand up and give an answer, it would be more embarrassed stammering, the seconds ticking by without a complete sentence ever coming out. The class moved quickly from learning the twenty-six letters to structures made from subjects, objects, nouns, adjectives, adverbs, and verbs. Some of my classmates were terrified of English from start to finish, and no matter how many reference books or old exams they studied, they never figured out how to change tenses. Our teacher told us, "Students, you have to imagine that English is a bicycle. If the chain slips or the tires leak, you need to give it a 'fix up,' repair it. Imagine that scene, students, imagine the sound of the words. 'Fix' looks a lot like a tool, and 'up' gives you a feeling of bouncing, of fullness, like if you fill your tires with air that's up, when it's all repaired then that's a 'fix up.' Let's try some more: if you repair your house, you've 'fixed up' your house; if your mama wants to do her hair then she could 'fix up' her hair in braids; if you want to make an appointment then you 'fix up a date.'" I understood—whenever I accidentally spoke Taiwanese in school, I'd get fixed right up too.

We were trained from the beginning to speak only Mandarin in the classroom. Taiwanese was only to be spoken secretly after class, out of earshot of detestable tattletales, if you wanted to avoid a fine. In the end we couldn't speak either one correctly. Starting in middle school we had to learn English. Of course, the hierarchy of languages went English→Mandarin→Taiwanese, our mother tongue on the bottom. When we went over to grandpa's house in the next village, he was always a bit disappointed that we couldn't understand him very well, and he wasn't very comfortable with our broken Taiwanese. Our Taiwanese was rusty from the beginning, and with even less chance to polish it later, it went to waste. But by then we were obsessed with the L.A. Boyz, back from America to put out their first record. We bought their tapes, tried their breakdance moves, and imitated their raps, which were in English mixed with Taiwanese (the English part we mostly just mumbled past), along with their none-too-standard Mandarin singing. Once, a couple friends and I brought some of the L.A. Boyz' English lyrics to our teacher, begging her to explain them. She took a look at them and said, "These words aren't all written out properly, there are a lot of abbreviations and shortenings. And since it's nearly all colloquial usage, it won't be too much like the grammar you're learning. But what's important is that you're taking an interest in English."

The only problem was that our interests never mattered as much as exams. One time, when my grandfather saw me struggling to memorize *Dixson's Idioms*, he said, "Grandson, if there's anything you don't understand, you can ask your uncle. He went to high school in the Japanese times, and he got good grades. I think maybe he could help, though even I know Japanese people's English isn't great." Later, when my uncle happened to stop by for tea, grandpa pointed at me, saying, "This little monkey can't get the hang of English. Give him some pointers." I only knew that my scrawny, dark-skinned uncle was the "intellectual" of the village, someone people respected and frequently asked for help settling some matter or other, but the truth was he hadn't even graduated high school. He took my phrasebook and started flipping through it, reading some phrases here and there. Wow, I thought, a bit surprised, his pronunciation is actually pretty good. He said, "I haven't read any 'American' for a long time. I already forgot it all. At this point, I don't remember much more than my ABCs." He told me he had a grammar book that one of my other uncles had bought, he would get it for me after he went back home. The book turned out to be a dark green, hardcover edition with no text at all on the cover, only the words "New English Grammar (Unabridged), edited by Ko Chi-hua, First Publishing" embossed in gold on the spine—the June 1981 revised and expanded 41st edition.

That younger uncle, whom I barely knew, had gone to Taipei for technical school, so I only ever saw him during New Year's holidays. This old grammar book, though, was covered with traces of its former owner, passages circled or underlined in pencil or ballpoint pen. As I read, I started to feel like English was a truly arcane subject. How could they write so much in just the first chapter, "Nouns"? Surely this was not written for middle school students. I shut the book and went back to my *Dixson's Idioms*.

Lesson 20: to hold still

When he thought of his confession, extracted under torture, he still seethed with resentment. His body had healed, but the scars held memories that swelled and split open. Repeated interrogation wore away his spirit until the language of deception and intimidation lodged itself in the deepest part of his mind, throbbing like shards of broken glass. Even if he could repress the memories from his consciousness, his sleep was still consumed by nightmares, so much that his wife kept a yardstick by the bedside, which she could use whenever she needed to bring him back to reality. When he came back home, it was right as one child was getting ready for the university entrance exam, while another was getting ready for the high school entrance exam. He was nervous for them and wanted to help them review English, while they were not only worrying over their exams but also learning uncomfortably how to live with a father they barely knew. His wife was trapped in the middle: on the one hand she needed to remind her husband that the children were used to managing for themselves, they knew how to manage the stress of an exam, he shouldn't worry too much, and on the other hand she had to explain to the children that their father had been away for so long, he was merely trying to make up for lost time in his own way. But all of them felt uneasy in this palpably awkward situation.

His wife wanted him to join her on her morning walks, but he was only interested in going up to the roof to take care of his tiny flower garden. He had already taken more than enough walks. Now he only wanted to free himself from his usual perspective by standing somewhere higher, to gaze out to the very edges of the city. He had always known he wouldn't feel out of step with society; after all, he had read many more books, newspapers, and magazines during his years in prison than his peers living on the outside. He was used to negotiating the world of the printed word; it was facing his children, who had grown up so suddenly, that left him feeling at a loss. He could only keep on working on English reference books for students—it was the only thing that hadn't changed, despite the seventeen years that had been stolen away from him. The spelling of a word, a sentence in the past perfect tense, the basic structure of a language, no one could take that away. The English language was not susceptible to torture; no one could force English to confess to a nonexistent crime. It was in the world of letters and punctuation marks that he could relax completely. English would never betray him.

Nor had music betrayed him. Now that he was finally safe at home, he found that the notes that played when the needle scraped across his record of Dvořák's *New World Symphony* matched his younger memories exactly—they surged out of the speakers like the ranks of an invisible army. Music was like the flesh of the fruit, wrapped tightly around the stone inside. He tried to imagine what Dvořák must have been feeling when he traveled the great distance from eastern Europe to America, that led him to compose his ninth symphony. As the second movement began to play, visions of the past streamed forth, voices singing "Goin' Home" swirled around in the drawer of his memories. Looking back at younger days from this side of life's midway point, he felt something like the longing for a distant home, far off across the sea.

As he felt a desire to control his own life as much as possible from this point forward, he learned to drive a car. The first day of driving lessons, after the instructor introduced the names and functions of the different parts of the car—as he tentatively sat in the driver's seat, started the car, and grasped the steering wheel—it was like grabbing hold of unknowable fate. Once he bought a car, wherever he drove, he liked holding the wheel, shifting the gears, stepping on the clutch. It was like every road led to freedom. And if he took good care of his car and drove it correctly, it would never betray him either.

LESSON TWO: I Have a Dream

(National Translation House, High School English vol. 6, 1987)

I nearly forgot to mention, there were also our English textbooks. My high school English teacher was practically a sales rep for Ivy English. Our syllabus followed along with *Ivy English Monthly*, with assessment exercises from the magazine as our quizzes and grammar and vocabulary references published by Lai Shih-hsiung as supplemental materials. My teacher was constantly afraid that our vocabulary lists weren't long enough, our assessments weren't frequent enough, our textbooks weren't thick enough. Textbooks we bought at the start of the term often didn't get used until close to finals, with our teacher moving through them at lightning speed. Cramming three textbook lessons into one period of class time meant we could polish off an entire fourteen-lesson volume in just a week.

My recollection of Dr. Martin Luther King Jr. is that his portrait in my textbook featured a mustache, gap teeth, and horns, courtesy of my classmates. At the time, we just quickly flipped through the text of the speech and determined that the English wasn't too hard. Our teacher, however, slowed his usual fast pace and uncharacteristically spent an entire class on this one lesson. He brought out a portable stereo, so we could listen to Dr. King's voice. The classroom resounded with the strident tones from thirty years before, interspersed with the sounds of the crowd cheering and clapping. Every word Dr. King spoke was creating meaning, every sentence, every paragraph telling of injustice, crying out for freedom. For the fifteen or so minutes of the speech, our teacher just leaned against the wall by the blackboard, listening along with us. When the recording ended, he said, "Maybe you couldn't understand all of it, since there were some references to the Bible. But all of you should be able to sense Dr. King's charisma. The first time I heard it, I felt goosebumps over my whole body when he cried, 'I have a dream today!' After that is when he begins using parallelism, creating a pattern of rhythmic repetition. This is the part most people know best. Students, learning English is not easy. It isn't our native language, and we don't live in an English-speaking environment. There are some things we will never really understand. Don't you think it's strange that your English textbook should contain this speech? Does your history teacher or your civics teacher ever mention the black civil rights movement in America in the 1960s? You don't recall? Then I should explain a bit."

This was the only moment in three years of high school when my English teacher's humanity radiated through. During that class, he spoke of Dr. King's struggle, explained that the part of his speech included in our textbook was ad-libbed, that the part he had actually prepared ahead of time had barely made it in at all. Clearly this minister was an infectious public speaker. For a moment, we forgot all about Dixson, forgot about Lai Shih-hsiung, forgot about assessments and college entrance exams. For the moment we were just a teacher and his students, trying earnestly to understand a slice of history from far away. After that, our teacher returned to his usual mode, and classes were once again filled with study points and practice tests.

Lesson 23: to clean out
Even though he had stopped making reference books for middle and high school English—he had since turned his focus to Taiwan's language, culture, and history, editing *A Bibliography of Taiwan Culture*—he would still occasionally flip through textbooks to look at their selections. He discovered that on the eve of the lifting of martial law, volume six of the national high school English textbook included Dr. King's "I Have a Dream" speech. He knew that Dr. King was a famous black American civil rights leader, but what he didn't know was that they were born the same year. The original date of the speech was a week before he went to prison the second time. He remembered reading the news of Dr. King's assassination while he was still in Taiyuan Prison, not long after he'd fought through a bout of tuberculosis to complete his revised grammar. He read through the text of the speech, doubting on the one

hand if Taiwanese high school students could really understand Dr. King's pursuit of fairness and justice, but on the other hand he was still feeling hopeful that after martial law, Taiwanese society might experience a new climate.

But he didn't trust the government that had repressed its people for so many decades, didn't trust that lifting martial law would produce any immediate changes. He still frequently felt that security agents were monitoring him; he could never let his guard down. No matter where he drove to in his car, or if he flew to Japan or America, he was no longer able to see things with naïve eyes. He'd spent his life wrestling with three languages—first Japanese, which to him was as familiar as a mother tongue; then Mandarin, after the war; and finally English, which he used to earn a living. Whenever he read or wrote Japanese, he would think of himself as a young man, when he loved to read all kinds of books, newspapers, magazines, when he was ambitious and competitive. Japanese enveloped his student years and war years; every youthful, romantic song he knew was in Japanese. The Mandarin that came after, though, was utilitarian and distant. The so-called standard pronunciation sounded to his ears overbearing and invasive. His familiar Japanese was displaced by the Mandarin that he was required to speak and the Chinese that he was required to write. It was the language that spoke interrogation and forced confession, that wrote intimidation and imprisonment, that left him no choice but to stand up and resist. If Japanese was his first love, then Mandarin was an arranged marriage, and English was the family property that paid the bills. He could love a language even as he hated the country that spoke the language. As a result, his three children all went to study in America, his daughter even settling there to marry and raise children.

After he completed his memoirs, written in Japanese, and said more or less everything he had to say, his memory began to resemble an English fill-in-the-blank exercise, with more and more gaps appearing. He saw the lyrics his hand was writing, recalled the melody, but could not think of the next line.

Kaori mo takaki hurusato no
oka no kokage no shirayui yo
ano hi no yuzata wa sono mama ni
ima demo kokoro ni saiteiru

(The fragrant white lilies in the shade of the trees on the hill in my hometown, their elegance still blooms in my memory)

He opened the cover of a grammar workbook he himself had written, already many years ago, and stared at the first set of practice questions.

Niao neng fei. _____ can fly.

Ta laizi Zhonghua Minguo. She comes from _____ _____ _____ _____.

Ribenren shi qinfen de minzu. _____ Japanese _____ a diligent _____.

Xingqisan zai xingqier yu xingqisi zhijian. _____ comes between _____ and _____.

He couldn't answer a single one.

He began to forget his wife's instructions. Sometimes when he went out for a drive, he forgot to drive back home. When his wife laid out a pair of socks for him, he would put both on the same foot and then frantically look for the missing sock. When his wife told him to sit in the kitchen and wait for her to prepare dinner, she would find him eating the raw ingredients before they went into the pan. Once, when his wife took him to the doctor to treat a cold, he slipped out and walked home alone, wearing just the flimsy hospital gown. He gradually grew less talkative. On days when he didn't speak at all, people still came to talk to him. He just looked at them silently. In her later years, Lolita, on the opposite side of the world, looked at her family in just the same way. The words she had accumulated over the course of her life went away without a trace, like freed slaves. This was a return to an original way of facing the world: without language, things had no names, and history was yet to begin.

Notes

1. Author and political commentator Bo Yang (1920–2008) spent ten years in prison when his translation of a *Popeye* comic, in which Popeye and his son Swee' Pea declare themselves rulers of a desert island, was interpreted as a satire of Chiang Kai-shek's regime in Taiwan.

5

BEEF NOODLES

Li Ang
(translated by Sylvia Li-chun Lin)

He was arrested as a political dissident and sentenced to death, later commuted to life in prison. One day during his twenty-three years of imprisonment, he had a craving for beef noodles.

That was a time when beef noodles were actually available in prison. Not free, of course, but neither were they so expensive that they were beyond the means of the average prisoner. Basically, anyone with a little money who was willing to spend it could enjoy a bowl.

Despite the fact that he was a political prisoner, his family was able to send him money regularly, and he could afford a bowl of beef noodles whenever the craving hit, though he knew he mustn't overdo it.

He ordered them by filling out a form at five in the afternoon, as stipulated by prison rules. They were delivered at nine o'clock. While he was enjoying his late-night snack, on this night, he noticed that the man across the way, also a political prisoner, was staring hungrily until he finished the last drop of soup.

It occurred to him that he ought to treat this fellow prisoner to a bowl, since the man had never had a visitor and, of course, no money to buy his own.

He made up his mind to do just that.

The next day he failed to place an order, for no particular reason (he tended to gloss over why, but if pressed for an explanation, he'd say he was on the toilet at the time). One day can't make a difference, he assumed, since time was one thing they had plenty of. He'd place an order the next afternoon, and it would reach his fellow prisoner that night.

Shortly after daybreak the next morning, before he had a chance to order the noodles, the man was taken out and shot.

After the passage of many years, even after he'd become an influential politician, crowned with glory and honors, he still could not forget the bowl of noodles he'd failed to order.

Beef Noodles
The dish usually comes in the form of noodle soup and is so named because beef is the main ingredient.

After chunks of beef are slow cooked with a packet of spices, the meat and soup are poured into a large bowl, to which are added boiled noodles and some sprigs of greens. A sprinkle of thinly sliced green onions tops off a bowl of steamy hot, aromatic beef noodles.

A layer of grease floats atop the rich brown soup. Steam sometimes escapes from the oily surface to expose white, tender noodles bobbing amid rust-red chunks of guileless-looking meat. The heat brings out the gamey smell of the beef, but, with the amelioration of spices, only an aromatic meaty fragrance remains.

Beef Noodles

It is a heavy fragrance.

It has an authentic, delicious flavor.

Many years later, when the sinister shadow of the White Terror was a distant memory, or even further back, when mass arrests and torture were common—after all, the White Terror era lasted nearly half a century—people (including his enemies, to be sure) had expressed their reservations, publicly and in private: "Political dissidents could buy beef noodles in prison? Obviously, being in prison wasn't as bad as they said."

He put up a mild defense: "But that was only during temporary detention at the Garrison Command's Military Court, and they weren't free."

People usually stopped at that point because he had referred to the notorious place where prisoners awaited sentencing and execution.

Giving the condemned one last decent meal was a practice of the people who had come from the far-off mainland to rule this place. Even children learned early on that before being executed, an intrepid man would wolf down big chunks of meat and gulp bowls of liquor before declaring: "Beheading just means a bowl-size scar. I'll be back in twenty years as a brave man again."

Liquor obviously bolstered the courage of the condemned, but why did they find it necessary to give them meat? The new rulers came from the Yellow River region up north, a landlocked area far from the ocean; decent-sized fish were a prized commodity there since fish that live in rivers and ponds are usually small. And they tend to be bony, so no one could possibly expect a condemned prisoner—who faced this meal with tears in his eyes (or a blank stare)—to carefully pick out the bones in the dim light before eating his fish.

Beyond that, chopsticks aren't very useful in picking out bones from river or pond fish, because they cause the irreparable separation of the pale meat and the backbone. Only with wild saltwater fish, such as the prized yellow croaker, can one pick off large clove-like chunks of tender white meat that remain intact, glistening and translucent. With most other fish, the meat falls off the backbone in a white mushy glob that is barely connected to the dense fibers.

Trying to separate the meat from the backbone usually ruins a fish to the point where it completely loses its shape, for the backbone breaks into pieces, from head to tail, taking every one of the pin bones that support the fish with it.

The preferred method is to cook the fish until its bones turn mushy. Well known for their fine cuisine, the people coming to rule this place from the mainland created a famous dish called "slow-cooked carp with green onions." A talented chef could prepare a palm-sized, bone-filled carp until all the bones were soft, but instead of making the meat lose its texture or taste, the fish is infused with the aroma of pungent green onions.

(Even though green onions and carp are inexpensive ingredients, it ought not to be given to a condemned prisoner for his final meal, for it is time and energy consuming.)

Meat is the best choice.

And so, a bowl of beef noodles was what was available to him while he awaited sentencing at the Garrison Command's Military Court, and where his fellow prisoner was waiting to face the executioner.

It was beef noodles.

The Garrison Command's Military Court, a legendary place of mystery, has been compared to the Bastille in Paris.

After his arrest, he suffered through nearly two years of interrogation and was confined in several detention centers to prevent a confession in collusion with others, before finally being brought to this place to await sentencing.

Transported in a windowless surveillance van, he saw a row of simple prison cells upon his arrival; he only later learned from cellmates about the high walls, barbed wire, and guards. No one could verify or refute their descriptions of the place, since the only ones who ever walked out of the cell block and actually saw other sections of the prison were those taken out to be shot or sent to other prisons after sentencing.

(No one could or would want to look back.)

In the cramped prison cells, they shared information gathered from here and there in order to describe the Garrison Command's Military Court—its location, the surrounding area, and what it was like, inside and out. No one could contest anything that was said, but such discussions were essential to convince themselves that they still existed, that they hadn't just vanished, and that they hadn't been forgotten.

(No one could ascertain the veracity of their speculations; to prevent jailbreaks, the guards, the only people with whom they came into contact, were forbidden from giving out any information.)

Finally, one day during his seemingly interminable wait, he was moved to a different cell block, where he was allowed to let his family know his whereabouts and, later, for them to visit him.

His family gave him reliable information about his current location. He was indeed still in Taipei, the capital city of the KMT, which had come from the mainland to rule this island. He remained in Taipei but on the outskirts.

With the money his wife brought on her first visit and the two hundred New Taiwan dollars she would send each month afterwards, he was finally able to pay for his daily necessities.

The prisoners were given three meals a day, but they had to buy their own toothbrushes, soap, towels, and toilet paper. Before a steady supply of these necessities was available to him, he must have lived in fear of having no toilet paper after relieving himself, which was why he always carried with him a bag containing a towel, some toilet paper, a toothbrush, and a certain amount of cash, even after he became a former political prisoner and was crowned with the acclaimed label of dissident.

He was waiting for a verdict that had no definite date of arrival; it would be a prison sentence, or the death penalty, the only possible outcome for someone found guilty of sedition, as stipulated by the "Temporary Provisions During the Period of Communist Rebellion."

Taking a prisoner out to be shot—in other words, carrying out the death penalty—usually took place on a Friday. Shortly before daybreak, when the sky was a dusty gray, the light would go on in the guard's room, signaling to everyone that it was a day for execution. They would not, however, know the identity of the condemned until they saw which cell the lead guard was walking toward and heard the name he called out.

Since Friday was execution day, all the prisoners enjoyed a special meal the night before—that is, their Thursday dinner had an additional piece of pork about three inches long plus a cake of tofu.

Prisoners awaiting verdicts looked forward each week to that piece of pork and cake of tofu to satisfy both their taste buds and their hunger, with added nutritional benefits. Finally, to their bland, dreadful food was added a piece of meat—a tiny, three-inch piece, but meat nevertheless. When they bit down, grease oozed through their teeth, and they could almost hear the happy shouts of pork fat. Then the grease flowed, first moistening dry teeth and gums before reaching other parts of the mouth. Wow, the whole mouth...

Seeping oily grease.

For those sentenced to death, each Thursday night's three-inch piece of pork and cake of tofu could very well mean his "last, sumptuous supper."

After notification of a death sentence, the condemned men slept only during the day. Their cellmates volunteered to do their chores for them. Why only during the day? Was it because it was impossible to sleep during the seemingly endless dark night as they awaited the execution that might arrive with daybreak? Or was it to cherish their remaining days on earth? Or maybe because it simply felt better to stay awake in the hours before sunrise?

No matter what, at least they had the three-inch piece of pork as well as the tofu and the previous night's dinner in their stomachs while waiting for what could be their last daybreak. Prison food was bland, with moldy rice, wormy flour, and vegetable stalks so thick they could choke you to death. Everything else would likely already be digested, so they had nothing but the three-inch piece of pork in their bellies as they waited for the bullet.

For the others, who awaited sentencing, over the following week the piece of pork often became the topic of discussion in cramped cells for prisoners who had no place to go.

"Why did he get a bigger chunk of pork this time?"

"Why does he always get better meat? Why is his always lean?"

"This is the third time in a row I've got nothing but skin. I can barely bite through it. It probably came from some old sow that had given birth to hundreds of piglets."

(Has he done anything to his prison mates? Whom did he sell out to get special treatment? A large piece of pork every time.)

In any case, pork was a welcome addition to their meal. Sometimes they even joked about it: "There were bristles on the piece I got. Lots of them standing straight up, like that you-know-what down there. Ha ha ha."

"Is your you-know-what as skinny as a pig's bristle?" someone would ask in jest.

Fortunately for them, there would be another Thursday, when they could hope to get a larger chunk from the better part of a pig, with more lean meat.

Those awaiting sentencing were basically sharing the pork prepared for those who would be executed the next day (usually with a bullet), and they might well ask: "Whose pork are we eating this time?"

With his family's 200 NT each month, he had more than the Thursday pork to look forward to; if he was careful with his expenses, he could enjoy beef noodles once or twice a week.

(A bowl of beef noodles cost 5 NT in prison.)

At the Garrison Command's Military Court, there was more to the policy of making beef noodles available to prisoners awaiting sentencing or execution than people might think.

All prisoners were given three meals a day; the rice might be moldy, the flour wormy, and the vegetable stalks thick enough to choke you to death, but the meals were delivered on time. The beef noodles, on the other hand, had to be specially ordered at five in the afternoon and consumed at nine the same night.

Which meant that, in addition to the five-o'clock dinner with the extra three-inch piece of pork, the prisoners, especially those waiting to see if they would be taken out to be shot at daybreak, might, if they could afford it, order a bowl of beef noodles.

It would be delivered at nine. Nine at night, closer to the time of execution.

The northerners, those who had traveled from the far-off Chinese mainland across the Taiwan Straits to rule this land, were staunch believers that a person must not die hungry. In particular, those who died a wrongful death must have a full stomach when they breathed their last, for a hungry ghost is hardest of all to appease.

Just before execution, the condemned must be given a decent meal with the basic necessities of pork and liquor; but since this is the most difficult moment in their lives, few manage to swallow the food. Only

Beef Noodles

a tiny minority even take a sip of liquor, thus depriving the last supper of its significance.

Was this why the Garrison Command's Military Court, the much-feared Bastille, delivered the beef noodles at nine at night? Since six or seven hours remained till executions were carried out in the morning, was it more palatable to someone who might be taken out at daybreak to be shot?

Naturally he had thought of ordering the noodles for his fellow prisoner because the man had been condemned to death.

He would never forget how the man pressed up against the steel bars across the way to hungrily watch him eat his noodles. He watched until the last drop of soup was gone, and then swallowed over and over, his Adam's apple bouncing up and down.

He also knew why this particular man craved beef noodles—it was for the spicy pepper sauce, something he was addicted to.

The man's preference for spicy food was a marker of his origins; he had come to Taiwan around 1949 with the KMT regime to rule Taiwan.

(Since he was one of "their own," how had he come to be sentenced to death? Shouldn't the KMT have victimized only the "others" on the island?)

Owing to its subtropical location, with hot, humid weather, most of the island's residents do not eat spicy food. Only those who live farther south, in the tropics, need hot peppers to help them sweat and cool off. The KMT regime came from temperate or cold areas and "their own" ate Chinese red peppers, garlic, and chili peppers to ward off the effects of the island's high humidity and damp chill.

So, the prisoners back then could be roughly divided into those who ate spicy food and those who did not.

And by the slogans they shouted before being led out to be shot.

To be sure, they no longer shouted:

"I'll be back in twenty years as a brave man again!"

What they might yell instead was:

"Long live the Communist Party! Long live Mao Zedong!"

"Long live the proletarian revolution!"

"Long live the People's Republic of China!"

If their legs weren't so weak that the guards had to bear them out under the arms, they would walk and sing "The Internationale" along the way, but usually only a few lines or a few notes before the guards' rifle butts cut them off.

(These were the spice eaters—they ate garlic, Chinese red peppers, and chili peppers.)

He and the other native-born Taiwanese political prisoners had not gone to jail for their "red" beliefs. Their crimes were more likely:

Planning to organize a Taiwan independence alliance.

Planning to organize an Asian alliance.

So they shouted:

"Long live Taiwan independence!"

"Stand up, Taiwanese!"

"Long live the Republic of Taiwan!"

(There were fewer of them, and they generally did not eat spicy food.)

To be sure, there were notable exceptions: Some non-spice-eating Taiwanese were jailed for their "red" beliefs, but in those days hardly any of the spice-eating people who had come over with the KMT supported Taiwan independence.

So, when he figured out that his fellow prisoner was addicted to spicy food, he realized that the two of them had come from different places and had been imprisoned for quite different reasons and different political beliefs.

But as political prisoners, their situation was essentially the same. Back in the 1950s and '60s, spice eaters with red beliefs and non-spice eaters who advocated Taiwanese independence sympathized with each other and shared common slogans:

"Down with the evil KMT!"

"Down with the Chiang Kai-shek regime!"

He even felt even especially sorry for his spice-eating fellow prisoner.

It was bad enough that Chiang Kai-shek ruled the Taiwanese with an iron fist, but it was far worse that he treated those who had come with him from China in a similarly ruthless manner.

Could that bowl of beef noodles have become a signifier of their shared misfortune, the compassionate act of a local Taiwanese toward a fellow political prisoner from a far-off place?

But what is the relationship between beef noodles and spicy peppers?

Beef Noodles in Clear Broth Vs. Braised Beef Noodle Soup
Noodle soup with beef as its main ingredient should, in fact, be divided into two types:

Beef noodles in clear broth, and braised beef noodle soup.

The former is made with a clear soup (or, simply put, water), in which chunks of beef are slow cooked with green onions, ginger, and rice wine. Just add noodles.

Following the same steps, but adding broad-bean paste, soy sauce, and a spice packet produces braised beef noodle soup.

The latter has a sunny shine to its light brown soup, with beef chunks that are an oily golden brown. If you add oil made from hot peppers, a bright, rosy sheen overlays the steam just beneath the surface. The soup, with its calm, watery surface, gives the impression of a sunset on water, peaceful and serene and yet irresistibly enticing. So, unconcerned, you take a big mouthful, and ah! the spicy heat ...

Oh, it's killing me!

His dissatisfaction with Chiang Kai-shek's KMT regime, whose army slaughtered the Taiwanese, compounded by advocacy of Taiwanese independence, had landed him in prison with a life sentence. Beef noodles were the only extra food he could order there, and he was convinced that his fellow prisoner, brought by Chiang Kai-shek from China, along with his addiction to spicy food, would want a bowl of it before he was executed. But he felt like asking:

Why would the Garrison Command's Military Court offer beef noodles as the last supper for the condemned, even though so many of the prisoners were local Taiwanese?

Was it to satisfy the tastes of those prisoners who had come from China with the Chiang regime, the so-called mainlanders, such as his spice-addicted prison-mate?

At that time, the island people of Taiwan were mostly farmers who considered water buffaloes a major contributor to their livelihood because the animals worked to till the land. They helped feed the family and were treated like part of it, which was why most Taiwanese back then did not eat beef—it was a way to show their gratitude.

"Eating buffaloes and dogs will land you in hell" was a popular saying on the island. Parents taught their children that when they walked by a slaughterhouse where buffaloes were being killed, or even when they just heard the animal's cries, they were to shut their eyes and put their hands behind them to mimic bondage, in order to show that they were themselves bound and unable to help release the animals, though they would if they could. Later, when they stood in front of the King of Hell, Yama would not criticize them for not saving a dying animal.

Beef Noodles

During fifty years of colonization, the Japanese introduced Westernization to the island, making available such things as steaks, which could be ordered at Western-style places like the Railway Hotel. But when they visited Japan, most Taiwanese would not even try the soup in beef hotpot dishes.

(How could anyone imagine a condemned Taiwanese holding a bowl of beef noodles and saying it was a good send-off meal?)

If it was important to include meat, why not pork or chicken? For instance, the three-layer meat from the back of pigs, which is boiled and sliced to serve as a common sacrifice to the ghosts, had been a required item in the "last supper" for condemned Taiwanese in years gone by.

If not that, fish would do fine. The island is surrounded by water teeming with big, fat saltwater fish like swordfish, shark, mackerel, snook, and more, weighing as much as several kilos, all cheap and tasty. Besides, since large fish have fewer bones, they lend themselves to many cooking styles—stir-fried fish filets, steamed fish belly in clear broth, fish tail soup, and fish balls made of mashed flesh.

If a soup such as that in beef noodles was a requisite, then saltwater fish turned into fish chowder was the answer. Say, for instance, mackerel chowder, a popular local dish filled with island flavor reminiscent of mother's cooking.

And why *noodles*?

The island, with its subtropical climate, has three rice harvests each year. The hot weather is inhospitable to the growth of wheat, which naturally has made the residents rice eaters. And yet, it was wheat noodles that saw them off "on the road" and provided them with the energy to travel down the path to the underworld.

It would have been a ruthless curse if, based on the many taboos dealing with death in the island's traditions, the dead would be burdened with more crimes and never granted rebirth just because they had eaten forbidden food (such as the water buffaloes that were so deserving of their gratitude) before they died.

The KMT regime that came from the far-off mainland did not merely control the island, the administrative capital Taipei, and the Garrison Command's Military Court, which was responsible for imprisoning dissidents. In fact, the KMT regime's area of control reached far beyond, all the way to the people's stomachs.

(And included even the place they traveled to after death.)

Nearly three decades later, owing to political changes, the KMT regime, which had come from the far-off mainland to rule Taiwan, fell from power. Accordingly, he was turned from a highly regarded dissident into a politician with real power. And still he often mentioned the bowl of noodles he'd failed to order.

People could tell he genuinely regretted his failure; it was not an act. The kindness he had not been able to demonstrate back then was a lasting regret, which convinced people that he had not lost his passion.

Then one day, developments in cross-straits politics made it possible for him to visit the mainland, though naturally he was forced to travel under the label of "returning Chinese" by the PRC government. Believing that his twenty-three years of imprisonment were sufficient proof of his unquestioned love for the island, he crossed the Taiwan Straits in search of a "major reconciliation," hoping to open up space for both sides to engage in a peaceful dialogue.

(His fellow former political prisoners, on the other hand, were convinced that he was scheming to reap political gains, that he had betrayed the ideal of Taiwan independence and abandoned his fellow Taiwanese out of a desire for power.)

When he arrived in Sichuan, China, he asked for something he had once enjoyed in Taiwan, a bowl of braised beef noodles.

Beef Noodles

Feeling that, as a "guest" from afar, particularly a so-called supporter of Taiwan independence, he ought to show how broad-minded he could be by not dismissing the Sinicizing influence on Taiwan by the KMT regime. And to show good will toward the local residents, he explained enthusiastically, "We call braised beef noodles Sichuan Beef Noodles."

Then he added, "The dish came to Taiwan from Sichuan after 1949 and has retained its original flavor, which is why we call it Sichuan Beef Noodles."

But no matter how hard he searched throughout the province, no one could produce the Sichuan Beef Noodles he described. The locals were actually amazed to learn that something called Sichuan Beef Noodles had crossed the Straits to reach far-off Taiwan.

At first, he thought they had lost track of pre-revolutionary Sichuan Beef Noodles because of all the major political upheavals and campaigns launched by the Communist Party. But after exhaustive research, he was surprised to learn that no one in Sichuan had ever heard of the Sichuan Beef Noodles popular in Taiwan, let alone the particular type he had once failed to order in prison.

He did, however, find something called Red Beef Soup, a spicy beef soup with Chinese peppers, but it was drastically different from the Sichuan Beef Noodles eaten in Taiwan. The most obvious difference was the lack of broad-bean paste, that and the pepper used to give the soup a numbing spicy sensation. The Sichuan Beef Noodles he'd been used to eating in Taiwan included spicy oil made of hot peppers, plus the spicy broad-bean paste, so the noodles were spicy but not numbing.

(The pepper from the South Pacific did not arrive in China until midway through the Qing dynasty, or no more than two hundred years ago.)

A more important difference was that people in Sichuan would never add boiled noodles to beef soup to make so-called beef noodles, no matter what they were called. In Sichuan, beef soup is beef soup and noodles are noodles; they do not mix.

He had to admit that he was shocked. For over four decades he had assumed that the Sichuan Beef Noodles available everywhere in Taiwan had come from Sichuan. But now, having arrived in Sichuan to search out the eponymous noodles, he learned that they do not exist there, and in fact originated in Taiwan.

At that moment, he experienced a keen sense of temporal and spatial displacement, as a myriad of images and events flashed before his eyes, including the bowl of beef noodles he had failed to order many years earlier in prison. He had thought that his stomach was under KMT control during all those fearful, desperate years in his tiny prison cell, those twenty-three years of suffering caused by his belief in Taiwan independence.

What exactly had Taiwan become in the wake of the massive cross-strait migration in 1949? Would things have been different if he'd known that his beef noodles came not from Sichuan, but from the hands of army cooks, making them a "Taiwanese" concoction?

(Are there more of these "Taiwanese" products in Taiwan? If so, how will we deal with them in the future?)

Years later, Wang Qifang, a so-called writer (according to her father), would write a biography of the former political dissident, and she would be particularly moved by the bowl of beef noodles he had failed to order.

After conducting research, based upon the consensus views of gourmets from all over the island, she reached a conclusion that has become a shared understanding of "beef noodles" on the island:

There are Taiwan Beef Noodles, and there are Sichuan-Style Beef Noodles

In 1949, after a resounding defeat at the hands of Mao Zedong, Chiang Kai-shek had fled with his government and army to the tiny island of Taiwan across the Taiwan Straits, bringing with him thousands of ordinary people. Some of the discharged non-commissioned officers

Beef Noodles

(NCOs) settled in Fengshan, on the southern tip of the island, where, calling upon recollections of hometown specialties, they began making broad-bean paste, some spicy, some not.

They made braised beef soup by adding broad-bean paste and a spice packet to beef soup, then dumped in boiled noodles to create their famous beef noodles.

During the immediate postwar era, when the island was plagued by pervasive poverty, some beef noodle shops shredded pickled greens to spice up the soup for their customers. That started a fad of adding all sorts of things to the dish: spicy hot oil, pickled greens, garlic, and more.

The creators of the beef noodles, the NCOs from Sichuan, were experts in spicy beef noodles, which lent the dish its moniker, Sichuan Beef Noodles. Noodle shop owners who were not from Sichuan cashed in on the popularity of the dish by calling theirs Sichuan-Style Beef Noodles. It did not take long for beef noodles to gain popularity all across Taiwan, and it no longer mattered whether it was called Sichuan or Sichuan-Style, since personalized variations, such as Old Zhang's Beef Noodles or Li Family Beef Noodles, burst onto the scene to meet demand.

When the island's economy took off, people became increasingly particular about food. Clear broth and thin soup, with its bland flavor, no longer appealed to diners' taste buds, so a refined process was created by adding beef bones, beef tendons, sometimes chicken bones, which were slow cooked to make a rich stock.

Studies and experiments then got underway to improve the broad-bean paste and spice packets. The paste from Fengshan in southern Taiwan was generally recognized as the best. Some producers even spiced the dish up with red wine dregs, not only to add flavor but also to give the soup a lovely red glow, tender as a virgin, instead of the bland brown of the stewed beef. Likewise, close attention was paid to the spice packets.

These packets could include peppercorns, anise seeds, cinnamon, cloves, nutmeg, and fennel to mask the gamey smell of the beef and give the soup a seasoned flavor. In time, some considered the anise overpowering and cloves dominating, so the quantity of both spices was reduced or eliminated altogether. More people stressed the fact that no MSG was used, replacing it with licorice root, which, according to the *Compendium of Materia Medica*, has a natural sweet taste and provides a good counterbalance to the toxicity of the meat.

Grade-A beef with its slightly chewy texture is top choice. Farmed beef tends to be soft and cannot withstand hours of slow cooking. The best meat comes from the front shank, which, when cooked, shows attractive transparent streaks of tendon.

So, the rich stock, the spice packet, red wine, and chunks of beef are slow cooked over a low fire until the flavor of the beef is fully brought out and the soup is just right. The noodles, whether thick or thin, must be handmade and cooked al dente. Some people have even experimented with Japanese udon noodles (but no one, apparently, has tried using spaghetti).

Whether to add chili peppers, spicy oil, garlic, or shredded pickled greens is left up to the diner.

In the 1990s, when trade opened up across the Taiwan Strait, some Taiwanese went to the mainland to open beef noodle shops but were unsure how to advertise the dish. It seemed inappropriate to call it Sichuan Beef Noodles. So, they listed it on the menu and shop sign as Sichuan-Style Beef Noodles.

Others simply called it Taiwan Beef Noodles.

These days, even restaurants in Europe and America call the dish Taiwan Beef Noodles to distinguish them from their mainland counterparts.

6

Disappearing Manhood

Wu Chin-fa
(translated by Chris Wen-chao Li)

1

When Wilfred[1] chanced to spot a feather concealed under his right armpit, it did not strike him at first as anything out of the ordinary.

Turning to take a closer look, he could see that the protrusion on the smooth folds of skin under his arm was no ordinary human hair, but instead possessed a hard shaft long and slender, out of which grew fabulous barbs of royal blue. This was a bird feather alright!

So it must have rubbed off from some bird—no big deal, he thought to himself as he raised his arm and turned to expose his armpit to the spray of the shower. Jets of water blasted the spot where skin meets feather, but the feather did not budge, remaining firmly attached to the flesh. He pulled at it with his fingers, and when he did, the shaft of the feather tugged at the skin beneath, bringing a wince of pain.

To think, it was sprouting from beneath the epidermis!

As this bizarre thought flashed through his head, it was as if he was struck by lightning. Wilfred stood there stunned, his jaw dropping wide.

Cascading streams of water inundated his head and his mouth, leaving him unable to open his eyes briefly.

Feathers growing out of human flesh—how crazy is that? He wasn't dreaming, was he? He put a finger to his lip and bit on it hard—the excruciating pain, not unlike that of a snakebite, was as real as can be.

"Oww!" he yelped, darting out of the bathroom like a flushed quail, diving straight into the safety of his bed, where, wrapped in a heavy blanket, he shuddered as he sought cover beneath the sheets.

But, but...how could this be? The mere thought sent a chill up his spine, slithering like a snake up his back until it reached the base of his scalp, where, without warning, his hairs started to bristle.

Time to go see a doctor, Wilfred told himself after quivering in the sheets for a good long while. He quickly jumped out of bed, hastily changed into his clothes, and, before long, was out and about on his motor scooter.

He cruised the streets for quite some time, unable to decide what type of physician to see. Was it internal medicine or surgery? Or perhaps the job called for a dermatologist. But no—abnormal hair growth had everything to do with hormonal imbalance, so what he needed, really, was an endocrinologist. He headed straight to a well-known private hospital and secured a walk-in appointment to see an endocrinologist

"What's this?" The elderly physician looked baffled as he examined the filament with a magnifying glass, and then, all of a sudden, turned to his nurse, who was standing in the dispensary preparing to administer medication to another patient.

"Miss Chen, come take a look at this. I have never seen anything like it in my years of practicing medicine."

The attractive nurse giggled as she put down her syringe and approached the doctor, giving Wilfred a quick glance before bending down to examine his armpit carefully.

Not used to having a young woman stare so intently at his underarm, he grew completely flushed and was forced to look away.

"Good heavens!" yelled the nurse. "It's the feather of a b-b-b-bird!"

So piercing was her scream that the patients in the waiting room outside were clamoring to get a look.

Wilfred quickly lowered his elbow and slipped back into his clothes, irked that the nurse had created such a scene. It was as if his most private parts had been laid bare before a gaping audience.

Aware she had misspoken, the nurse blushed as she turned and headed back to the dispensary, albeit glancing in Wilfred's direction every now and then as she prepared her syringe for injection.

"When did you first notice this?" The doctor smiled as he put down his magnifying glass.

"Today," Wilfred answered, his voice quivering. "I returned from birdwatching and was in the shower when I saw this, this..."

"It's alright." said the doctor, patting him on the back. "Growing a feather is no big deal—I mean, what harm could possibly come of it?"

"But I gotta tell you," he continued, "without an understanding of the cause, I'm at a loss as to how to treat it. You should seek the opinion of a dermatologist."

The message was perfectly clear. Wilfred had little more to say and headed out the door.

2

That evening, Wilfred took a leave of absence and did not show up at the newspaper office for his late shift.

Instead, he removed the feather from his armpit with a pair of scissors and spent his time pouring over tomes of Chinese- and English-language publications on birds, hoping to find a species whose feathers matched that found under his arm. After having spent the good part of the evening perusing field guides, he stumbled upon a section on water fowl, which included pictures and descriptions of the loon, with which he was intimately familiar—and there, among the various color photos, were images of an exotic subspecies that made him shudder, the most memorable of which was a shot of a bird spreading its wings on the shores of a lake in Siberia—in the picture it was clear to see that the plumage of the bird was identical to the feather growing on the side of his chest.

This was disheartening. Wilfred could not, for the life of him, understand how something so monstrous could befall him. How could the feathers of a loon grow on the flesh of a human? Still reeling from the shock, he placed his field guides back on the shelf and lay petrified in bed, quivering every now and then at the thought of this abomination.

Then, eerily, a scene from a film drifted into his consciousness. He remembered having seen *An American Werewolf in London*, about a man possessed by the vengeful spirit of a wolf. Come full moon night, the protagonist would transform into a werewolf and roam the streets of London to kill and feed on the blood of humans. "Which is to say, now that I am growing feathers, am I possessed by the spirit of a bird? Am I ultimately doomed to shape-shift into a werebird?"

As the word "bird" crossed his mind, it was as if his world was rocked by a giant explosion, as if, without warning, he was struck in the head with a baseball bat. Twitching uncontrollably from the shock, he soon found himself perspiring profusely. Before long, his clothes were soaking in a deluge of cold sweat.

Apprehensive as ever, he got up to fetch a new change of clothes. As he was switching into his tank top, a persistent itch in his left armpit was starting to grow unbearable. He couldn't help but scratch with his right hand, but the prolonged scratching did little to relieve the itch, which only grew more intense, like it was coming from deep beneath the skin. He turned to look at the affected area: the skin had turned red and was now covered in a rash. But even more troubling was that over the rash he could detect faint traces of blue—fine little barbs that looked ready to break the surface. "Oh my God," he gasped and fainted on the spot.

3

Wilfred took the next few days off and did not show up for work at the newspaper.

He kept busy though, seeking treatment from different specialists. What with more and more feathers growing on both sides of his chest, he was starting to panic, and sought help from doctors with different specialties, only to be told that they had "never seen anything like it before," which worried him even more. The thought that he would turn into a bird drove him crazy. Though he had once dreamed of flying like a bird, it was a mere passing thought—the product of birdwatching, where the sight of a bird soaring through the sky made him wish he could do the same. But this was different—his chest was now blanketed in feathers —and unless he could identify the problem and seek timely treatment, chances are he would go crazy as a loon.

He sought treatment from various medical experts, all to no avail, after which he was referred to a noted mental health specialist. The doctor's name was Dandy—a graduate of University College London who, it was said, not only possessed expert knowledge of psychiatry but also dabbled in spiritualism. Known for his unorthodox approaches to treating mental illness, the word was he once miraculously cured a patient of schizophrenia by performing an exorcism. He is dubbed "the witch doctor" by his colleagues in the field. They're probably thinking, why would a University College–educated psychologist want to have anything to do with demonic possession?

Wilfred did not care, however, what kind of medicine he practiced. The rumors about his eccentricity only fueled his hopes of a miracle cure.

"Unorthodox maladies call for unorthodox methods." Wilfred told himself. "Dandy's probably the only physician in the world who knows how to treat my condition."

Filled with newfound hope, he hailed a cab to the clinic in the suburbs. Dandy worked at a major hospital in the day and saw private clients only in the evening, in the comfort of his own home. By the time Wilfred arrived, it was already eight.

And unorthodox the doctor was indeed, judging from his eccentric sense of fashion. A pair of oversized distance lenses hung over his long, bony face as he stood with a mahogany pipe in his mouth. He looked to be thirty-five or thirty-six years old at most, but sported a Hitler Youth cut, and, hidden behind the pair of gigantic magnifying lenses were a set of mysterious yet boyish-looking eyes. As if it couldn't get any more jarring, he was dressed in loud, patterned boxers, from which a pair of long, crane-like legs protruded, covered completely in dark, curly hair. He wore white knee-high socks and bulky yellow brogues that appeared a size too large. "Can he actually walk in that thing?" you'd be tempted to ask just at the sight of the ridiculous proportions.

The man is truly difficult to fathom, Wilfred thought to himself, and yet at the same time could not help being drawn in by his boyish smile.

"Come in, come in." the doctor urged in a welcoming tone.

Wilfred didn't know how to answer, so he simply removed his shoes at the foyer and entered the premises with his head hung low.

"Have a seat." The doctor showed him to the living room and gestured for him to make himself comfortable on the couch.

As Wilfred was about to sit down, he surveyed his surroundings and found the walls decorated with freakishly disturbing paintings: one of the head of a horse, another with the skull of a bull, and yet another depicting a large human cranium attached to a long serpentine neck—the mouth was open wide, as if grimacing in pain—it was as if you could sense the quivering tongue beneath the surface, howling from the throaty depths of the canvas.

Perhaps because it was already dark, the sight of these chilling images staring at you from the living room walls made for a surreal experience and was particularly unsettling.

"These are all by my mental patients," the doctor explained with a gracious smile, as if sensing his unease. He sat down across from him, removed the pipe from his mouth, and gently emptied its contents in an ashtray.

At the mention of "mental patients" Wilfred grew particularly anxious and couldn't help fidgeting with his hands.

"So, Wilf Lee, is it?" the doctor asked as he scraped at the inside of his pipe with a copper reamer.

"Yes." Wilfred answered detachedly.

"I know you!" The doctor smiled and cast a reassuring yet piercing glance from behind the lenses of his spectacles.

"You do?" Wilfred asked in surprise. His fingers stopped twiddling.

"Yes, it's probably slipped your memory, but seven or eight years ago, before I left for the UK, we had met once at the newspaper office you work at."

"We've met at the newspaper?"

"Yes, I worked closely with the senior editor of your literary supplement. I used to write under the name Ffynnon Dandy[2], and would translate poetry from Africa and Latin America..."

"Fine and Dandy—yes, I remember that name!"

"It's all coming back to you, isn't it?" The doctor laughed hard as he picked up strands of loose tobacco from a box on the table and packed them into his pipe.

"To think, seven or eight years can go by just like that, in the blink of an eye. I remember you were still an assistant editor back then..."

"And I still am."

"You're not going to believe this, but over the years, I've been reading a lot of your poetry. I'm a big fan!"

With the chamber packed, he brought the pipe to his mouth, lit the tobacco, and sipped on the lip, then exhaled a puff of smoke.

"That comes as something of a surprise—I don't know what to say. But, to think, you've changed so much since then—I really wouldn't have recognized you if you hadn't told me who you were!"

"And if you hadn't told me on the phone earlier your name was Wilf Lee, I wouldn't have been able to tell it was you. It's only because I've been reading your poems that I feel as if I know you so well."

"Uh-huh..." For some reason, the idea that the doctor "knew him so well" made him jittery. Lately he'd grown wary of anyone who claimed to "know him."

"Your poems really strike the right chord." the doctor commented, removing his pipe and pointing to the paintings on the wall, "you know, like these artworks here, depicting human suffering in its rawest form—which is why I've always been fond of your writings."

"Is that so?" The analogy made him queasy, for what writer would enjoy hearing his work mentioned in the same breath as the doodles of institutionalized patients?

"You know, I haven't published any poetry for close to two years now."

"I know, you've turned to birdwatching, haven't you? I've read your articles on birds," the doctor mentioned in passing, which left Wilfred flabbergasted, outraged that another individual could follow his life in such great detail, and a mental health expert at that. To have someone who studies psychiatric disorders for a living keep tabs on every aspect of your life, to him, was mortifying, akin to being forced to strip bare in front of a crowd.

As the conversation grew cold, the two sat facing each other in silence.

"Well," the doctor remarked, sensing the awkwardness in the air, "what a terrible host I've been, all preoccupied with talking and forgetting to ask what you would like to drink." He rose and walked toward the refrigerator, from which he fetched a glass of ice water.

"Um..." Only after hanging his head and deliberating for a long while did Wilfred slowly begin to speak.

"Dr. Dandy, I came all the way here because I'm actually suffering from a...from a condition...which I was hoping you could help with."

"Oh?" The doctor smiled reassuringly as he returned to his seat and set down his pipe. "What kind of condition?"

"What I would like to know is, from the perspective of psychiatry, would it be possible at all for a person to, well, like, change into a bird?" The words crawled haltingly out of his mouth, until they reached the end of his utterance, when they suddenly flew into a loud high pitch.

"Say what?" The doctor appeared blindsided by this question.

The look of surprise on the doctor's face left Wilfred unable to respond. He quickly turned his gaze away.

"Do you mean fantasize about turning into a bird?" The doctor asked again with his signature smile after regaining his composure.

"No, I mean—literally—turn into a bird." With that he gathered himself and turned to look at the doctor.

There was a long silence. From the look in his eyes, it was evident the doctor was deep in thought.

Wilfred stared unflinchingly at the doctor, hoping to get an answer.

"How long have you had this urge?" the doctor inquired in a soft voice as he picked up his pipe and took a slow sip, gazing upon his patient with a look of pity.

"It's not a mere urge, it really is happening to me!" Wilfred explained with some irritation, his lips quivering ever so slightly.

"So you're saying…"

"I'll show you," Wilfred offered, staring at the doctor as he removed his shirt and bared his chest and abdomen. "Take a look at this."

As Wilfred removed his clothing to reveal the large patch of feathers to the side of his chest, the doctor was dumbstruck.

After recovering from the shock, he anxiously leaned over the lucite coffee table to get a good look at the aberration, examining the surface up close, and even reaching to stroke the patch of feathers.

As he pulled on the feathers to make sure they extended from beneath the skin, his hand began to shake.

"Dr. Dandy—" Wilfred protested as he shrank away from the doctor's touch and sank back into the upholstery of the couch, jittery as ever.

At a loss for words, the doctor returned to his original position, staring silently at the patient.

"So, can a human turn into a bird?" Wilfred repeated his question.

"In theory, no, but…" The doctor replied cautiously after an extended pause.

"But what?" Wilfred kept on pressing.

"But pathologies of the skin brought about by psychosomatic factors are quite common in the psychiatric literature…"

"Are there any recorded cases of humans growing feathers, like me?" Wilfred pressed on, eager for an explanation.

The doctor did not answer, but he squeezed out a smile and tried hard to present a façade of sangfroid.

"Take it easy—let's see what we can do for you."

As Wilfred awaited eagerly, the doctor continued, "Humans growing feathers I haven't heard of, but some years ago there was a case in the US that, I believe, bears some similarity to yours…"

"Which was?"

"According to the literature, the case involved a G.I. who, after having been trapped by the Vietcong for ten days, was rescued by his comrades, only to lapse into severe psychosis, after which he believed himself to be a bird. He lost his ability to speak human language and would flap his arms and chirp all day, as if he were a bird, becoming an avianthrope in the truest sense."

As Wilfred listened to the account, a chill ran down his spine, making him shiver all over.

"But," joked the doctor, mindful, perhaps, of the consternation on the face of his client, "you don't look to be on the verge of psychosis—you're not turning into a bird anytime soon!"

"But why—from a psychiatrist's point of view—would something like this happen to this poor veteran?"

"Well," responded the doctor matter-of-factly, after pausing for a minute to think, "it's a flight response, you know, turning yourself into a bird so you could fly high and flee the clutches of the enemy."

Upon hearing the word "flee," it was as if his cranium suddenly ruptured. His head ached like never before as he drifted out of consciousness. With his arms wrapped around his head, he let out a piercing scream and passed out on the couch.

"What's the matter? Are you alright?" asked the doctor, startled out of his wits as he sprung up and skirted the coffee table to tend to his patient, holding him up and trying to shake him conscious.

4

After who knows how long, when Wilfred finally came to his senses, he found himself lying on a surface in the doctor's examination room.

As he opened his eyes, the doctor slowly came into view, holding a syringe in his hand as he stood next to the examination table, looking genuinely worried.

"Awake now?" asked the doctor as he gently reached to touch his forehead. "How do you feel?"

Unable to speak, Wilfred made an attempt to sit up, but found himself drifting in and out of consciousness as aches and pains plagued every inch of his body, and he was forced to lie back down.

"Take it slowly," urged the doctor, "You may want to lie flat for a little longer—I just gave you a dose of muscle relaxant." After putting down his syringe, he retrieved a wet towel from the refrigerator and placed it above the patient's brow.

"What just happened to me, doctor?" asked Wilfred, sounding clearly distraught, his voice still feeble.

"You were far too anxious and overexerted yourself," answered the doctor, smiling as he adjusted the towel on Wilfred's forehead.

"I felt as if...as if I had just walked...or rather, as if I had just flown a great distance."

"Is that so?" The doctor moved his stool closer to the bed and listened intently to what Wilfred had to say.

"It was an epic dream—I dreamt I was flying: from up above, the city, the rivers, and the mountains all appeared so small and insignificant..." Wilfred rambled on in what resembled a somniloquy.

The doctor smiled and quietly excused himself. He walked toward his desk, where he pressed the record button on his voice recorder and discreetly brought it back with him.

"I was flying so high—it felt so good! As I lifted off the ground and ascended into the air, the chill of the wind brought a tremendous sense of relief, as if I were free of all my baggage. How wonderful it would have been to have just kept flying. I could go on like this for..." His eyelids started to droop as he mumbled his story in an ever more indistinct tone, until he himself couldn't make out what he was saying and gradually drifted back into sleep.

When he woke up a second time, he was feeling much more relaxed. His head was a tad dizzy still—a side effect, perhaps, of the muscle relaxant. He sat up in his bed and checked the time on his watch: it was already past eleven o'clock—more than three hours had elapsed since he arrived at the hour of eight.

Seeing no sign of the doctor, he walked out of the examination room into the living area, where he found his physician chatting with the cab driver he had hired.

"What took you so long, boss?" asked the cabbie, rising from his seat to complain about the delay. "You didn't tell me I'd be waiting beyond eleven—I need to hand my cab over to the driver on the next shift."

"I am so deeply sorry!" Wilfred was profusely apologetic. "I lost track of time—I'll pay you for the extra hours. I can't tell you how sorry I am."

"You kept me waiting for hours outside the clinic—what choice did I have but to come in and look for you?"

"Yes, you're right. It's late. Let's get going." Before stepping out, Wilfred turned to look at the doctor. "So, is there any way to treat this… this condition of mine?"

The doctor gave him a pat on the shoulder. "I wouldn't think too much of it. Just take it easy for now—you've told me quite a lot in your sleep, all of which I've recorded. I'm going to bring these recordings to a specialist and see what we can do for you. Come back in a day or two, and we'll take it from there. Sound good?"

"I guess," Wilfred accepted grudgingly. He reached into his pocket and asked, "How much do I owe you? For today's session, that is."

"Oh, forget about it already." the doctor laughed as he walked them out the door. "We've known each other for so long, not to mention I wasn't of much help today—even if I was, it's the least you would expect of a friend, wouldn't you say?"

The exchange went back and forth until Wilfred finally conceded and turned to board his cab.

After Wilfred was gone, the doctor returned to his examination room, where he placed his voice recorder on his desk and, with a stern look on his face, scrolled back a few clips as he sat back in his chair. As he pressed the play button, the speakers began to broadcast in a muffled, dreamy voice:

"How wonderful it would have been to have just kept flying. I could go on like this for—"

After which all that was audible was "squawk, squawk, squawk"—the sound of a human emulating the caw of a bird—which cackled on for a good five minutes.

"Squawk, squawk, squawk, squawk…"

The more he listened, the more concerned he grew, until his entire face went pale and was covered in pearl-sized beads of sweat.

Disappearing Manhood

5

It was half past midnight when Wilfred finally got back to his apartment.

After the ordeals of the night, he felt grimy all over and headed straight into the shower.

He started by positioning himself beneath the showerhead and allowing its jets of fine spray to cleanse every inch of his skin. He then ran a bath and lay quietly in the tub, enjoying the comfort of a leisurely soak.

With the dizziness from the injection long gone, he was feeling sharp as ever.

With his eyes closed, he resigned himself to the soothing pleasure of a calm, relaxing bath. But the restfulness did not last, for, while fully submerged in water, as his fingers brushed past the feathers extending from his waist, his worries surfaced yet again.

"It's a flight response." he remembered the doctor saying.

The urge to flee transformed the Vietnam vet into an ornithoid human. So am I sprouting feathers because some flight response has been triggered in me? What am I fleeing from? What is it I fear?

He turned these thoughts over in his head.

The vet came under attack from the Vietcong day in, day out, to the point where he simply lost it and hallucinated that he was a bird to flee the brutal reality. But what about me? How did I end up with this predicament?

Then it was as if a light bulb suddenly went off in his head, striking fear in his heart as he stared up at the ceiling with eyes wide open.

Could it have been that…that incident that triggered these hormonal changes and led to my condition? How could this have slipped my mind? If only I had told the doctor. Back then, yes, I…I was indeed overcome with an irrepressible urge to change into a bird and flee the circumstances, exhibiting instincts much like those of the G.I.—could the trauma of entrapment have triggered this abnormal growth? Could this incident lie at the root of my illness?

It all happened a month or so ago.

Like every other day, he was armed with camera and binoculars as he scoured the estuary looking to take pictures of migratory birds. He would spy a raft of loons through his field glasses one minute and be photographing their gorgeous plumage the next, noting their numbers and their foraging routes in relation to tidal cycles, jotting everything down in his notebook.

He had been regularly tracking this asylum of loons for over a month now, since they arrived at this estuary back in October. He kept a close watch on the birds, spending his waking hours observing and recording their every move. Like clockwork, he would arrive at this spot at eight every morning, where he would park his motor scooter under a tree and begin his meticulous study of bird behavior.

His observations were not limited to loons, of course, for the small mangrove patches along this mile-long stretch at the confluence of fresh and salt waters was home to migratory birds of all species. Large flocks of rare and magnificent avian species make a stop here on their migratory journeys, turning the area into a paradise for birdwatchers. He would often bring his own lunch and spend the greater part of the day here, feeling at ease and completely in his element.

Ever since he swore off poetry, in his mind there was no greater purpose in life than birding—which came as a surprise, considering a mere two years ago he didn't have the slightest clue about birds and knew nothing of birdwatching. Back then his calling was poetry—he was a devotee of literature and the politics of identity. As a sociology major, he naturally found identity issues compelling, but he didn't confine himself to the sociological angle and soon found himself dabbling in literature and poetry, going so far as to conclude in his writings that "the only salvation for the soul of our degenerate society is through poetry."

This bold statement was what he was remembered for back in the day in the literary circles of Taiwan.

Hyperbole, no less, but few took issue with it, as such melodramatic slogans were the rule rather than the exception in the local scene—not to mention poets of his caliber were generally afforded greater artistic license.

Within two years of making his appearance, he had become a fixture in local poetry circles, publishing several collections of lyrical verse that had remained on the best-sellers lists for years. His poems were stylish and catchy, and they spoke to the ills of society—a welcome departure from the staid platitudes that had come to dominate the local poetry scene. Like a bomb going off, his writings disrupted conventional literary practices and created a frenzy among the cultured classes. Among his most devoted fans were starry-eyed college students, who would photocopy his verse and tack them on campus message boards. Many were moved to tears upon reading his work, as if they were brought to an epiphany.

Alas, a crime it was to be blessed with such God-given talent, not to mention adored by so many bright young things, but his greatest sin, perhaps, was that he had the audacity to go on book tours, where he would expose the underbelly of society in all its gruesome glory. His supporters described him as a "swan in a pond full of ducks"—yet what duck in the right frame of mind would tolerate a lone swan in their midst without plotting to do him in?[3]

It all came to a head after he edited the *Yearly Anthology of Poetry* for a major publishing house the year before, where he took the bold step of excluding many established names. The backlash was swift, as he was given unsavory labels and denounced by critics in all the mainstream papers and journals. He would break into a sweat in the middle of the night, shuddering as he read review after scathing review, overcome with a sense of impending doom. Only then did he begin to see the vindictiveness of his fellow poets, just as a professor had warned many years ago, "Beware the tyranny of petty writers, not least the wrath of small-minded poets!"

"Like I give a bird's ass—," he cussed in a fit of anger as he grabbed his manuscripts and tossed them into the fireplace, swearing never again to write poetry. Not long after, for reasons he could not explain, he became enamored with birds.

"Go to hell!" he would answer, turning irate every time he is asked why he no longer writes in verse. "Apparently my poems and commentaries on the human condition offend people, so I'm keeping company with birds."

A flight response, perhaps? You got that right! Abandoning poetry and turning to birdwatching is a cop-out, but what can you do? In this day and age, writers have been known to seek solace in mysticism, religion, and pornography, among other things. What is so unthinkable about turning to birdwatching?

Wilfred tried hard to convince himself—the sight of his fellow authors turning to otherworldly pursuits somehow justified his daily visits to the watershed and made him even more adamant that birdwatching was his path to salvation.

In fact, he was able to glean lessons from the behavior of birds that he would never have drawn from the study of literature. The various survival mechanisms that allow birds to flee their predators, for example, he found outright fascinating.

He once found an injured loon near the watershed, lacerated in the most unexpected of places: it had a festering wound over its anus, covered with a sticky film, showing signs of infection. Puss oozing from the gash made the feathers stick together.

Feeling sorry for the bird, he brought it home with him and took it to a vet.

As it happened, the veterinarian was a seasoned member of the birdwatching club. Seeing the loon, he explained with a smile, "He's going to be okay. You know, when loons come under attack, they shed their body weight in order to flee—often this involves discarding their excretory organs. If not for the bacterial infection here, wounds such as these heal very fast, but we can easily fix that with some hydrogen peroxide and antibiotic ointment."

"Shedding their excretory organs?" Wilfred exclaimed in surprise. This was the first time he had ever heard of such a thing.

"Well, you, too, are an expert on birds. Haven't you heard of auto-mutilation in the animal world, especially in times of distress? This is quite common among reptiles."

"Yes, but I never knew it was possible with birds."

Hearing Wilfred's response, the doctor looked secretly pleased—to come across as more knowledgeable than a fellow member of the birdwatching club is no small feat.

"Well, birds evolved from reptiles, so it wouldn't be surprising for certain reptilian survival mechanisms to have carried over, especially among the water fowl."

"Say again?"

"Even more amazing is the fact that not only would they shed their excretory organs, but even their reproductive organs have atrophied to oblivion. Teeny pecker, no balls—what a price to pay for the capacity of flight, wouldn't you say?" the doctor reflected with some sentimentality.

Wilfred was tongue-tied, completely stunned at the explanation. Having studied birds for over two years and read all manner of ornithological works, it suddenly dawned on him that he had barely scratched the surface and that his knowledge of bird anatomy and bird behavior was lacking in a very big way.

So, loons self-mutilate to escape their predators—how so very clever! Once their flight instincts kick in, they discard a crucial part of their anatomy and take off, then find a safe place to hide out and grow back their organs, so that their lives may be spared. Loons, it would appear, are true masters of survival to which humans can barely hold a candle.

This was how Wilfred began his fascination with loons, which he had grown to respect deeply after learning from the doctor of their survival tactics.

In the period that followed, he would spend all his time at the watershed observing loons and studying them.

The more he understood of their behavior, the more fascinated he became—never before had he seen a bird species so dignified and so graceful. Their beauty, it turned out, was manifest not only in outward form but also in their calm demeanor: their foraging patterns, their mating rituals, and their family bonds all attested to a nobility of character.

"If only humans behaved in the same way." Peering through his binoculars, tears started to stream down his cheeks as he reflected on the comparison.

The trouble was that humans were seldom as honorable and peace-loving as he imagined them to be.

That afternoon, as he was hiding in the brush, enjoying his time among the birds of the estuary, a jeep burst onto the scene, out of which a handful of men dressed in blue and armed with rifles stepped forward to confiscate his equipment and take him into custody at a military base near the mouth of the river.

Once there, it became clear he was brought to a coast guard field station, where agents led him into a small interrogation room and slammed the door.

There he sat all alone, with a growing sense of unease, unable still to process what had happened to him. Back in the vehicle, he was furious and demanded to know why he was brought in, only to be ignored by his poker-faced captors.

He was left unattended for some time before the door opened again, and this time, an officer in a lieutenant's uniform entered, holding in his hand a blue plastic binder.

The officer grabbed a chair and sat facing him. Across the tiny desk he politely inquired of his name, his age, his profession, and his place of employment—information which Wilfred duly provided. It wasn't until the officer opened his binder and starting jotting everything down that Wilfred began to sense something was amiss.

"So, what am I in here for? What's going on?" he asked the officer nervously, who only smiled and proceeded to produce sheets of paper from his binder, on which were diagrams etched with a ballpoint pen. Wilfred recognized them immediately—they were foraging routes he had charted—initial drafts that he had torn out and discarded, only to have them end up here.

"We've been watching you for a while now. You've been surveilling the place, taking pictures, and drawing maps..."

"I've been watching birds, for God's sake!" Wilfred shouted before the officer could finish his sentence as he started to gain a sense of what was happening.

"Birds, eh? I don't see any birds around. I'm here all day and never noticed there were birds," the officer countered in a serious tone.

"Don't you see, there are birds everywhere!" Wilfred could barely hide his exasperation.

The officer was silent, glaring intensely with his eyes fixated on Wilfred.

Wilfred did not back down but stared straight back at the officer.

"So, birdwatching, eh? What are these diagrams, then?"

"They're foraging routes and distribution patterns of the water fowl I'm observing. It's data I've collected for research..."

"You call this data? Looks more like smuggling routes to me..."

"No, no, no...you've got to be kidding," Wilfred protested, yelling with equal parts fear and indignation.

"Why the tide charts? What's that got to do with birdwatching?"

"I'm looking into possible correlations between tide fluctuation and bird movement patterns."

At a loss for words, the officer went silent for a while, then, after regrouping, resumed his questioning in spurts.

"So...you say you work at a newspaper office?"

"That's right."

"What does your work for the newspaper have to do with birds?"

"Nothing. Birdwatching is a hobby."

"A hobby? Now, come on, what's there to watch, anyway?"

"What I choose to do in my spare time is none of your business," Wilfred snapped, slowly losing his patience for this absurd line of questioning. "It's my personal freedom."

The officer quietly stared at him for a while, then, just as suddenly, shut his binder and got up to leave.

"Hey, when will I get my camera and binoculars back?"

The officer, who had already reached the door, turned to look at him, "That'll depend on how soon we can get the negatives developed and what we find in the pictures!"

"You have no right to do this to me—" Wilfred stood up and shouted.

The officer ignored his protests and simply walked out.

Interrogations continued for the remainder of the afternoon, with the same line of questioning repeated by different officers, some friendly, others hostile.

One of the officers threatened, "You're accused of a very serious crime, do you understand? We found pictures of classified military facilities in your negatives. You better start talking now, or God knows where they'll send you."

"I want to call my employer," Wilfred demanded, but his pleas were dismissed.

The interrogations ended at six o'clock sharp, after which he was left by himself in the tiny room.

It was then that it occurred to him to turn into a bird. At the height of fear and anger, he shut his eyes and began to grow woozy, experiencing a dizzy spell as the world around him spun topsy-turvy. Seemingly lost in hallucination, he experienced a floating sensation, during which odd, random images progressed through his head, like a film projector showing frames out of sequence, all of which contained headshots of birds, each larger than the next, slowly picking up speed, until he couldn't help but cry into the void.

"Arghh—" he screamed, instantly opening his eyes and finding himself lathered in sweat.

"Let me out of here!" he yelled at the top of his lungs, but to no avail.

He remained captive in the interrogation room until a little past nine, when the door eventually opened. In burst the lieutenant together with Associate Editor Wang from the newspaper.

"It's all a huge misunderstanding!" the editor pleaded with the officer, fawning and nodding with every word.

"Our bad," answered the lieutenant, smiling and firing a short but spirited salute at Wilfred.

The incident was brought to a close just as tensions were poised to rise. Wilfred's diagrams and negatives were confiscated, but his camera and binoculars were returned to him.

"These assholes!" Wilfred cussed as he left the barracks, "All that fuss over something as benign as birdwatching."

"Can you really blame them?" the editor shrugged, patting his colleague on the shoulder. "They recently busted an arms-smuggling ring operating in the area and mistook you for one of its members."

"Now, come on, do I look like an arms smuggler to you?"

"Arms smugglers aren't going to have 'trafficker' tattooed across their foreheads. But, you know, forget it—consider yourself lucky to have been let go. No more birdwatching in these parts, do you understand? Find something worthwhile to do with your life! I don't want to have to come here and bail you out again."

"Find something worthwhile to do…" This off-the-cuff remark from the editor irked him more than a little.

"Hmm…something worthwhile to do." Soaking in a warm bath, he shut his eyes and quietly explored his options.

Writing poetry—now, that, surely, qualifies as something worthwhile. But where did that get me? Smeared and labeled all sorts of nasty things for simply speaking my mind. Yet as a writer, how can you be taken seriously if you don't speak your mind? And if you cannot speak truthfully, then what is there worth doing? This is why I chose the company of birds over people. Harmless enough, you would think, but little did I expect I'd be accused of offences against the state even for birdwatching!

As he allowed his mind to wander, the water in the tub gradually cooled. He got up and wrapped himself in a towel, losing himself in thought as he wiped himself dry.

A flight response. The doctor was absolutely right! All this time I've been dodging the charges brought upon me, certain one day I will flee. Is the will to flee behind the recent spurt of feather growth? Am I sprouting the feathers of a loon because, like that American G.I., I am hallucinating

I am a bird to escape these inhospitable times? But loons can mutilate themselves to get away, whereas I—what can I do?

The more he pondered, the greater the pounding in his head. Again, his world began to spin. He forced himself to snap out of his reveries and rushed out of the bathroom after having barely put on his pajamas.

6

It was three in the morning. Wilfred sat shaking at the edge of his bed, having just awakened from a terrifying dream

Once again he dreamt of turning into a bird, but this time in much more vivid detail. He was standing in a bed of reeds at the river's mouth, slowly growing feathers and transforming into a loon.

It began at his armpit, where bright blue feathers started to appear, extending downward toward his abdomen, where the plumage turned an ashen gray. As they reached his buttocks, there appeared a tuft of down in black and white, following which his arms began to sprout feathers of a light brown color. His neck then started to itch, but as he reached out to scratch, he saw that his hand had atrophied—at which point he heard "plop, plop, plop" as one feather after another started to surface on his neck, like flowers blossoming at the height of spring. Surprised to be dreaming in technicolor, he could see the feathers on his neck were brown, and that the hair on his head had, in the shortest time, morphed into a patch of green feathers. Other than his still human face, the transformation into water fowl was complete. Unsure whether to mourn or rejoice, he spread his wings and, before he knew it, was airborne.

From this point onward the dream took a decidedly unpredictable turn. One minute he was flying over glistening fields of snow; another minute he was gliding over stormy desert sands and boundless ocean waters. Each setting was more disorienting than the next; in each scene the open space was immense: the fields of snow were vast beyond measure; the deserts stretched on without end, and the oceans extended to the edge of the earth. Flying high, he searched in vain for a perch, and was about to die of exhaustion when suddenly…

A bird of prey, its wingspan wide enough to blot out the sun, descended from the clouds and hovered above him. The predator's pointed beak and sharp talons were in clear view, causing him to shriek in terror and flap forward with all his might. But it was of little use, for the eagle proved even faster, and was soon casting its ominous shadow over him, sending him into spasms of fear. As the monster reached out with its claw, he found himself beginning to self-mutilate: first his legs dropped away, then his tail, and, finally, his vital organs were egested through his anus—which, oddly enough, produced no pain. Like a sequence in a silent film, parts of his anatomy fell away like crumbing plaster on a dilapidated façade, drifting off into the wind.

He was ultimately unable to escape the clutches of his nemesis, which left him frustrated, fearful, and full of regret. In the end he was forced to abandon his wings, after which he descended into freefall. As he spiraled earthbound face down, the eagle did not let up, but tumbled after him in a circular motion. He could feel the huge bird closing in, its shadow looming ever larger, until the moment its talons grasped his body, at which point the predator shapeshifted into a gigantic label maker[4] that obscured the light of day.

He woke up screaming.

Reeling from the shock, he sat up in bed, his hands shaking as he attempted to wipe the sweat off his cheeks, only to see his palms fully covered in feathers. He was likewise astounded when he tore off his pajama top to find his entire torso coated in bright feathers. In a panic, he got out of bed and removed his pants—and was stunned to discover himself blanketed in feathers of ashen gray from the navel all the way to the soles of his feet. As he glanced between his legs, he noticed something even more disturbing: there was nothing dangling from his crotch! His manhood had somehow shriveled into oblivion.

"Holy cow!!! I've turned into a man with no balls!"

As the thought flashed through his head, he could no longer contain his angst. "Argh!!!"

Screaming and bawling, his cries of desperation rippled through the night.

He leapt out of bed, and, with his arms wrapped around his head, bolted straight out the door.

His morbid cries echoed across the dark skies as he raced past street after street, traversing distant suburbs before disappearing into the darkness of the night.

"Argh...Argh...Aaugh...Aw...Caw...Caw"—the piercing shriek echoed in the streets as he zoomed by, rising in pitch until they no longer resembled the utterances of a human.

7

Epilogue

Curiously, from that evening onward, the poet Wilf Lee was never to be seen again, nor was anyone aware of his whereabouts.

After his parents reported him missing, the police had yet to develop any promising leads, although they had discovered a pile of shredded pajamas, together with the poet's Telux watch and a likeness of the goddess Matsu he had worn on a chain since birth in an empty field in the outskirts of T. City. It would appear this Taiwanese male had disappeared without a trace, vanishing into thin air, like vapor before the rays of the rising sun.

After his disappearance, friends from his writers' circle launched a massive search, after which they imagined a range of possible scenarios, all of which were as far-fetched and as absurd as the plots developed in their works of fiction:

A

That he had disappeared—which was not uncommon in the day. People disappeared when they ran afoul of the mafia, or when they got on the wrong side of the authorities—either of these could have happened to their fellow poet.

B

That he had taken his own life, but his body had yet to be found.

Suicide could not be ruled out, for friends had discovered the following lines penned in his journal just days before his disappearance:

> ...
> *From western sands to eastern docks,*
> *Quaint fishing town to city blocks,*
> *Shared sensibilities years apart*
> *Send sojourners home with weary hearts.*
> *As Grandma used to tell us, wryly,*
> *Few look on learned folk so highly;*
> *Yet, here we are, two men of letters,*
> *Father long dead and I, no better,*
> *Standing in this solemn hall*
> *As plumes of incense rise and fall,*
> *Where a plaque erected in your name*
> *Beckons me near and urges*
> *That I aspire to the same...*

C

The most preposterous of conjectures was that he had, well, turned into a bird and flown away.

On the night of his disappearance, near the location where his personal effects were recovered, a farmer tending his crops in the wee hours witnessed a scene so disturbing he raced home to tell his loved ones he had seen the devil himself.

In his statement to police, the farmer said that he was draining his field by moonlight when he saw a figure charging at him from the distance, squawking and cawing as he ran, until he was 20 to 30 meters away, at which point he turned into a mammoth-sized bird and ascended into the air. The bird, with a wingspan of 10 to 20 meters, hovered in the air above the field, bawling like a baby, circling three times before soaring off, seemingly with a hint of regret, wailing as it took off in a southerly direction.

(The characters and events depicted in this story are fictitious. Any resemblance to actual persons, living or dead, is unintentional—or not.)

Notes

1. In the source text, the lead character is given the unusually punny name Li Iok-pun 李欲奔 (Mandarin Li Yuben), the elements Iok 欲 ("to wish; to desire") and pun 奔 ("to run; to flee") of which are, together, strongly suggestive of the theme of flight pervasive throughout the story. In the translation we replicate this arrangement by assigning the name Wilfred Lee, shortened to "Wilf Lee" in the recollections of his eccentric psychiatrist, to foreshadow the fact that, in the end, the protagonist "will flee."
2. The source text gives the name of the psychiatrist as Denn Nga 鄭雅 (Mandarin Zheng Ya). The component characters Nga 雅 ("elegant; sophisticated") and Deng 鄭 (homophonous with Mandarin 正 "proper," or slang "attractive"; "stylish") are both suggestive of key features of his appearance. In the translation we parody this effect by assigning the name Ffynnon Dandy, reparsed as "fine and dandy" in the recollections of the protagonist.
3. The source text uses the Chinese idiom *hèlìjīqún* 鶴立雞群 "a crane among a brood of chickens," normally taken to mean standing head and shoulders above one's contemporaries.
4. The source text has the eagle transforming into a gigantic "hat," a pun on the Chinese idiom *dài màozi* 戴帽子 "to force a hat onto someone," meaning to apply a derogatory label or to bring unsubstantiated charges against a person.

7

My Second Brother, the Deserter

Wu He
(translated by Terence Russell)

1

It was while I was in my first year of university that Second Brother began his career as a deserter. After his Lunar New Year's leave, just four months after he was called up, he didn't report back. One day at the crack of dawn, the doorbell rang. It was the "hunters." With nothing but his underpants on, he went out to see who it was. Just as he opened the door a crack, the hunters smashed their way in. He turned and ran, thinking that he could jump out the window onto the neighbor's corrugated roof. He made it halfway up the first flight of stairs when one of the hunters grabbed him by the leg and another one gave him a vicious karate chop. As he slumped over on the steps, one of the hunters went up and straddled his head.

This first episode in his career as a deserter lasted thirty-five days and nine hours. It wasn't a spectacular record, but it was nothing to be ashamed of either. Most don't make it more than three to five days before they fall into the clutches of the silent hunters. And Second Brother wasn't about to give in. He claimed that were it not out of consideration for his newly wed and pregnant wife, he would never have been so brainless as to go and answer the door himself. If not for that, by the time the hunters made it to the foot of the stairs, he would have been long gone, flying over the tract of corrugated roofs and down into the street below. Back inside the camp compound, Second Brother made this claim as he walked along the path between one trough latrine and another. He had just got out of the brig and returned to duty. Because I was the only one in the family to get into university, Mother wanted me to go and give him some guidance. He led me along, chattering away as, one by one, he inspected the latrines. I could hardly get a word in edgewise.

Several years later, at the training center for new recruits, I was able to gain a deeper appreciation of trough latrines. In order that my eyes, so accustomed to reading fine literature, should not be assailed by the sight of turds in the latrine trough, it was my habit to peel off my glasses and put them in my pocket before squatting down. But one time, just as I was squatting down, my glasses fell into the trough, lodging on who knows who's brownish-yellow pile of shit. For twenty or thirty seconds I just stared at my glasses, unsure what to do. All the while the pile underneath them was slowly eroded by the stream of water. At the same time, newly arrived clods kept piling up, creating a nest of shit that cradled my glasses. I wasn't sure if I should just give up on my defiled glasses, or if it was more important to be able to see clearly—then, impulsively, I thrust my face down and reached to scoop the glasses up. In the process, the latrine trough relieved me of something resembling my self-respect.

My Second Brother, the Deserter

2

As I was fishing out my feces-covered glasses, Second Brother was embarking on his third desertion. On the path between the latrine troughs, he had mentioned that he was just waiting for a reason to desert; a reason, not an opportunity—a reason that would make it easier to explain himself to others. He found that reason soon enough, less than a month and a half after he returned to the ranks. He was lingering in his bunk as roll was being called after the afternoon nap. When the duty officer found him, he, the officer, gave the bunk a swift kick which prompted Second Brother to leap up and deliver a punch that knocked his antagonist to the ground. Mother was willing to accept this reason. What if the kick had landed on Second Brother's vital parts? She would have raised a son for nothing. But Elder Brother, who worked in the taxation office as an inspector, didn't see it that way. He said that deserting the army was like being delinquent on your taxes; both were examples of people getting addicted to the illicit pleasures got through bad behavior. At the time I wasn't sure if I should applaud him or not, but afterwards when I joined the army myself, I was also involved in an altercation during which I knocked a man down with a single punch.

It happened a few days after I had been dispatched to a unit at the foot of a mountain. During the evening roll call, the company commander issued an urgent announcement: "Tonight a riot has broken out in Kaohsiung. While the rioting continues to widen, our unit must intensify preparations and vigilance…" Standing in the cold night air I could feel the heat of the disturbance, and in the succeeding months we found ourselves engulfed in its flames. Study session after study session was screened on the television. There were panel discussions and then more panel discussions. The political warfare officer, who was a graduate of a vocational college, appointed me to produce a summary of events. I talked about how all things happen for a reason, but I couldn't find any reliable evidence, that sort of thing. He rebuked me saying that I had wasted my time reading a lot of useless books and wasn't using my head because everyone could see that the evidence was "unconvertable" (probably what he meant was "incontrovertible"). The evidence was clearly "unconvertable." All the same, he applauded my magnanimous view. When a child misbehaves, the parents need only give the child a bit of spanking, and that should be the end of it. All the more so for a government like ours that is so devoted to benevolent governance. He boldly predicted that most of the miscreants would be given no more than three to five years, and most likely they'd get six months, or two year's suspended sentences. On the "Political Warfare Day" after the judgments in the Kaohsiung cases were passed, I declare that this government can't even pass a fart. They're determined to force plugs up people's assholes—pull them out! The junior political warfare officer bellowed, "Pull them out! Pull those deviants out and disinfect their thinking: Those are problematic words spoken by someone with problematic thinking."

Second Brother's second attempt at desertion didn't even reach twenty days. The hunters tracked the baby carriage and captured the young father waiting beside a fence in the tiny zoo. I wrote at least twenty letters to him during his second stint in jail. He wrote back only once, saying that his downfall had come from being too attentive to his wife and child, but the day would come when he could run rampant like a wolf. He used the expression "run rampant" to imply that he would move with the ferocity of an eagle in flight. The second time that he returned to the ranks he only hung around for four days. Then, like an eagle, he flew over the low wall surrounding the camp. During the time that I was stuck at the foot of that mountain under thought surveillance, I had no idea where Second Brother was running rampant.

3

For several years afterwards there was no news of my second brother for long periods. We had grown accustomed to that. When the family got together, we didn't mention him. I am pretty sure that his wife knew where he was, but we didn't ask. If we had asked her, she wouldn't have given us a straight answer.

Late one night, Second Brother's "Long March" brought him to my house. He had a prostitute and a young girl with him. The prostitute was probably thirty or forty. My new bride whispered in my ear: "It's Seventh Lord from the temple of the City God." I took a good look—Second Brother actually looked more like Eighth Lord.[1] That evening, after enjoying my wife's thin fish congee with condiments and two bottles of Shaoxing rice wine, Eighth Lord, the girl and Seventh Lord squeezed into our little four tatami mat-sized guest room. We both wondered how they were going to sleep, then my wife turned over and fell silent. It took me the longest time to get to sleep, imagining Eighth Lord's coarse, powerful body squaring up against the girl's delicate frame.

...After being placed under thought surveillance, I was spared guard duty. They didn't dare let anyone with a warped mind handle a gun in case they took it off base to sell. Or they might go off and try to make a living with it themselves. You probably noticed in the martial-law bulletins that once in the middle of the night some guy with a warped gourd had taken an automatic rifle and opened fire on his bunkmates...For my part, I was happy to be able to sleep through until daybreak. The men who had to stand sentry in the freezing mountain air got chilblains on their hands the size of their balls from clutching the magazines of their rifles. To soothe the ranks in their resentment over this, Lieutenant Commander Jiang Zhihong explained, "...by not letting him have a rifle we are preventing him from becoming a soldier, and he won't be able to fulfil his sacred duty as a man-at-arms. He'll be unworthy of being called a soldier. You could even say he won't be worthy of being called a man..." And since I wasn't a real soldier, I could only be assigned work for those who aren't real soldiers. Most of the time this meant temporary assignment to latrine duty or to the vegetable garden. The latrine supervisor was a social deviant who had also been placed under surveillance. His responsibility was for the first-round inspection of the latrines. He inspected to verify that the temporary worker (me) had satisfactorily cleaned them. Then he waited for the second-round inspector, a higher-ranking duty officer, to come by every so often and verify that his first-round inspection had been satisfactory. There was a flush toilet occupying pride of place, first in the row of latrines. Four words were painted in red on the wooden door planks: "For Officers' Use Only." The social deviant soldier's butt also only used the officers' toilet. As for me, although I cleaned the latrines hundreds of times, I never dared use the one reserved for the butts of officers. Because there wasn't much water pressure, regular flushing often became irregular flushing, resulting in turds piling up beneath the butts of the men using the last three latrines. So, the enlisted men preferred to unload in makeshift field latrines, and that meant an additional duty for me: twice a day, once at the break of dawn, and again at dusk, I wobbled out to the vegetable plot with a shoulder pole loaded with buckets of night soil. Back then my greatest ambition was to become the vegetable-plot supervisor. I watched as the current supervisor stood, plastic hose in hand, spraying a cascade of water that the sunlight turned into a dazzling rainbow. It was as though the ground was being showered with shining crystal. I thought to myself that I would be happy to make this my life's work. But that was impossible, just as it was also impossible to be the latrine supervisor. Someone under thought surveillance was not allowed to have fixed work or fixed anything. If he ever had extra energy, who knows what kind of heretical thinking might spring into his mind? At the same time, someone under thought surveillance could not assume sole responsibility for a job. He had constantly to be under observation by his colleagues—Why were the screws in the base of the flushing toilet always broken? You had to be careful that nobody put chemicals into the night soil that would produce deformed cabbage. My superiors were most considerate in ensuring that I had no potentially dangerous energy to spare. They gave me three temporary duties: occasional latrine cleaner, morning and evening vegetable-plot night-soil carrier, and then in the afternoon there was the once-a-day pigsty cleaning. With the latrines as my central base, the pigsty, vegetable plot, and field latrines formed a

My Second Brother, the Deserter

perfect equilateral triangle around the outskirts of the camp. At irregular times I holed up in the central administration office for the latrines, and regularly went out on assignment to the borderlands. On my way I took in the outline of the mountain ridges highlighted in the morning and evening light and listened to the chirping of the forest birds—ah, the joys of being a stooped, hunchbacked foul-smelling pig-man who didn't at all resemble a military man. But occasionally something would jump out at me, blocking my way. I didn't need to look to know that it was my political warfare officer. He would start by sternly ordering, "Stand up straight. A good soldier has to look like a soldier, not like damn riff-raff." Then he would do an ad hoc inspection of all my pockets. The main purpose of this ad hoc inspection was to collect any texts, book notes, or slips of paper on which anti-government manifestos or secret plots to subvert the nation might have been written. Most of the time checking two pockets would be enough, but in emergency situations the political warfare officer would scrupulously check six in the summer and nine in the winter. After he pulled everything out and had a look, he threw it emphatically on the ground then made you crawl around picking it up. I once went on a hunger strike to protest this kind of coercion. I avoided thought issues and aimed my attack at the banal topic of "steamed buns or blocks of tofu," something that required no thinking at all. According to army regulations, sleeping quilts must be folded into a perfect cube, like a block of tofu. After we got up in the morning, the first matter of business was squeezing the "tofu." You squeeze and squeeze to show you can endure the discipline. But every day my handiwork with the quilt was judged to more like a round steamed bun. So, during afternoon naptime I had to do "steamed bun" exercises. With my quilt held above my head, I had to run a lap around the long slope in front of the warehouses. If I didn't make it in five minutes, I had to do another lap. I didn't eat lunch and didn't turn up for the "steamed bun" exercises. Instead, I hid in the empty warehouses on the other side of the mountain, walking randomly around between one warehouse and another. After missing dinner I snuck back, only to be pulled into the political warfare office.

"You're starting to have extreme thoughts again, aren't you?" were his first words. I steadfastly maintained that it was just a question of tofu blocks or steamed buns. "If your thoughts aren't problematic how could steamed buns or tofu blocks become a problem?" I confirmed that my tofu blocks were handmade, and there was no way they could be like machine-made steamed buns: If your thoughts aren't problematic, blocks of tofu won't be mistaken for steamed buns and there won't be any problems. "Be careful of your thoughts." The junior political warfare guy's face clouded over. "A hunger strike is like problematic thinking with a fake exchange policy." The next morning, the director of political warfare from central command came to inspect the base. I was summoned for a routine chat, "A hunger strike is genuinely problematic thought." He affirmed repeatedly: It's very, very genuine. You could also say that it's like problematic thinking with a fake exchange policy...I've heard that you're determined to go on a hunger strike. I hope you'll shape up and change your mind. The army isn't like society. There can be no compromise when it comes to this kind of thinking. So you had better give up on this pointless war of resistance. Save your precious energy for the army and the nation. Feeling a lot of empathy for this idea, I replied that I also was anxious to give my lifetime of energy to the army as well as the nation, but unfortunately they made me waste my energy in the pigsty. "Ah ha!" The director suddenly saw the light. "So that is what the war of resistance is about—" In that case, it's a lower order of problematic thinking. All the same, raising pigs is ultimately for the benefit of people, so you can't say it's a waste. You have to correct your decadent thinking. Being a pig-rearing soldier is like a being a screw in a machine. Without that screw, the great machine that is the army cannot run properly, never mind the nation. I was much gratified: If raising pigs was like raising people, then wasn't it the same as nurturing soldiers, and by extension nurturing the whole army and nation!? I took this opportunity to mention my ambition: My ambition was to become a full-fledged military pig-management engineer. "A military engineer managing pigs?" The director thought deeply for two and a half seconds.

My Second Brother, the Deserter

"We will carefully consider your request...but there can be no problematic thought." "The pigsty is an excellent place for thought reform." I pressed my point. The director heaved a sigh of appreciation, "The pigsty is an excellent place for thought reform." An excellent political warfare slogan! I lowered my voice, "Making us do 'steamed bun' exercises in the hot sun is extremely inhumane." The director was caught off guard, "But soldiers aren't simply people, so something inhumane isn't necessarily unmilitary." But "whether 'steamed bun' exercises under the hot sun is military or not," that's a thought problem worth discussing. The wise eyes of the senior political warfare officer were all perceptive: because if I could identify with the reality of tofu blocks, you could say I could identify with this great and promising organization of ours. At best, mine was a kind of "intra-organizational war of resistance." Clearly, in terms of thought, I still had hope of reform. The director asked me to stay behind to join the base bigwigs for lunch. I temporarily took on new duties: bringing the dishes to the table of the big brass, filling their rice bowls one by one, respectfully placing the chopsticks at their places. Through all of this, the director offered earnest instruction: "Your presence in the military clearly has existential value. It provides us with a negative example and gives us an opportunity for deliberation and self-reflection. I hope that you will report what you see, hear and think to us for our reference..." That noon the "steamed bun" exercises were nowhere to be seen. The junior political warfare guy was summoned to base command. He returned with a steely expression on his face and announced that from now on "steamed bun squats and jumps" will replace "steamed bun running." My "steamed bun" quilt also began to be evaluated as a block of tofu. After all, once a person's thinking has been stabilized, the problem of "steamed buns or blocks of tofu" is no longer a problem. He gave me special permission not to speak on Politics Day. I was the only man who did not have the pleasure of taking part in panel discussions, nor was I encumbered by the entreaty, "Everyone must speak—this is both a privilege and a duty." Instead, my superior officer urged me to eat more to build up my diseased body, my "deformed intellectual" physique was completely unsoldier-like...

I tossed and turned until the sky turned a fish-belly white before I managed to get to sleep. For lunch, my wife made grilled milkfish belly, steamed milkfish backs with fermented black bean, and milkfish head soup with juliennes of ginger. We joked that Second Brother must miss the flavors of home. He was "temporarily stationed" with us for three days and two nights. When he left, he said only that he was headed south to continue his long march. He might even go to the Spratly Islands. I gave him $2,000[2] for the road and my wife picked two bags of guavas from the back garden for him to take on his travels. After he left, both my wife and I felt depressed for over a week. She said she really couldn't stand a man who didn't have a taste for meat and she vowed that she would never again cook for Seventh Lord, although she had genuine respect for Eighth Lord who didn't make a sound the whole night.

4

The third time that Second Brother was captured, he was in a small theatre not far from his wife's house. The little theatre screened both local kung fu movies and Western romances which attracted large audiences of men even on winter afternoons. The instant the lights went on after the end of the romance movie, Second Brother discovered that to his left and right as well as behind and in front of him sat hunters with cold smiles on their faces. Mother sighed that Second Brother just couldn't forget his wife and son. Even real men feel strong attachment to their children. Elder Brother conjectured that it was the habit of fugitives to hide in dark dens for sexual dalliances, and naturally the hunters are well aware of the fugitives' habits.

The third time that he deserted the army, he held out for almost six years. Mercifully, the military court only sentenced him to three and a half years. Standing before the court martial, Second Brother said that during the past few years, in order to support his wife and son, who

My Second Brother, the Deserter 255

lived with his mother-in-law, he had drifted all over doing odd jobs. He had just returned from a little seaside village on the east coast called Jingpu. After giving the money to his wife, he had collapsed from fatigue in the theatre. His wife vouched for the truth of his story. I took my mother's place and responsibility for going to the military prison to visit Second Brother. Several times during the visits, he recounted bits of the story of how he had been stationed on the beach at Jingpu for a few days when one morning he looked out over the ocean and suddenly remembered the oyster omelets of Anping in Tainan. He immediately set out to return there. After eating an oyster omelet with oyster soup, he only had enough money left for a movie ticket. Before he went to Jingpu, he had been stationed the entire summer at the bottom of rocky cliffs in a river valley and hardly had to spend any money at all. He was so tired that he just drowsed off. Otherwise, his nose, fine-tuned over many years, would never have missed the scent of the hunters, although truly professional hunters can be right under your nose and you wouldn't be able to tell that they're any different from ordinary people like you or me. He missed those dazzling, passionate films. The first thing he did when he got out of prison was go to that theatre and watch movies to his heart's content. He had become exhausted by his life as a drifter. He thought it wouldn't be such a bad idea if they let him rest and recuperate for a while in prison: that place that is more like an army base than an army base. "Talk about your life as a soldier," Second Brother gave a rare smile, "an outstanding recruit like yourself."

I couldn't keep myself from trembling. With quivering hand, I reached to stroke the hair of the woman in the seat in front of me. I was on the bus back to the base, a holiday afternoon. Strands of hair hung down from the neatly arranged bun, covering the smooth white nape. I fixated on the neck and its white flesh as sunlight filtered in, creating highlights and shadows. I reached until I could clasp the tips of my fingers over the ends of her hair. After trembling a moment, I let go, then took hold again, moving upwards on the strands. In the instant that my fingers touched her neck, the woman inclined her face toward me, and I sensed how sticky my fingers were—I began to report what I heard, saw, and thought to the national authorities for their reference. My reports were in the form of personal letters sent to a functionary in the political warfare division of base command. Inside the base, the combat officers had a taste for pornographic videos. They frequently took a couple of grunts along with them, locked themselves in the reception room, and made war from late at night until dawn.[3] Any visitors who came for a meeting the following day were assaulted by the rank stench of the previous night wafting off the chairs under their butts. Two weeks later a military inspections officer arrived and made the reception room his temporary interrogation room. After a number of people had gone in for individual consultation, the inspection officer instructed that from then on the duties of the gate sentries should include keeping watch over the television set. After nine o'clock, watching TV would be strictly forbidden and no one was to be allowed in. A week later, the combat officer was reassigned to be a training officer. I let my left elbow drift upwards just slightly, letting my right fingers slide under my left armpit to give the young wife pretending to sleep in the seat beside me a poke in the nipple. Then I quickly withdrew. Under her light yellow t-shirt, her nipple exuded the warm, fragrant tranquility of a gardenia flower in a church courtyard. In the evening darkness on the bus, my hand probed toward the schoolgirl beside me. It hesitated for a long time at the side of her leg, then crept upwards. The girl's expression didn't change. At first my palm lay completely still on her thigh, then it began to slide up and down. When the bus arrived at the terminal the girl walked in front of me as we disembarked. She was a high school student on her way to a school in the city. Suddenly, she stopped and turned around. With her eyes lowered she said, I like your uniform, why do you have to be like that? Inside the base there was always a hidden, floating gambling ring. Sometimes, late at night, it was beside the stoves in the kitchen. In the daytime it was in the spare-parts room of the second-class maintenance workshop. A few times it traveled to the empty warehouses behind the mountain, and sometimes it moved to the tangerine orchard or the chicken farm outside the base. When the guys who ran the ring were in the mood, they snuck out of the base after evening roll call. There would be a taxi waiting for them outside to take them to the town to drink and whore around until daybreak. Then they would hurry back for morning roll call. The junior political warfare officer, whose specialty was developing an intelligence network, must surely have known about this, but there was no war going on, and besides, it had nothing to do with thought. In my private missives I drew a detailed flowchart of the gambling ring while pointing out that the junior political warfare officer was "the black hand who saw nothing" in order to take a cut. Within a month, he made his first raid on the gambling den in the second-class maintenance workshop. Two days later, he broke up another gambling den in a corner of the pig pen. The company commander comforted the political warfare guy while reprimanding everyone in general, "It isn't that soldiers don't gamble. It is the professional responsibility of soldiers to stake their lives in service of the nation, when the nation requires us to do so..." The junior political warfare officer's face turned ashen, "I'm not afraid of whoever ratted on me." Growing angrier, "Fuck the son-of-a-bitch who did this. He's a rotten back-stabbing rat!" My cane poked at the woman's fulsome breasts. When she felt it, she stiffened her elbow and pulled it tight to her body. My cane poked left and right so that she had no choice but to clasp her purse under her arm for protection. The tip of the cane pushed, then relaxed, feeling her purse clutched to the undulant slope of her breasts. The crotch of my pants stuck out and pressed against the skinny buttocks of a farmer's wife as we swung back and forth with the movements of the bus. When the driver hit the brakes, I deliberately bumped up against her butt with enough force to make her feet leave the ground. She turned her head and saw only a smart green army uniform. Commander Jiang doted on his youngest son, often bringing the boy into the base to eat and sleep with him. We addressed him respectfully as "Commander Junior," but behind his back we called him "Little Commander SOB." We had no idea who was responsible for the "Commander Junior's" provisions. The base's senior political warfare officer's pampered wife came out to the country to check on her husband's workplace. They locked themselves in the officer's quarters and for three days and two nights there wasn't a peep out of them, although her rouge-colored panties could be seen in the distance, hanging in the sunlight by the back window. Strangely, soldiers who climbed up to work on the roof of the warehouse always seemed to drill their holes in the wrong place. The taciturn, grim-faced base commander always got the hots for the lady emcees from the evening variety shows that came to entertain the troops. And when he walked, grim-faced and wearing his green cap, into the fruit and shaved-ice shop run by a woman, all the little kids in the village lined up at attention and saluted him. The troop carrier finally came to a stop in a remote forested area. The driver got down to reconnoitre. "It's better to shoot your wad than to do target practice." Those were the training officer's famous words. We hadn't done target practice all year, but in the report that he submitted the date for target practice was clearly indicated. As usual, bullets were counted out and shells counted in. On Thursday, Politics Day, the troops got a break from work. After the men took turns giving over-ripe bullshit speeches on politics, they hung around shooting the breeze, or took the opportunity to get a bit of rest and relaxation. One time during a televized instruction session, a mob of rioters with slogans on their headbands appeared on the screen. One of the military guards shouted out, "...take 'em out and shoot 'em all..." The junior political warfare officer immediately got up and stood beside the screen, "We don't need to waste the nation's bullets on them. Those bullets are there to deal with those other disgraceful scum. As for these people you can all see here, we have to think of some way to reform them. When you return to your regular lives..." I privately sent a missive to the higher command saying: "Didn't our ancestor, Sunzi, once say that being compassionate to your enemies is being cruel to yourself? A political warfare officer like this can only weaken our resolve in battle, never mind what happens when we go back to regular life...Besides which, he even encouraged us all to go get circumcised. Never mind if that could be called preparations for war or not, what is the point?"

Second Brother smiled and said that he hadn't been in the ranks long enough to run around getting himself circumcised. For about six months, he was the man in charge of transportation for the mobile gambling ring near a freeway interchange. Aside from the phrase, "Report complete!" he couldn't remember saying anything else while he was in the service. He had made "long marches" to Indigenous villages, like Dalai and Ali, in the mountainous region of Pingtung where he made the acquaintance of a young Paiwan guy. They soon became bosom buddies because whenever they talked every sentence ended with, "Report complete!" His plan was to start up a gambling ring as soon as he returned to the ranks. He would regularly take a forty percent cut to pay for tip-offs. When the heat was on, he could raise that to sixty, or even seventy percent. That way even an artillery barrage couldn't touch them, never mind political warfare. I told him that Mother begged him to finish his service no matter what. He replied that if the gambling ring went smoothly, the remaining two and a half years wouldn't be a problem. It might be necessary to break up the ring temporarily, but he couldn't give up on his brothers-in-arms. Once, standing on a pier in Nanfang Ao, he bet someone that the oil slick on the surface of the water was thick enough to support a man who weighed at least eighty kilograms. He won himself some seafood snacks that way. Mother hoped that he would at least see his son who was gradually growing to adulthood. "Me, I'm a secret sleeper-cell member dispatched by the army." Second Brother's voice suddenly turned shrill. He was part of a sleeper cell attached to military command who was in training as he spoke. His mission was the long-term investigation and monitoring of the hunters who pursued him. Did they really hole up sometimes in the fruit and shaved-ice shop to flirt with the young wench who ran it? Did they really drift over to the little theatre after lunch to take a nap? He had once been apprehended when, by coincidence, he run into some hunters taking their naps. When they took their naps, the hunters always arranged themselves in the form of a trap.

I always worried about Second Brother's gambling ring. Even though alcohol and gambling weren't prohibited, could the gambling ring stand up to the formidable powers of political warfare? One evening his wife was worried and came by my place after she finished work at the factory. Six months before, she had visited Second Brother in military prison. It was only eight days before he was to be released, but afterwards she lost all contact with him. We comforted her. Maybe he had been deployed to some distant, strategic outpost of national defense and it wasn't convenient for him to come home. She said that had never happened before. Leaves for second-class soldiers like Second Brother were short, but for many years those had been the only times when the two of them could properly enjoy life as a couple. She had recently bought a color television and replaced the wooden bed with one with a spring mattress. I agreed to look for her husband. It was pretty obvious that he was a fugitive again, unless he had been deployed to the moon.

5

I spoke to four of Second Brother's sworn brothers. One of them stood in the doorway and told me straight out that he hadn't seen him for a long time. He wouldn't let me set foot over the threshold. Another one pulled me inside and prattled on for an hour and five minutes about their heroism of bygone days. Yet another said that Second Brother no longer respected him and hadn't come to see him for years. The last one told me that I shouldn't go looking for trouble because sworn brotherhoods dated from before the Nationalist period.

Every Monday I placed a missing-persons notice: "Second Brother, if you see this, contact me." With the addition of my name, it made a total of nine words. I was sure that if he read the newspaper in his spare time, he would eventually see the notice. Late one night, close to one o'clock, we got a phone call: "...if you want to find your brother, come to Taipei and give me a call..." It was a very peculiar female voice, unusually low. After she repeated the phone number she hung up, but that voice, rich and strong like well-aged Shaoxing wine, lingered with me for a long time. My wife was certain that it was just a trick, some sort of honey trap. I said that I was just a poor teacher and a faithful husband, so they'd have a hard time trapping me. Besides, nobody could just guess my phone number out of the blue, although who knows, eh? It could have been one of my past lovers who had a sudden urge to revive old passions. My wife was jealous. She scoffed that they shouldn't mess with her. Didn't they all have husbands now? We thrashed it out until daybreak. But after she vented her belly full of envy she relented and reassured me, "I know you're doing it for Second Brother. Be careful, that's all."

Just like in a detective movie, I followed the instructions that I got over the telephone and found my way to a massage and barber shop. I said I was looking for Number Twenty-two. "There's no Number Twenty-two here. We only have eighteen girls." A rich, full voice spoke from the darkness, "I'm Number Two." It wasn't until midnight, after she had emerged from that black cavern, that I got a good look at her. Her cream-colored suit was stretched tightly over her large-boned frame. She had high cheekbones and her eye sockets were unusually deep and dark. "You can call me Second Sister." As we crossed the street, out of habit Second Sister slipped her arm under mine. "I knew who you were as soon as I laid eyes on you. You're from the same mold. Your brother says you're more posh—and even worse than him." We crossed two streets. Second Sister bought two skewers of grilled chicken butts from a sidewalk hawker, as well as two boxes of sushi. We turned into an alley, then cutting past the cul-de-sac, we turned into another lane. "This is it, the apartment complex." We then returned to the street and bought two bottles of Paolyta-B tonic wine at a general store, which she asked me to carry. "These are your brother's supplies." Back in the alley again, Second Sister checked in all directions before we entered the apartment complex.

Only ten *ping*, about 350 square feet, the suite was filthy—mounds of crap were scattered around like tombs in a graveyard. Second Brother sat cross-legged on a bed-mound amid the stench of meat stewed in bitter gourd. "I hear you've been looking for me." Second Sister gathered a pile of clothing in her arms to reveal a beach chair underneath. "How come it took you so long to get word of me?" I gazed over at Second Brother's bloated face. The flesh on his chest had also started to sag. "I haven't been outside for nine months."

He passed me a glass of the tonic wine. "Nine months and two days, no, now it's nine months and three days. When I was in the can..."

"...You swilled rice wine," I continued for him, "but on the outside you get the 'fancy good stuff', Paolyta-B."

He laughed. "It's not as if I can't afford good wine."

Second Sister brought me some ice cubes. "Once when I was walking along, bringing her a bottle of Black Label, I just took a little swig and fell into the toilet." Second Sister ate her sushi.

"There's some rice gruel," said Second Brother, "and the stewed beef is done."

"He can make pork trotters with peanuts, too," Second Sister giggled. Slightly drunk on Paolyta-B and rice wine, Second Brother heated up his stewed beef, pork trotter with peanuts, and gruel in a rice cooker. Unfortunately, he couldn't use the cooker to fry things, otherwise he would have liked to learn how to make braised eel. He had another famous dish as well, Second Sister reminded him, don't forget to have your brother try your mystery fish poached in rice wine.

When he escaped the base, he fled directly to Second Sister's bed chamber. One winter he was stationed in the bed chamber of a Daoist nun behind the great temple on Dagang Mountain. There he found genuinely warm winters and cool summers. When considering the basic needs of the common people, you can't forget the importance of Daoist sexual practice and the refining of inner elixirs. It was just the incessant tap, tap, tap, tap, of the "wooden fish"[4] accompanying the chanting in the middle of the night. The sound carried into the bed chamber and made

My Second Brother, the Deserter 263

things extremely dreary. He had decided to mend his ways and retreated to practice the Dao and refine his inner elixir. But unexpectedly, one day when requesting "tribute rice" from the nun she mentioned something about how she had to get up early on the day after the Spring Festival plays. That was because there were men coming up the mountain to check household registrations. On a sweltering, restless night in military prison, he suddenly remembered Second Sister's chamber: Thigh meat, medicinal wine, and porn flicks. He had lived in ruined buildings, empty buildings, and buildings under construction. He wandered free and easy on herbal wine and fueled himself with dreams of beautiful women everywhere he went. The only problems were the mosquitoes and the occasional reek of urine wafting around. Slowly, he came to the realization that perhaps he could just shut himself away in Second Sister's bed chamber. For a time, he was stationed in an air-raid shelter, but the moldy, rancid smell was ten times worse than the smell of urine. And in the darkness, he sometimes touched or bumped into the bones of who knows which dead people. He had a friend in the can who was so restless that as soon as he got out he took his lover and hid, terrified, in an air-raid shelter on a slope beside a road. The forensic investigator said it was because of a lack of oxygen, but the fact is he had died from the overwhelming stench. He loathed his life of long marches and short sojourns. No matter how long the marches, the hunters were always right there on his ass. He knew for certain that he would be caught on one of his short sojourns. But he also knew that he had plenty of stamina, and the tricks he learned while languishing in jail all those years had stood him in good stead as he holed up in Second Sister's bed chamber. Separated by layers and layers of reinforced concrete, his heartbeat was lost in the heartbeat of the city.

I could feel that heartbeat—the heartbeat of a deserter. Tipsy on rice wine mixed with Paolyta-B, I told my brother that once I had also deserted, but first I wanted to talk about rifles. I was finally able to get my hands on the rifle that had been assigned to me. "When he arrived, he really wasn't a man." Commander Jiang praised me in front of everyone. "The army made him strong..." The first time that I lifted a rifle from the locker, the flames of gratitude, resentment, revenge, love and hate all coiled together, scalding the palms of my hands. I dipped my fingers in the gun oil and carefully stroked the rifle. I wished that my hand could forever be a rifle-polishing cloth. I would peel a long strip of skin from my palm, press it to the rifle barrel, then rub back and forth a million, zillion times until the barrel gleamed and flashed like lightening. I was a natural born rifle-polisher. "I recommended you for my position a few times." The firearms officer inspected my rifle. As I carried the rifle back to the locker, I reached to press my fingers into the sandy soil. Tiny clumps of oily dirt formed on my fingertips. Then, like hailstones falling on a sunny day, the clumps showered into the barrel of the gun. Late at night, while on sentry duty in the carpark, or the pigpen, my rifle barrel inclined toward the black vault of the Milky Way or the assholes of the pigs. One night, the junior political warfare officer angrily reproached us, "In the future it is prohibited for two men to sleep under the same quilt—What the hell are you doing under there?" That same night I rested my rifle butt on the top of the pig enclosure so I could rub my anus on the muzzle. The front sight left a scar on my rump bone that took forever to go away. Breathing in the smell of pig or human shit and piss, I became aware that a gun is built to work like a penis. But the bullets that eject from the muzzle bring an end to the life that sperm brings. The army is like a huge penis that the state puts on open display. Countless sperm bullets spew from its rifle barrel outward at foreign targets and inward against the nation's citizenry. The little penises of ordinary men must all shrink with impotence in the shadow of this huge penis rifle's stock. And you never know when you might find it thrust up your anus. Apparently, while I'm being ass-fucked to death it's all right to reach out my hand in a pathetic gesture-seeking mercy—to grope any woman I can.

"Ah, yeah." Second Brother sighed: Men all lust to grope any woman they like. There was one night when, after pulling off its sheath, I stuck my bayonet into the ground. Then I took off my uniform and hung it over the butt of the rifle with my helmet covering the anus. I leapt over the wire mesh fence in my undershirt and underpants. From the other

My Second Brother, the Deserter 265

side of the barbed wire, I stared for a time at the physically and mentally upside-down rifleman trapped in the dark cave of the national pigsty. Following a path that ran beside the camp, I descended for a few minutes. Suddenly I stopped and stood stunned—was it really this easy to leave the steely hard military behind and return to the disorder of humanity? I would flee back to disorder. They would immediately dispatch the steely hunters. I thought of Second Brother. How could a disordered life stand up against such steely resolve? I turned around and started to trek back toward mid-mountain—what if you pitted the steel of an individual's resolve against the steely resolve of the group? The night was very dark. I passed by the tangerine orchard, mushroom sheds, and a bamboo forest. As I climbed the steep banks of a ravine, the powerful shafts of light from the twin spotlights by the camp gate joined to form an arc whose murky image appeared, then disappeared under my crotch. Looking up, the mountainous interior was clothed in starry pearls that seeped down to greet me. I waited for three nights and four days at mid-mountain on a mesa two and a half metres square. I went down to the orchard a couple of times to get some tangerines. There was a winding mountain stream that dripped past the base of the rocky cliff behind the mesa. I munched some succulent chayote tendrils, washing them down with water from the stream. In the distance I could see the smoke of cooking fires curling up from the base. In the kitchen they were using water from the same stream to poach chicken Cantonese style. Early in the evening, as the mosquitoes started biting, I realized that basically, the only form of self-redemption is complete rebellion. I only regretted that I hadn't brought any mosquito coils with me. On the second night, as I scratched my swollen, itchy bites, especially the ones on the inside of my thighs and under my arms, I realized that the military conscription system was a bastard that had to rape each and every virgin male, leaving behind the scars of its defilement on their bodies. My almost empty stomach churned and cried out for one of those big steamed buns that they served at breakfast. I swallowed a mouthful of water and gazed at the vast sea of stars. Why does every person have to belong to a nation as soon as they are born? Why has no nation ever asked whether you really want to be its citizen? Waking up on the third day, I made my way down to the orchard. My legs were rubbery, and my head was in a fog. When I got there I just stood and stared at all the tangerines. The orchard was really only a pathway. In my sleep-befuddled mind, I wound my way in the direction of...the base. I made a laborious ascent up the mountain with five or six tangerines in my arms. Clambering over the boulders in the stream, I dropped a few of them. When I got to the mesa, I collapsed limply on the ground. On the third night my mind went completely blank, and I woke up twice with the dry heaves.

After returning to the base, the first thing I ate was rice gruel with luffa gourd and dried shrimp. To this day, I always ask my wife to cook up this dish every time there is a national holiday. "For me it's...pumpkin vermicelli with steamed pork." That's the dish Second Brother most missed from his army days. The junior political warfare officer insisted on transferring my case, but according to Commander Jiang's broad interpretation, the entire mountain area behind the camp was within the boundaries of the base. That way it was just a breach of discipline, not a case of desertion. In a telephone call, the senior political warfare officer conditionally agreed with the commander's view. "Motherfucker..." Slightly tipsy on rice wine and Paolyta-B, Second Brother conditionally agreed with the junior officer's view. He claimed that everyone thinks about deserting, but not everyone deserts, and back then, if I had been able to desert properly, my life today wouldn't be as monotonous as it is. He used "monotonous" to describe my life now. I was escorted to command headquarters for three weeks of confinement. Once the three weeks were up, I was immediately dispatched to a newly established unit on the coast. The social deviant soldier was sent along with me. A little high on rice wine and Paolyta-B, Second Brother judged my experience as a deserter to be like a foot soldier riding a horse: If the horse lost a hoof, he wouldn't even realize it. At the very least, if I was going to climb the mountain, I should have taken food and some clean clothes. The first time he jumped over the wall and deserted, he went and got the civilian

My Second Brother, the Deserter   267

clothes that he had hidden in clump of grass on his last leave. I gazed at my brother lying spread eagle on his bed. With his deathly white face he looked like a recently buried corpse. I recalled that the first time he deserted he had just forgotten to return after the New Year's holidays. Was he talking about the second time that he deserted?

   Tipsy on his Paolyta-B cocktail again, Second Brother mumbled away in some cryptic language. Since Second Sister worked the evening shift, he mumbled until midnight and then bothered her until daybreak. If Second Sister worked the graveyard shift, he would mumble until daybreak and then bother her until almost noon. "I work long shifts," said Second Sister, "so it's a good thing he invented a way to talk to himself." The reason he called it a "cryptic language" was because he didn't want anyone else to understand it. If nobody understood it, there was no fear of secrets being leaked. If there was no fear of leaks, it meant that he could speak freely whenever and wherever he wanted, and days of freedom were the happiest. Once the Paolyta-B and rice wine had taken effect, Second Brother began his speech. His cryptic language was completely unique and constantly changing. He had developed it gradually while he was in military prison and was working toward the day when he was completely fluent. Then he was going to take off for the place where they spoke that language and never come back...

6

I thanked Second Sister and asked her to continue looking after Second Brother. Second Sister smiled poignantly and said that this was the first time that she had a man all to herself. As we said our goodbyes at the entranceway to the alley, tears glinted silently in her deep-set eyes. I passed my remaining days gazing at the glow of ocean waves at night. It occurred to me that walking into the ashen-blue watery glow was the only way to find complete freedom. Mother said that you have to start learning patience from the time you are born. Elder Brother maintained that the system tests people's endurance, and those with the greatest stamina are the ones that succeed in the system. Could Second Brother's stamina overcome the system? On my days off, I got a ride from the fishing village into the city where I wandered around aimlessly in the dark alleys. I would follow the ass of some lady of the night and end up crashing in who-knows-who's damp, moldy bed.

I told my wife that it really was a kind of trap. For two days and one night I looked without success for that woman with a deep, sultry voice. Second Brother was at that moment perfecting his art of life. I told his wife and asked her to help complete him. When was it that I started drinking vintage rice wine? My wife sneered that maybe I was drinking it in search of immortality. High on rice wine vinegar, I imagined reenacting Second Brother's life as a deserter. I had spent several months hanging about the bars in Wanhua. In the mornings I slept in a corridor behind the main hall of Longshan Temple and ate the pastries and fruit from the offering tables. In the company of the family of an old beggar named Song, I travelled to a bunch of temple fairs in the north and in the south. But they ditched me in the crowd of worshippers at the Lu'er Gate because they didn't like how fat I had gotten. It wasn't good for their image as beggars. As I followed the gully of some nameless stream, trudging to the foot of the mountain, I thought I saw a tender-faced deserter sitting hunched over at mid-mountain. I shouted to him, "Come on down. What are you afraid of—there are enough serious deserters in the world." He just kept sitting there in his safe tower, not moving a muscle. I had diarrhea for two days straight, but I managed to drag myself down to the Tamsui pier. In a daze, I looked in the distance to the evening sun inlaid on the mouth of the breakwater, all the while thinking that I had come to the end of my life. Feeling helpless, I turned around and fled to the apartment of my lover. My lover only said, "We're both just degenerates at the end of the earth." We buried our faces in our hands and wept. I told my lover to knock on the door six times in a row, then ring the bell three short and one long. Otherwise, no matter who was there, I wouldn't open up. Day and night, I kept the inky green blinds pulled shut. The only way that I could tell night from day was from the sounds and smells that seeped in.

My Second Brother, the Deserter

After not going out for three or four months, I was already pretty handy with an electric rice cooker. But I didn't stop there. Now I've learned how to make steamed dumplings. My lover says next time she'll ask to see if there's such a thing as an automatic dumpling steamer.

I love the life of long marches and short sojourns, even though you always have to be careful to wipe your ass clean. If you don't, that gang of eternal hunters can pick up the scent too easily. As for the life of confinement, "although I don't like it, I can accept it." Under my wife's constant gaze and under the influence of alcohol, I visualize my disappearance: in the instant that this person, "I," disappears, the guy holed up in his lover's bedroom can just open the door and walk away to live out his life using "my" identity. But planning to make myself disappear wasn't easy. I ran through the scenario over and over until I felt I had it under control, then immediately set out to rescue my life of confinement. That was during the bitter summer of the second year.

The lover's chamber is now occupied by a young couple who do stage shows. The guy says that the place was empty when he moved in. The woman scoffed—it was more like a garbage locker. I asked whether they found a rice cooker in the garbage. The woman pointed to the one placed beside the tulips by the doorway. The guy said they had checked to see if it worked, then decided to keep it for themselves. The lid of the cooker bounced and jiggled, exuding the aroma of shredded bamboo shoots and steamed pork. I wandered around the concrete, bug-infested forest, searching for a face I had known since childhood. I stood and looked up at a beehive window in a great mansion: that face was focused on the red-bean-filled steamed bun in his hand. He had secretly learned how to make these from Mother—the red-bean filling was Mother's specialty. I bought a bamboo steamer basket and took it home to my wife. She said Second Brother was hiding in a place nobody would suspect, working as an apprentice dumpling steamer. One winter night my wife brought out the steamer and heated up some frozen *shuijiao* and pork *shumai* dumplings as a bedtime snack. I placed little cups of Eternal Spring herbal wine on the steamer lid to warm them up. Having survived until the arrival of spring, I resolved to accept this imagined reality: There was a client who fell desperately in love with Second Sister. He secretly followed her to where she lived. A few hours later the hunters arrived. Knock knock knock knock knock knock knock. Second Brother got out of bed naked and went to answer the door. "It's not me," Second Sister hissed. "I'm here!" He opened the door a crack just as the hunters were about to break it down. As quick as a flash Second Brother said in an icy voice, "Don't bother," then opened the door and walked out, a detachment of hunters following right on his tail ...

Notes

1. Seventh Lord and Eighth Lord are figures from Taiwanese folklore. Seventh Lord is very tall and has a white face, Eighth Lord is short and has a black face. They are believed to reside in the temple of the City God and are in charge of rewards and punishments in the spirit realms.
2. At the time, two thousand Taiwan dollars were equivalent to about US $50.
3. The expression "grunts," a North American expression referring to a low-ranking soldier, is used here to render the slang expression "*pi bing* 屁兵" which literally translates as "butt soldier" or maybe "fart soldier." They "made war" satirically refers to the fact that they were "combat officers." This is the author's invention.
4. A "wooden fish" is a hollow wooden percussion instrument often carved to resemble a fish.

About the Editor

Ian Rowen is Assistant Professor of Sociology, Geography and Urban Planning at Nanyang Technological University, Singapore. He earned his PhD in Geography from the University of Colorado Boulder, and was a Fulbright Fellow and postdoctoral fellow at Academia Sinica. His work on Taiwan's culture and politics has appeared in *The Journal of Asian Studies*, *International Journal of Transitional Justice*, *The New York Times*, the *BBC Chinese*, and elsewhere. His translation credits include *Tibetan Environmentalists in China: The King of Dzi* by Liu Jianqiang (Rowman & Littlefield, 2015), and several international award-winning Taiwanese films such as *Splendid Float* and *Spider Lilies* directed by Zero Chou.

About the Translators

Howard Goldblatt is Emeritus Professor of East Asian Languages at the University of Colorado, subsequently Research Professor at the University of Notre Dame. A Guggenheim Fellow and founding editor of the journal *Modern Chinese Literature*, he has received honorary degrees from Hong Kong and British universities. Author or editor of more than a dozen books, in Chinese and English, he is the translator of more than fifty Chinese-language books, including ten by the 2012 Nobel Laureate Mo Yan, and two winners of the Asian Booker Prize. He has co-translated nearly two dozen with Sylvia Li-chun Lin, one the winner of the Asian Booker, another recipient of the Translation of the Year Award from the American Literary Translators Association. He has published a collection of flash fiction entitled *A Night in a Chinese Hospital* and is coeditor with Sylvia Li-chun Lin of *A Son of Taiwan: Stories about the 1940s and 1950s*.

Sylvia Li-chun Lin, a native of Tainan, Taiwan, earned a doctoral degree in Comparative Literature from the University of California at Berkeley. She was Associate Professor of Chinese at the University of Notre Dame before resigning to become a full-time translator and writer. Author of *Representing Atrocity in Taiwan: The 2/28 Incident and White Terror in Fiction and Film*, she is professionally and personally invested in fictional works dealing with this part of Taiwan's past. She coedited *Documenting Taiwan on Film: issues and Methods in New Documentaries* as well as *A Son of Taiwan: Stories about the 1940s and 1950s*. Besides translating fiction from Chinese, she is also writing a series of essays on food in cross-cultural exchanges.

Brian Skerratt is an assistant professor at the Graduate Institute of Taiwan Literature and International Cultural Studies at National Chung Hsing University, Taiwan, where he teaches modern and contemporary poetry, comparative literature, literary translation, and ecopoetics. He was a Fulbright Senior Scholar at National Chengchi University. He received his PhD from Harvard University. His publications include articles such as "Born Orphans of the Earth: Pastoral Utopia in Contemporary Taiwanese Poetry," "Hsia Yü Buys a Computer" and "Zhu Guangqian and the Rhythm of New Poetry." His translations of Macanese writer Un Sio San's poetry, *Naked Picnic*, are published by CUHK Press, while his translations of Taiwanese poetry and fiction have appeared in *Taiwan Literature: English Translation Series* and *The Taipei Chinese Pen*.

Chris Wen-Chao Li received his doctorate in general linguistics and comparative philology from Oxford University and currently teaches linguistics and translation/interpretation at San Francisco State University. He is the author of *A Diachronically-Motivated Segmental Phonology of Mandarin Chinese* and *The Routledge Course in Chinese Media Literacy*. His writings have appeared in such scholarly journals as *Language and Communication*, *Diaspora Studies*, and *Target*, while his translations have been published in *Renditions*, *The Chinese Pen*, and *Asia Pacific Translation and Intercultural Studies*.

Terence Russell is a senior scholar of Asian studies at the University of Manitoba in Winnipeg, Canada. He holds a PhD from the Australian National University, and an MA and BA from the University of British Columbia. Dr. Russell's work has included studies of many of Taiwan's modern authors and has a special focus on Indigenous writers. He has done full-length translations of *September Fable* and *Seven Kinds of Mushrooms* by Shandong writer, Zhang Wei, and most recently translated Husluman Vava's *The Soul of Jade Mountain* for the Cambria Press Literature from Taiwan series. Dr. Russell is coeditor of the journal, *Taiwan Literature: English Translation Series*.

Cambria Literature in Taiwan Series

General Editor: Nikky Lin
(National Taiwan Normal University)

A Taiwanese Literature Reader edited by Nikky Lin

The Soul of Jade Mountain by Husluman Vava, translated by Terence Russell

A History of Taiwan Literature by Ye Shitao, translated by Christopher Lupke

A Son of Taiwan: Stories of Government Atrocity edited by Howard Goldblatt and Sylvia Li-chun Lin

Transitions in Taiwan: Stories of the White Terror edited by Ian Rowen

Queer Taiwanese Literature: A Reader edited by Howard Chiang

www.ingramcontent.com/pod-product-compliance
Lightning Source LLC
Chambersburg PA
CBHW031724230426
43669CB00007B/233